1985

SO-AZE- 769

PRIVATE PRISONER

PRIVATE PRISONER

An astonishing story of survival under the Nazis

Robert Gayler

Patrick Stephens, Wellingborough

First published in 1984

British Library Cataloguing in Publication Data

Gayler, Robert
Private prisoner.
1. World War, 1939-1945—Prisoners and
prisons, German 2. World War, 1939-1945
—Personal narratives, British
I. Title
940.54'72'430924   D805.G3

ISBN 0-85059-724-2

*Patrick Stephens Limited is part of the
Thorsons Publishing Group.*

Photoset in 11 on 12 pt Plantin
by MJL Typesetting, Hitchin, Herts.
Printed in Great Britain on New Edition Book Wove
Vol 17.5 80 gsm, and bound, by Woolnough Bookbinding,
Wellingborough, Northants, for the publishers, Patrick
Stephens Limited, Denington Estate, Wellingborough,
Northants, NN8 2QD, England.

Contents

This manuscript was checked for authenticity by
my three companions, George, Steve and Gerry,
before publication.

1

May-June 1940

In the summer of 1940, Major the Baron de C. Chimay was probably the only Belgian aristocrat who was adjutant of a British regiment. He was a glorious sight as we passed him in our Army lorries; his cap badge shone, his boots glistened and his uniform was immaculate. As I type these words I can still picture him standing there by a hedge, but chiefly I recall his expression. He looked as grim as I have ever seen a man and exhausted beyond endurance. The men in the lorries with me were not quite as smart as the Major. We had no batmen and no spare uniforms to change into. Not one of us had had our clothing off for the last three weeks and during the past few days there had been little time for washing or shaving — or for eating or sleeping for that matter.

It was the wonderful summer's evening of June 11 1940, and we, 'D' Company of Kensington Regiment, machine-gunners attached to the 51st (Highland) Division, were part of the British Expeditionary Force in France. We did not know much of what was happening in the war in which we were fighting. All we knew was that the rest of the BEF had been evacuated from Dunkirk already, that the Germans were advancing, and that the French were retreating. By this time the Major probably had the additional information that we were the only British division left on the Continent and that we had been ordered to hold up the enemy advance for as long as possible so that feverish preparations could be made in England to combat the expected invasion. In addition he was likely well aware that no aircraft could be spared to aid us, as the defence of London would need every man and machine. No wonder the Major looked grim.

The immediate past had been a nightmare for the Kensington Regiment. Within a fortnight of landing in France we had been in action in outposts eight miles in front of the Maginot Line and four miles from the German Siegfried Line. We had been very optimistic then, for we had been on actual German soil. Every night the battle patrols of the Highland Regiments penetrated behind the enemy lines, coming back past our gun emplacements at dawn with an occasional prisoner, sometimes pausing to give our men a swig of rum. After an interesting,

7

although only mildly exciting spell of front-line duty, we had been sent back behind the Maginot defences to rest. Everything had seemed fine.

Then the trouble started. It began for us with heavy German air activity. Waves of planes passed over us to bomb Metz. The first time they passed above us I asked a French NCO if they were Boche, whereupon he shrugged his shoulders gloomily and said, 'Mais naturellement'. Two days later we got orders to move and the demoralising retreat across France began. At first we moved west, nearly to Paris, then we turned north to the Somme river, there facing a highly mechanised and active enemy army. We were amazed to find that the Germans had penetrated so far into France and with my particular friend George Lang, I studied a map in an old French newspaper we had found. George was short, dark, slightly built and highly intelligent. Looking first at the map and then at me he grunted, 'If we can't hold the bastards on the Somme they'll be on the Seine within a week'. They were.

Two thousand years ago Caesar's cohorts had fought on the Somme. Two hundred years ago Napoleon's legions had fought there. Twenty years ago our fathers had fought and bled in this cockpit of Europe. Now it was our turn. From then on we followed a 24-hour routine. In the evening we left our lorries and dug slit trenches, holding them all night against the advance of the Nazis. Just before dawn, if possible, we got into our trucks and withdrew, sometimes fighting as we went. This performance was repeated day after day, night after night, during which time our losses were caused mainly by air attacks from German dive-bombers. The only Allied aircraft we saw during the whole of this period were six Morane fighters of the French Air Force and even they were not in the air, but were standing unattended on an airfield outside Paris.

It is impossible to give a chronological account of those days, but in spite of our position our morale was surprisingly high. Once we gained a local success and pushed Jerry back a few miles, but we were not allowed to follow up and received the usual order, 'On trucks and withdraw!' Every day our NCOs had to call the roll of their platoons though we always had an unofficial check-up before this ceremony. The convoy would halt, an NCO would stick his head into each truck and ask, 'Any missing?' and cross off the names he was given. Then we would get out and the roll would be called only of those present, thus we avoided the names of the dead being called and not answered. It was strange how few wound cases we had. A man was either alive or dead.

On one particular occasion, we were very hard pressed. Enemy patrols had penetrated a hundred yards to our rear on either flank. We had our guns in a ditch by an iron crucifix which, we realised too late, would give the Germans a clear target for their range-finders and artillery. I remember saying to George, 'Well, if your religion is true we will know all about everything in ten minutes time, but if we rationalists

8

are right we won't be aware of anything!' George, a devout Roman Catholic, grunted as he looked along the barrel of his gun. However, at the last minute we escaped as some French light artillery behind us opened up a barrage.

The nightmare continued. At one place the convoy halted and we went into a deserted farmhouse, switched on the radio set and got the BBC six o'clock news. It started, '"This is London calling. The BEF has been successfully evacuated. . ."' We could not believe our ears for here we were sitting in France. Almost at once somebody shouted out that it was probably only a fake bulletin broadcast by the Germans on our wavelength to dishearten us and he reminded us that thousands of Canadians were being rushed up to support us from Bordeaux. Our spirits revived a little, though those of us who had any doubts had the sense to keep quiet as we prepared our gun positions for the night. Later a rumour circulated along the convoy that in England the Fascist leader, Sir Oswald Mosley, had been arrested. This was celebrated by our Quartermaster, a Jew, by the issue of all the rations he had left; one bar of chocolate per man. And so we fought and ran, day after day, harried from the air and butchered on the ground by an enemy far superior to us both in numbers and in armament. Finally, in the early evening of June 11 we passed Major the Baron de C. Chimay as he stood by the roadside.

2

St Valery

We passed the Major, rounded a corner and there the lorries of my platoon left the convoy, turning off to the right and stopping. With the skill of experts we camouflaged the vehicles, as we had done so many times before, then carried our guns and ammunition to an orchard some half-mile away and prepared for action. We had not been in position long when some refugees came down the lane beside the orchard. We had seen so many of these poor wretches recently that we scarcely took any notice of this typical group of working-class women and children and old men (all the young men were in the army). Pushing children's prams piled high with their most valued possessions, pots, pans and blankets, they were a pathetic sight. They seemed to have no destination, just a hysterical fear of the advancing Nazi army. One of the old men, whose hand was bandaged with a rag, came over to us in panic and pointed down the road, saying that 'millions' of German tanks were coming. We put a field dressing on his hand and told him to hurry after his family.

At 10 o'clock we got orders to return to our trucks and withdraw but at midnight we were suddenly halted. We clambered out, each man with his share of equipment. It was pitch black and chilly. By the leading truck we could hear the voice of our Company Commander, Major Dodge. He greeted us cheerfully, 'Well lads, thank God we have a Navy!' We laughed for none of us had a very high opinion of ourselves as an army. The Major pointed down the road and, as we strained our eyes in the darkness, we found that we had reached a crossroads at the head of a valley. At the other end of the valley, some five miles away, a battle was going on. We stood in silence, huddled together, looking at the artillery flashes and fires on the horizon. 'That', said Major Dodge, 'is a town on the coast called St Valery. The Navy is coming in on the tide tomorrow morning at about 06:00 hours to evacuate the whole division. Our job for the next couple of hours is to stay here and form a rearguard. At 02:00 hours you will get in your lorries and descend to the town. In the trucks you will have your guns mounted on their tripods with a swinging traverse as parts of the road may be in German hands. Good luck, and I'll get you all drunk in London tomorrow night!'

'Blow this for a game of soldiers!' said somebody in the darkness, and once more we mounted our guns in a nearby field. Another man said, 'Well, if I get my lot tonight, at least I've had a jolly good time while it lasted'. I wondered if I could say as much for myself. Someone else commented, 'We'll be OK tonight and tomorrow. It's after midnight now and the 12th of June, but you wait until the 13th comes! We're the 13th Platoon of the 13th bloody City of London Regiment!' There was silence for 13 was considered the most unlucky of all numbers. In spite of our danger most of us dozed, but then came a shake and the whispered message, 'Get on the trucks!'

There was only a little Scot in our lorry with George and myself and in silence we mounted the gun so that we could engage the enemy on either side of the road. A moment later our driver came round to the back of the truck and warned us that if he came to a road-block he would be crashing through it at full speed. Then, with no lights, we were off and roaring down the dark road to St Valery. The little Scot, crouching behind the gun, murmured, 'This bloody well can't be bloody well real. It's too much like a bloody film!' We had reached the outskirts when we had to slow down behind a French convoy. For the first time we began to hope that we would reach St Valery in safety. In the French truck in front of us a shell-shock case was laughing and screaming hysterically. We heard the blow and a thud as somebody knocked him out.

Our lorry stopped. We had got through safely. We were now in a very narrow lane with high banks on either side. The large number of men and lorries made us feel worried as, a few nights previously, a German patrol had lobbed mortar shells into a similar lane, killing most of the men trapped there. Pushing the incident firmly to the back of our minds we gathered round our Platoon Commander, Lieutenant Lavington. We each carried a gun, tripod or ammunition box in addition to our usual pack and rifle. Lavington then ordered our drivers to wreck the engines of our vehicles, so that they could not be used by the Nazis.

At first we waited and then, in single file, we followed a Black Watch NCO who led us down the lane and into the town. The whole of St Valery was in flames, but nobody paid any attention to the burning buildings and nobody attempted to put out the conflagration. The streets were crowded with French and British soliders. Although there was fighting in the town, the rattle of small-arms fire and the thud of artillery seemed to surround us, while from all directions streams of tracer bullets whizzed overhead. In a narrow alley a burning lorry blocked the way. Ammunition in the truck was exploding at intervals and, one by one, we had to sprint past to safety. George, who was in front of me, gave a wonderful performance. Silhouetted against the flames, bent double, his rifle slung over one shoulder, with a huge box of ammunition in either hand, he made a picture I will never forget. I swear he touched the ground only once in thirty yards!

We came to the end of an orderly queue which, we were later told, was over a mile long. 'Wait here for Blighty', said our guide as he left us to escort another party through the town. We waited for about an hour. Wounded were being pushed and carried past us to the head of the queue and after they had gone, I had to wipe some blood from the butt of my rifle with the cuff of my tunic. Apart from the passage of the wounded our wait for Blighty was strangely uneventful, and we were so exhausted that in spite of the eternal crash and rattle of the fighting around us, we dozed off. Once I woke up to see the door of a house near us open and an old man shuffle out. He looked up and down the road, urinated into the gutter and returned to the house. He was the only civilian I saw that night. Soon after a shout went up, 'Tanks coming!', and we all dived for cover, but nothing came of it. At about 4 o'clock in the morning we were ordered to leave the queue and were sent to rest as best we could on the side of a deep cutting outside the town. It started to rain lightly, but we got down in the mud and fell asleep at once. An hour later we were woken, still bone weary. The rain had stopped and it was a bright clear day. As I was soaked, I took off my battle-dress jacket and put on a fatigue tunic that I found in a deserted lorry.

We retraced our steps through the town, which by now was not burning quite so furiously, and the gunfire had died down considerably too. We reached our lorries and mounted our guns in a nearby ditch at the edge of a field. By now a rumour was circulating that the Navy could not get in to evacuate us as the Germans had field guns all along the cliffs on either side of the town. Hoping that 'something would turn up' we studied the field of fire from our position, which looked across the valley. We had our sights trained on the skyline opposite, in anticipation of an enemy attack which we expected from that direction at any moment. I was behind No 1 Gun with an old reservist, two other man were behind No 2 Gun and the rest of our platoon was arranged as an ammunition supply line though many of the men had dropped down on the ground where they stood and were now sleeping. In the same ditch to our left were Scots infantry armed with Brens. Suddenly a bugle sounded down in the town. 'Christ!' said the reservist to me, 'D'you know what that was, son? That was "Cease Fire!"'

'It's a German behind our lines blowing it then!' I said, and we continued to stare at the skyline, my thumbs lightly resting on the thumb-piece of the gun, the safety-catch lifted. A few moments later there was a confused noise from the direction of the town and a procession of French soliders came along the opposite side of the valley half-way up the slope, some of them waving white flags. 'Who the hell are they?' somebody shouted.

'Bastards who are giving themselves up,' came the reply.

'Then shoot the bleeders!' came a voice — and we all opened up at once. I like to remember that I did not alter the elevation of my gun and all my bullets went high over their heads, to the horizon. The Jocks with their Brens were more accurate.

After this things were quiet for some 15 minutes, when suddenly Lieutenant Lavington appeared, looking very haggard. 'Destroy your weapons', he said. The four of us behind the guns could not believe our ears. Some of the Jocks got out of the ditch and stood looking at him with their mouths open. He repeated, 'Destroy your weapons, the General has ordered us to surrender!'

'Not fucking likely, you yellow bastard!' came the reply.

'You aren't a bloody rabble', Lavington said coolly, 'you're disciplined British soldiers and you will obey the orders of your officers. I have personally heard General Fortune give the order for immediate surrender.' As he spoke a huge tank appeared in the field behind him. It had a black Maltese cross on its side, and a young German soldier was standing up in the turret with a Tommy-gun in his hands. We looked from the tank back to Lavington and silently turned to our guns to smash them. The man with me attacked the water-casing with a pick-axe while I dismantled the intricate firing mechanism and scattered the pieces in every direction. The Nazi watched from the tank and jeered. Then we went over to the rest of the platoon who were still asleep on the ground. I poked George gently in the ribs with the toe of my boot and as he sat up rubbing his eyes.

'Sorry old man, but you have just been captured!' I said.

The German shouted out and everybody turned to me and asked, 'What's he saying, Bob?' I did my first job as interpreter. 'He said, "Now see what Chamberlain has done for you!"'

The German shouted again and we all crossed over to the field on the other side of the lane. The field was now surrounded by tanks with their guns trained on us. We joined a mob of French and British soldiers. Some were wounded but all were dispirited. Everybody was busy destroying anything that might be of value to the enemy. I saw one man burning a large wad of English bank-notes, 'They may be in need of foreign currency', he said, importantly. I was standing next to the driver of our lorry and asked him anxiously if he had put it out of action. 'Sure!' he said, 'and as soon as the swine lift the bonnet a hand-grenade will go off!'

We were amazed to find a French prostitute standing near us in the crowd, the only woman any of us had seen in St Valery. She was, I supposed, the only camp follower who was too stupid to have left earlier. When she saw us looking at her, she looked round furtively, pointed to the tanks with an expression of disgust on her face and opened her handbag to reveal a pathetically small spanner, with which she apparently intended to defend her honour!

As we had no kit, George and I started to hunt for anything that might be of use to us. There was rubbish everywhere — rifles with broken butts, cap badges, web equipment, torn up documents. I picked up a mess tin which seemed unusually heavy and found it was full of French money. I was about to throw the money away and keep the tin when George hissed, 'Let's keep the notes.' I objected, knowing that the Nazis would devalue the franc, but George pointed out that the money would still be worth something, however little. The notes would weigh next to nothing, may prove useful and could easily be destroyed if the Germans tried to confiscate them. Thus converted, I sat down and we sorted out 180 francs. The pile of coins we left.

By now the Germans were swarming everywhere. We began to move slowly to the gate of the field and out into the lane. The march had begun.

No. MX/C/25'/40
(If replying, please quote above No.)

Army Form B.104—83
RECORD OFFICE
25 JUN 1940
ASHFORD
19

SIR ~~or Madam~~,

I regret to have to inform you that a report has been received from the War Office to the effect that (No.) 6846484 (Rank) Ple

(Name) GAYLER · ROBERT · JOHN ·

(Regiment) ~~1st PRINCESS LOUISE'S KENSINGTON REGIMENT,~~ THE MIDDLESEX REGIMENT.

was posted as " missing " on the 12 JUN 1940

The report that he is missing does not necessarily mean that he has been killed, as he may be a prisoner of war or temporarily separated from his regiment.

Official reports that men are prisoners of war take some time to reach this country, and if he has been captured by the enemy it is probable that unofficial news will reach you first. In that case I am to ask you to forward any postcard or letter received at once to this Office, and it will be returned to you as soon as possible.

Should any further official information be received it will be at once communicated to you.

I am,

SIR ~~or Madam~~,

Your obedient Servant,

for Officer in charge of Records.

IMPORTANT.
Any change of your address should be immediately notified to this Office.
(6546) W1.25451/1287 80,000 9/38 A.&E.W.Ltd. Gp.698 Forms/B.104—83/3

On June 25 1940 the War Office notified Robert Gayler's family that he had been posted as 'missing'.

14

3

The March

In the corner of the field near the gate stood a group of our staff officers. General Fortune was sitting on the stump of a tree gazing into space with tears in his eyes. He was in a worse position than any of us, for not only was he a prisoner but he held himself, in part, responsible for the fate of the men who were now marching past him into captivity. George and I 'flung one up' as we passed, but the General did not see us, one of his ADCs returning our salute in his stead.

Out in the lane we turned left over the fields. One man near me, commenting on our retreat right across France, said, 'The 300 mile run was easy, it was the 21 mile swim that beat us!' As we moved on, groups of Germans stood watching us pass and we regarded them with mutual curiosity. They were fine physical specimens of the celebrated *Herrenvolk*, and I was surprised to observe that their uniforms were not the field grey I had expected, but rather more blue in colour. We could not but notice that the equipment of these front-line troops was much more practical than ours. A British soldier was expected to go into action wearing all his equipment. Besides his basic uniform this consisted of a webbing belt and braces, a bulky gasmask (that hampered movement) on his chest, an anti-gas cape on his back plus a small pack containing washing and shaving kit, towel, boot brushes and polish, metal brushes, polish, mess tin, knife, fork and spoon. In addition to this he carried a rifle and he had two or more bandoliers of ammunition slung over his shoulder, while on his belt were pouches for more ammunition and a heavy metal water-bottle. As well as all this the machine-gunners had to carry either a gun or its tripod (each of which weighed 50 lb), or ammunition boxes, which were heavy and even more bulky. None of us could look at the Nazis without envy. They had a leather belt on which ammunition pouches and a water-bottle were hung, while over their shoulders they carried a light gasmask. They carried nothing else except their weapons and I imagine they would have been able to move twice as far, and three times as fast as we could. We were also amazed by the German mechanical equipment. They not only had huge tanks but also great grey lorries with caterpillar tracks and large-calibre mobile anti-

15

aircraft guns. As we passed these we tried not to look too impressed, but, compared with our 30 cwt Bedford trucks, this German equipment was magnificent.

As we came to a slight rise, we were able to see the column of prisoners stretching for miles ahead and behind us, and yet the Nazis seemed to be amazed that we were so few. Their own troop concentrations at St Valery must have been enormous, and we were later to discover that Rommel was their commanding officer.

We marched all that morning and well on into the afternoon, always southwards away from the coast. Once a British plane flew low over our heads and the German guns opened up against it. We all shook our fists, some shouted curses, for, at that time, we looked on the lack of RAF support as the chief reason for our capture, for British propaganda had convinced us that we had a huge air force. At the beginning of the march, I had a few words with my friend Len Stoppani of No 12 Platoon but we soon got separated in the crowd. Len had said that he thought that being a prisoner in the hands of these 'efficient rogues' would at least be interesting . . . We marched on in beautiful summer sunshine under a cloudless sky, and although it was warm I picked up an overcoat somebody had thrown away, feeling that it might be useful in the future.

Eight of us from No 13 Platoon tried to keep together, speculating about the future and commenting about the things we saw, until at 4 o'clock the Nazis directed us into a field. A stir was caused when General Fortune passed the field in a German staff car, under the escort of a Nazi officer. We all cheered, just to let the enemy see that we were still loyal to our officers. Later I noticed a British Captain speak to a young German NCO and was impressed to see the German stand to attention because he was speaking to an officer. After we had been resting in the field for half an hour a German shouted to us in English, 'All Tommies on the road!' It seemed that we were still not far enough from the coast for the German's taste so we formed up, leaving the French behind. We had been tired when first captured and had marched 20 miles before our stop. Already exhausted, we began to march again. A guard gave a Sergeant Major near me a heavy pack to carry for him and after we had been marching for an hour I felt I had to offer to take it from him, although I was very relieved when he grimly refused. I was disgusted to find that he thought we had lost the war, and he was busy trying to convince himself that the German invasion would only mean a 'new form of government' in Britain. Fortunately he was the only man I met who ever doubted our eventual victory.

Looking back I do not know how we managed to continue our march. Gradually men began to throw away their belongings and even those of us in need had not the strength to pick them up. We must have left a trail of army and personal kit behind us worth a fortune. Suddenly 'Chikko' Branton, one of our platoon, began to feel the strain. He began

16

to stagger and we had to hold him up to keep him going. At this moment a field-grey German car full of enemy officers came along and George wrenched open the door as it passed us at walking speed. Bundling Chikko in on to the knees of the protesting occupants I shouted out in German that he was seriously ill. Chikko rejoined us next morning, but could not remember what had happened to him until he came round in a German first aid post. We all felt quite paternal about Chikko, who was only 18, while we were mature 20 year-olds.

We marched until late evening. At one point a drunken German officer urged a fanatical-looking guard to chase us up a steep hill at the point of his bayonet, while he shouted at us in English, '"It's a long way to Tipperary" for you, "old boys!"' Wearily we reached a farmyard where we more or less collapsed, and slept where we fell. The yard was so crowded with prisoners that there was not an inch of unoccupied space right to the very brink of the duck pond.

We were awakened early next morning by a typical Nazi reveille for prisoners. A bull was let loose among us. There was a general panic as men scrambled out of the way and in the uproar I lost my precious mess tin. Although some men were hurt, order was eventually restored and we began to think about food, and we agreed to pool our meagre resources. I cut my emergency field ration into eight small cubes and distributed them. In a corner of the farmyard we found some old potatoes, which amounted to two each. These we rubbed clean and ate raw, as we had no means of cooking them.

The march on this second day of captivity was not quite so gruelling but soon we began to suffer from hunger and thirst. Everybody began looking for food by the wayside and my group strategically spaced itself throughout the column for this purpose. We were now marching, not across fields, but along roads and as well as guards on foot at the side of the column, special guard trucks were introduced at intervals amongst the prisoners. There were machine-guns mounted on these trucks and trained on us continually. However, we found these very welcome, as the marching guards tended to attach themselves to the trucks so they could talk to their friends and get their personal kit carried. Thus, by keeping well back from the trucks we were able to make sorties into the potato fields along the roadside without so much danger as when under the nose of the guard. The potatoes were not much good, however, rarely being much bigger than a halfpenny.

During the day the head of the column made a few halts, moving on again as soon as the rear caught up, so those at the end of the caterpillar never rested. That night we slept in an open field. The last thing I remember before I fell asleep was two guards talking. 'Well, we have a fine collection of Churchills and Lavals here', and then, seeing some black French Colonial troops, 'and a few Haile Selassies as well.'

Next morning we cut up the second emergency ration for breakfast. The Nazis were obviously anxious to get us further away from the coastal area and so we were moved by German army transport. While we waited in the field during the morning a number of Germans walked around amongst us and a young Luftwaffe pilot got talking to our small party. His father had fought for Franco in Spain and he himself had been through the Polish and French campaigns. He told us that we would be sent to Germany to do 'agricultural work and sport.' This sounded a much more cheerful prospect than the rumour that was circulating along the column, that the Germans were going to force us to advance in front of them during their attack on Paris. It was a story which found many believers at first.

About midday we discovered it was our turn to get on a lorry, which transported us about 30 miles south, though always under the eyes of watchful guards. These were tough looking fellows with metal plates shaped like new moons hung round their necks on chains, showing them to be members of the Military Police. We came to another field but this time it was surrounded by barbed wire and machine-guns. Here we spent the third night of captivity and received our first German rations. Having lost my mess tin I looked round desperately for something from which to eat and found a rusty tin-can about two inches deep and three inches across. This comfortably held the small ration of thin brown vegetable soup the Nazis gave us, indeed, it held every ration issued during the march without ever being more than half full.

Next morning we were aroused at dawn and marched again with hunger and thirst as our companions. We passed through a number of badly wrecked French villages in which the Nazis had already stuck up numerous pictures of Hitler and proclamations in French promising the restoration of democracy to the defeated inhabitants. The Germans must have had propaganda agents and equipment with their front-line troops, for when we passed through one village we saw brand-new enamel nameplates renaming the main street 'Rue d'Adolf Hitler.'

At the end of the afternoon, nearly crazy with thirst and with a merciless sun beating down on us, we halted in a deserted village named Formerie. Somebody dived into the cellar of a café that had been directly hit by a shell and came out with his arms full of bottles, shouting, 'Its full of wine, lads!' In spite of shots fired by the guards there was a mad rush and the Germans soon found that we were beyond control so they had to content themselves with preventing anybody from coming out of the cellar with more than one bottle of wine. If a man had more they were smashed. By the time our party managed to get into the place it was very nearly empty. Don Moss got the last bottle, but, as we were coming up the stone steps empty-handed I saw an uncorked bottle standing in the corner. I grabbed it and, nearly delirious with thirst, put it to my lips. My mouth and throat seemed to be full of molten lead. I had never imagined such pain and find it impossible to describe. I spat out a mouthful of blood, for the liquid was acid and my mouth and tongue were badly burnt.

Back on the road my exhausted friends carried my overcoat and precious tin-can for me, while two others supported me until we got to the halting place for that night, which was luckily just outside the village. As Don assisted me a Frenchman came up, snatched his bottle of wine from him and disappeared into the crowd.

In the field they put me down and I lost consciousness. When I came round a tall scholarly-looking German officer was bending over me and my friends were saying to him in simple English, 'He cannot walk, he cannot eat, he cannot breathe . . .' The German replied, 'Here we are in the middle of a field. I can do nothing. I will put him with the wounded.' I was helped to my feet, left my greatcoat with Chikko, who hadn't got one, and, clutching my tin-can, followed the officer. I was taken to the corner of the field where some sick and wounded prisoners were lying near a German machine-gun. A Frenchman got up and introduced himself as Emil, but when I could not understand him he tried again in German and I was able to reply in the same language in spite of the pain it caused me. I lay down, my legs suddenly beginning to twitch and kick in a most annoying manner and in spite of my efforts to relax. The Germans from the machine-gun came over and looked at my mouth and tongue, fascinated but sympathetic, except for one, who leaned over me and sneered in English the inevitable, '"It's a long way to Tipperary" for you Tommy'.

A French Medical Officer eventually arrived under German escort. He examined us all and Emil acted as my interpreter. I was told that I was lucky to be alive, for if the acid had reached my stomach I would have had a very painful death. The Medical Officer departed with his escort although he returned later with medical supplies from the wrecked chemist's shop of the village. He hesitated for nearly five minutes before giving me an injection and then presented Emil with a supply of medicine, probably an alkaline solution, which he said I must be given every hour for the next five hours.

Emil sat by me all night, talking to the successive guards who came on duty behind the machine-gun and giving me my medicine at regular intervals. Listening, I discovered that he was a German who had become a French subject after the First World War, when Alsace was taken from Germany. He had the German words 'Kein Glück' (No Luck) tattooed on his arm and because of this the guards assured him that he would be recognised as a German and freed as soon as he reached Germany. He told me privately that although he considered himself a German he was also a Democrat, and did not welcome recognition by the Nazis, as it would probably result in having to do service in the German army.

At dawn a field kitchen arrived to dole out minute portions of soup to the prisoners. There was some disorder as the men formed a huge queue for their rations. The guards near me fired a few bursts from their machine-guns low over the heads of the prisoners and roared with laughter as everyone in the field flung themselves to the ground. Emil managed to get me some soup, but although ravenously hungry, I was quite unable to swallow any. Suddenly, a lorry drew up and four of us were ordered in it with some German wound cases and a guard. I had only time for a few hurried words of thanks to Emil and a quick wave to George as the truck moved off. Our journey did not seem a long one and we soon arrived at a village called Arraines, where we pulled up outside the school and I was told to get off by myself.

The school was being used as a field ambulance post and had two 'wards' (simply the schoolrooms with mattresses on the floor). One room was for Germans and had a swastika stuck to the door, the other room was labelled 'KGF' or *Kriegsgefargen* (prisoners of war). There were two wounded Germans in the first ward, three Frenchmen in the prisoners' ward and so I stretched out on to the fourth remaining mattress, falling asleep at once.

I was woken up at midday by a French medical orderly with a bowl of first-class soup and I was delighted to find that I could eat a little without too much pain. I could also talk a bit and commented to the orderly, who spoke some English, that there didn't seem to be many Germans about. He said there were, in fact, two guards in the hospital who were rather 'trigger-happy'. There were a few German wounded, but the field post itself was being run by French medical personnel. He laughed proudly as he said that no German who entered the post as a patient would ever fight for the Nazis again. 'If a German has an ingrowing toe-nail our doctors cut the leg off above the knee!'

In the evening a party of Germans arrived to take over the post and as the only English inmate I was a centre of interest. They instantly assumed that I had attempted suicide and an Austrian medical orderly, who spoke English, was sent to question me. He blinked earnestly through his glasses and said, 'Prisoner of war no good. I am prisoner of war in Scotland in 1917. But we are alive and must think of our loved ones at home. Old father and mother and young wife and little children love us. We must be going home one day, not?' I heartily agreed with him and he seemed very relieved. Then he produced a Royal Army Service Corps cap badge from his pocket and pointed to the words 'Honi soit qui mal y pense', and said, 'This English I understand not.' I replied that it was old French, but one of the Frenchmen stared at it blankly and could not understand it either. My subsequent attempt to translate 'Evil to him who evil thinks' into German was not a great success as I could not remember the word for evil and talking still caused me pain. An attempt to explain the Order of the Garter and tell its story was not much better. From this esoteric topic we soon turned to the war. The little Austrian kept asking, 'Why you not attack in the first three weeks?' He argued that the whole German nation had been so demoralised at the prospect of another war that they would have capitulated without a fight, but that 'Whole nation wrong, one man right — Adolf Hitler!' As we were talking another German came in with the news that Verdun had fallen a week earlier without any real resistance. This excited both of the Germans for they had both been at Verdun in the First World War, when the German army had tried to take it for months without success. Now it had fallen, according to a letter from this German's friend, and within a matter of hours. Now I was to hear one of those strange political discussions which one got used to in Nazi Germany. In England, after a statement of political opinion has been made, I have noticed that somebody usually starts with, 'But the Tories . . .' or 'But the government . . .' yet these two Germans nodded at each other's remarks with, 'Yes! And Hitler . . .', 'Yes! And the SS . . .', always monotonous agreement.

Next morning I was classified as 'Fit to march' by a German Medical Officer, and I was indeed much better. The French medical orderly gave me a French NCO's overcoat, cap and jacket to replace the thin fatigue tunic in which I had been captured. I later discovered that he had filled the pockets of the overcoat with army biscuits for which I was very grateful.

I was sent to the local 'Prison field' which held at least 4,000 men. At this point the Nazis seemed to realise that the prisoners were incapable of marching without a rest, so everybody now spent a complete day resting here before resuming the march. I was fortunate enough to meet up with my friends again. They were delighted to see me again and to find me so much better. Chikko returned my British overcoat to me and I was able to give him my new French one in return and divided the biscuits up between us to supplement the meagre soup ration doled out by the Germans. When we were preparing for another night in the open a German announced, first in German and then in French, that an armistice between France and Germany had been signed. This was greeted by hand clapping by the French, who stupidly imagined that it would result in their immediate release. Bad feeling between the French and British prisoners grew rapidly after this, encouraged, it seemed, by the Germans.

So dawned the day that marked the end of our first week as prisoners of war. For breakfast that morning we had the 'novelty' of about half a cup of clear brown liquid per man. This was the infamous substitute coffee made from roasted barley. The great event of that day's march was the first sight of French civilians. Hitherto the complete country-side had been deserted, but from that time on people seemed to be attempting to resume their normal lives. It was in a little place called Domart St Leger that the miracle happened — the civilians, almost all women but with a few old men — not only stared at us but stood by the roadside and gave us food! One old dame had pointedly taken up her post with a basket of sandwiches under a German anti-British poster printed in French. This sort of incident became typical. Our 'syndicate' managed to get hold of some dry rolls and I slipped into a shop we were passing, when no guards were looking, to try to get some butter. When the girls behind the counter managed to understand me they handed me a large block but on offering them my French money they waved me away and one of them started to cry. As I stepped out of the shop I was seen by a guard who gave me a battering with his rifle butt, but he did not take the butter from me.

We marched all day and in the late afternoon reached the outskirts of Doullens where, as a change from fields, we were lodged in a gravel pit. Here George called me aside and produced two pathetically small cubes of milk chocolate, which he had found in the lining of his pocket. By now we were suffering seriously from hunger and for George to offer me half this fragment of chocolate was more than I should have thought any man capable of doing. Anticipating a real luxury I put my share of the chocolate in my mouth but was disappointed to find it tasted like a piece of cold hard fat. The acid had burnt all the taste buds from my tongue.

A Frenchman, who was a first-class linguist, was acting as interpreter here, and, under German orders made a public announcement that London had been badly bombed during the previous night. This was greeted with howls of abuse by the British and I am sure that the fellow would have been lynched if we could have got at him. This made me realise that the position of interpreter could be dangerous and a role to be avoided under these circumstances so I made up my mind to conceal my knowledge of German.

The following morning we marched again, hoping for more gifts of food from the Frenchwomen, but as we were passing through a sparsely populated area my party was unlucky. Still, we marched, talked among ourselves and found out all kinds of information about each other. Chikko Branton, for example, was forced to join the regular army at an early age by his home circumstances. His mother had suffered from sugar diabetes and the insulin that kept her alive cost his father over a third of his wages. In turn Don Moss told us stories of the men's outfitting trade, George talked of race horses and I held forth on books and libraries while the miles dragged by.

Our sleeping quarters that night was the race course outside St Pol. The first men there had shelter in the grand style but, as usual the rest of us slept in the open. We knew how much our welfare depended a great deal on the weather and congratulated ourselves on the days being dry, if a little too hot, and the nights being not too cold. Before we went to sleep two fighters flew low overhead. A German pointed at them with pride and started to boast about the Luftwaffe, when every gun in the district started firing; they were British planes!

The following day we marched on to Béthune and events on the road were unforgettable. The entire population of this mining area greeted us as a victorious Allied army rather than as defeated foreigners. The working-class women lined our path giving us food we knew they could ill afford. One old woman, who had already distributed all she had, put a bucket of water at her open door with some metal mugs from which we could drink. A guard, mad with rage at our reception, kicked the bucket of water the length of the passage and fired a shot through her front-room window. Many Red Cross nurses were also at the roadside handing out pencils and paper for us to write down the names and addresses of our next of kin. I wrote mine down many times and although I heard later that a few lists did get smuggled to England my name was not present on any of them.

The front of the column now consisted of British prisoners while the French lagged behind. This was partly due to our superior marching ability, but also because the French had been prepared for capture and so were laden down with kit, while we were practically all empty-handed. Three Frenchmen, however, were at the very front of the column, possibly put there by the Germans. They shouted to the civilians as they passed, 'Don't give anything to the English, your own men are behind!' The French women nearly all abused them for this and did not hesitate to help us. We agreed with each other that French men were swines, but that French women were wonderful!

At Béthune we were directed into a sports arena in the town itself and the only room our syndicate could find was on the cinder running track itself. Hungry and thirsty, George and I wandered about the dense mob of prisoners. Seeing some Frenchmen eating a large cheese we attempt-ed to buy some from them. They guiltily refused but as we turned away, looking pretty miserable, they called us back and insisted on giving us some, refusing our offers of money. We stayed with them while we con-sumed their gift for had the news circulated that they were parting with food they would have been trampled to death. They told us that they were Alpine troops and had been in action in Norway a few weeks pre-viously and they showed us some photographs of themselves there. As we left them they asked us not to judge all Frenchmen by the specimens we saw on the march who were, they said, the dregs of the slums of Paris.

Marching from Béthune next day we were encouraged in our march by the townspeople, who must have got up at dawn to give us food. One shop had a relay of helpers handing out paper bags full of hot chipped potatoes to the passing prisoners. In spite of all that these good people could do the amount of food they could provide for each man was pathe-tically small. On a typical day I remember being given two meat-paste sandwiches, one small cake and a cup of coffee by the civilians and one of the normal Nazi 'soup' rations. Nobody in our group fared better and although we were grateful for the extra food, we were marching over 20 miles a day, so our hunger grew. When there was no officer or NCO about the German guards sold rye bread to us. The price for a slice about one inch thick was a fountain pen, a ring, a watch or a cigarette lighter. If a man with a particularly good watch tried to bargain he was waved aside. Any guard who went into this business did a roaring trade for despite the exhorbitant prices charged there were always prisoners eager to buy.

At this point George went lame and a woman who saw him limping immediately handed him an umbrella from her hallstand. He stripped off the cover to make it as light as possible and not quite so ridiculous looking. It was a great boon to him. Later on the same afternoon we reached Seclin, after a day's march through intense heat. We were herded into the playground of a school where there was barely enough room for everybody to sit down. The latrines were blocked and from them little rivers of urine trickled across the playground and one had to be careful to avoid them as they ran through the thick crowd. That evening the thing we dreaded came to pass, it started to rain. However, somebody must have broken into the school, or maybe the Germans unlocked it, for George, Don and I managed to get in an overcrowded classroom where we had to sit upright on the floor all night with our knees tucked under our chins. One of the men in the room was a shell shock case and made various odd noises all night, but in spite of this and our cramped position we slept quite well.

Next day, George, Don and I kept together while the rest of our party split off into two separate groups. The original syndicate had been held together during the first days of captivity chiefly by the pooling of our emergency rations, but as these were exhausted, smaller groups would be more practical. That day we passed the Belgian frontier and for some reason I imagined our reception by the inhabitants was rather cooler than that of the French. For the last week rumours had circulated that 'tomorrow' we were to get on a train, but each day we resumed marching. Our first night in Belgium was spent at Tournai where we slept in an army barrack, a prison-like building which, to our eyes, resembled a palace. Having been marched onto the drill-square and halted we were told to 'fall out' and the mad scramble for sleeping places began. Our trio dashed off to the top floor of the furthest block, hoping to find some space, but a group of Scots were already coming down the stairs, saying, 'There's a bloody Froggie up there who won't let you in!' George and I told each other what we would do to anybody who got in our way as we made our way up the stone stairs. The 'Frenchman' turned out to be a Kensington from 'B' Company dressed, like me, in French uniform. He had been wounded and had arrived at Tournai early that morning by lorry. When the column of prisoners had marched in he had seen some of his Regiment among them and had 'reserved' a barrack room for us by sitting on the stairs and telling everybody in English, with an assumed French accent, that the Germans had put him there to keep all prisoners out. Now he told George to get in and occupy three beds for us, while Don and I went round and collected any other members of the Regiment we could find.

After we had settled in we found that there were some small holes

24

knocked into the outside walls of the barrack through which a few enterprising Belgians were selling the prisoners blocks of chocolate and at
very inflated prices. We managed to buy two slabs before the Germans
ruthlessly stopped this trade by shooting and killing a number of civilians and prisoners as an example. That night we had a cold shower in a
crowded wash-house, a shave with a borrowed razor, two thirds of a
block of Belgian chocolate each, and a good night's sleep on real beds!
Eating the chocolate, I discovered with relief that my sense of taste had
partly returned. However, our respite was all too brief as our march was
by no means over yet.

During the next day's march we were all very impressed with the
high standard of living in Belgium and with the fact that the people
were as pro-British as the French, despite my first impressions. Halting
at Renaix that night we slept once more in the open, this time in an
orchard. The owners of the orchard were living in a nearby house and
must have stripped their store-cupboard to feed us, but how far does
even the best stocked larder go between 2,000 men? Yet, the middle-
aged couple and their daughters worked for hours helping us, unmolest-
ed and unhindered by the Germans.

Another shorter march next day took us to Ninove and to yet another
open field. Every day at the end of the afternoon the men would ask me
to find out from the guards how much further we had to go. The reply
was always the same 'One more kilometer', even if in fact, it was nearer
nine or ten. It was during this day's march that our trio got to the very
head of the column, where a British interpreter was marching with
some guards and a German officer. During a halt the officer asked the
Englishman if he was married.

'Yes', replied the Interpreter.

'How long?' demanded the officer.

'Three years', came the quiet reply.

And again, 'How many children?'

There was a pause. 'None,' admitted the Interpreter rather sadly. At
this the German curled his lip and contemptuously turned away.

In the field that night we attempted to make some stinging nettle tea,
as we had seen others doing previously. Don made a fire with some
wood we had collected on the march while George and I searched the
field for nettles, but other prisoners had been there before us. George
then recollected having heard a speaker on the radio say that he lived on
a diet of grass. Rather than waste our fire we boiled some but it was
impossible to swallow, so we had to be content with chewing it and
drinking the green water in the hope that it contained some nourish-
ment. Some distance from us some Englishmen were sitting gloomily
around a small fire of their own on which they had cooked some quite
good meat stew. Seeing me looking over at them one shouted 'Like to
try some mate?' I accepted with alacrity but I have never tasted anything so revolting! Ravenous as I was, and with an impaired sense of

25

taste, I could not attempt to eat it. Spitting it out I asked what it was. 'Dog', said the man who had hailed me, 'but we don't know what disease it had.'

Another day's marching with its hunger and thirst followed and we spent that night in the barracks at Aalst, where there was a great pile of wooden clogs in the barrack square although nobody could think of an explanation for their presence. Having found a fairly empty barrack room we established ourselves on a bunk wide enough for three — George, Don and myself. I was lucky enough to find an empty cowhide pack on the bunk above ours and was able to put my overcoat in it, instead of having to carry it over my arm. We found that a group of British officers were segregated in one wing of the building and we were able to have a few words with Major Dodge and Lieutenant Lavington who were 'mucking in'. The Germans had erected a barricade across the entrance of the barracks and allowed the townspeople to talk to the prisoners over it. As George was the only one of us who spoke much French, Don guarded our belongings while I helped George to force his way through the front of the crowd that surged round the entrance. We managed to get to the front at last and George was about to address a middle-aged woman in nurse's uniform when she said, 'You may speak to me in English. I come from Bromley in Kent and married a Belgian boy in 1919.' At once we tossed all our French money over the barricade to her and asked her to buy all the food she could for us. She departed and we waited in the milling throng for nearly an hour until she returned laden with food, which she passed over to us under the envious gazes of the other men. Before we could thank her adequately she smiled and turned away to take an order from another man. We hurried back to Don to examine our package at leisure. There was a large rice custard gateau, two loaves of bread, some butter, some breakfast sausage, numerous tins of sardines and some bars of chocolate. We had given the nurse what remained of the 180 francs I had picked up at St Valery, but this feast had obviously cost her much more! We tucked into some bread and butter, sausage and the gateau immediately, but after that we had to strictly ration ourselves to one item between the three of us per day. That night we slept with the food stored away in my new pack wedged tightly between Don and myself to prevent it from being stolen. Every night we had to tie our boots to ourselves for the same reason.

The march next day was uneventful, and our trio was cheered by the knowledge that we had a reserve supply of food. As we passed through the small Belgian towns we remarked to each other on the quietness of the scene and how well-dressed the people were, when suddenly we realised that it must be Sunday and the people were going to church. I wonder if they prayed for the thousands of gaunt prisoners who were passing through their streets that morning?

That night we slept in a textile factory in a town near the Dutch frontier named Lockeren. Throughout the march there had been various searches by the Germans for 'warlike equipment'. Some of the searches were probably unofficial and carried out by individual soldiers after loot, although by now we had very little worth taking. At Lockeren there was a more efficient official search, but about the only things taken from us were the tin helmets that some of the men were using as eating utensils. My tin-can was examined critically but to my relief was thrown back to me. After we had settled down for the night a German guard, rifle on shoulder, passed by and an indescribable feeling of incredulity swept over me. I had never been an enthusiastic solider, but now, the fact that I was unarmed in the presence of one of the enemy aroused such powerful emotions in me that I realised sooner or later I must escape. I did not say anything of this to George or Don as I did not want to be responsible for them risking death, unless it was at their own suggestion. As I fell asleep I realised that I would have to be patient as we were far too weak to undertake an attempt at the moment.

On Monday morning we marched only a few miles to the Dutch frontier and could hardly believe it when we found ourselves in a railway siding and ordered to get on the long-promised train.

4

Into Germany

The train consisted of small open trucks and as many men as could stand upright were forced into each. After some delay, and a great deal of hysterical shouting by the guards who fired a few random shots into the air, we moved off. The sunshine was brilliant as, under the eyes of Germans who stood armed with Tommy-guns between each pair of trucks, we moved off wondering what the future held for us. Our train journey was only a very short one but not uneventful. During our journey we passed through a small town where the Dutch engine driver had to slow down to walking pace. Dutch housewives, who must have known we were coming, stood at the end of their gardens with supplies of food which they threw to us. In the packed trucks there was a mad scramble as the gifts landed amongst us. Don managed to get a packet of sandwiches done up so daintily in greaseproof paper that we gulped as we looked, first at them, and then back to the suburban housewife who had thrown them. She looked very near tears herself, obviously wishing she could have done more.

The train came to an abrupt halt in the open country and we were marched a few hundred yards down a main road to the banks of a river. During this short march we passed two Dutch policemen both of whom smiled brightly and lifted their right arms in the Nazi salute and shouted 'Heil Hitler!' as they passed each German guard. The guards ignored them while we grunted curses. On the bank of the river we were each issued with a loaf of German rye bread and a piece of sausage. As I received mine I asked in German how long it had to last and the Nazi NCO in charge held up his fingers and said 'Four days, so you had better tell your comrades'. I stepped out of the ranks and shouted out this information for all to hear. When I got back in line George was very worried in case I was kept behind as interpreter and so I agreed to be careful and conceal my knowledge of the language in the future.

We were sent to a landing stage and an English-speaking Dutchman informed us that we were to be transported into Germany by boat and that this river was the Rhine. As he spoke a tug came up river towing some huge empty coal barges for us. Some 800 men were boarded on each barge and our trio was lucky enough to be among the first men on ours. As the holds were huge and filthy with coal-dust we established ourselves on one of the gigantic covers that partly covered the barges, the later men aboard having to go 'below decks'. I observed that as the holds were not completely covered in, and as we were close to the edge of our cover, we ran the risk of falling down below in our sleep. Don replied wryly that it was better to fall 20 feet on top of somebody, than to have somebody fall 20 feet on top of you! Later we were told how, on another barge, a cover with many men sleeping on it had collapsed into the hold and some 30 men had been killed.

We had now been captives for three weeks and during that period none of us had been to stool more than twice, presumably because we had nothing to pass. Now our digestive systems rebelled and within 24 hours everybody was suffering from an acute form of diarrhoea caused, I imagine, by the heavy rye bread and strong sausage on our stomachs after weeks of near-starvation. This illness was accompanied not only by acute physical discomfort but by great mental distress caused by cramped conditions and lack of privacy for the only method of relieving oneself was to squat over the edge of the barge in full view of the people on the banks of the river. With the onset of dysentery my friends and I realised how lucky we were to have positions on deck, as in the holds the conditions defied description. One French negro fell overboard from sheer weakness and sank without a struggle and the Scot who dived in after him was only rescued with difficulty.

We spent two days and three nights on the barge, passing under the ruins of great steel bridges, wrecked during the German advance through Holland. We saw the names of many famous British engineering firms on the twisted girders and were greatly cheered by the friendly waves we got from the people on the banks of the river. During the first day the Dutch Red Cross managed, with German consent, to distribute a little food to us. On my barge it amounted to one teaspoon of honey per man. By this time we had exhausted almost all our private food reserve so, at George's suggestion, we rationed ourselves to half a bar of chocolate each day between the three of us.

Slowly crossing Holland we were pleased to note that the Rhine, the Highway of Europe, was practically deserted, our barges being the only shipping on it. During our second night we left the Rhine for the river Waal and passed a huge factory, surprisingly labelled in English, 'Blue Band Margarine'. We stopped for some time at Dordrecht where some Dutch Boy Scouts were permitted to distribute a little food to us. They seemed to have no Scouters in charge of them but were working under the Patrol Leaders. I was very moved by their conduct. Although young and excited, their bearing towards the enemy was pathetically dignified, and I have never been more proud of my own association with the movement than I was at that time.

At last we reached Emmerich, the first town over the German frontier. The whole place was a mass of Nazi flags and banners celebrating the fall of France. We got off the barges without regret and, as we disembarked, were given one loaf of bread between seven men by immaculate Nazi storm-troopers. This was done in full view of the civilian population of the town and was blatant Party propaganda — 'See how well we treat our prisoners!' The local people regarded us silently, with expressionless faces. Having read for years in the British press of the shortages in Nazi Germany we were surprised by the high quality of the clothing, the well-fed air of the civilians and the general atmosphere of prosperity. As we waited to move off an old man, sitting on a roadside seat under some trees, looked furtively in both directions and whispered sadly in English, 'No ham and eggs for breakfast now!'

We were marched to a sports field near the railway and there waited for some hours with the sun beating down on us. Eventually we were put into closed cattle trucks for a two-hour journey to a town called Bockholt.

The train stopped outside the town and, as we clambered out, we found an impenetrable evergreen hedge some 18 feet tall running parallel with the railway. We were lined up in twos and marched through a gap in the hedge only to find another exactly the same beyond it, and turning right, we marched along a narrow cement path between the two towering hedges. We were marched past a stone memorial dominated by a great eagle with a swastika in its claws. The German inscription read, 'Erected by the National Socialist German Workers' Party to the Heroic Memory of our Comrades who were murdered during the Struggle for Power'. Reaching the end of the avenue we turned left and saw an open gate in a great barbed wire fence. Over the gate was another German inscription, 'Always be proud that you are German'. We marched slowly in, counted by guards. George and I looked at each other in silence. We were in Bockholt Concentration Camp.

5

Bockholt

As we looked anxiously around us we were very relieved to see no Nazi Party uniforms, for all the Germans were in the now familiar field-grey of the army. We realised that the Party had evacuated the political prisoners and had lent the place to the armed forces for use as a reception camp for prisoners of war.

The camp itself was surrounded by two fences of barbed wire, 18 feet tall and with a tangled mass of more wire between them. In turn the great double hedge surrounded the fence on three sides, the fourth side totally cutting us off from the outside world by huge buildings outside the barbed wire, (which we thought must be the offices and living quarters of the staff of the camp). At intervals along the fences and at each corner, were guard post towers which dominated the camp. In each tower there were two guards on duty day and night. They were equipped with searchlights and machine-guns, and were in close telephone contact with the guard-room. Within this double fence the camp itself was divided into large compounds by less elaborate fences of barbed wire. The earth was so sandy that it was impossible to run on and, in our weakened condition, walking on it was a major effort. There were no buildings whatever to accommodate the prisoners although the Army had erected large marquees in each compound for us. However, before we were allowed into the marquees we were thoroughly searched. As we lined up two German soldiers informed us that all valuables would be confiscated and any attempt at concealment would be punished. So, we would be wise to hand over our fountain pens and watches to them! These very obvious racketeers actually did deceive some men who quietly gave them their valuables. The official searchers got my fountain pen which I regretted not having sold for a slice of bread on the march, but I did manage to smuggle out a silver propelling pencil in my boot, the one which Dorothy, my girlfriend in England, had given me.

In the marquee, into which we were herded, there was a mass of straw scattered over the ground. We arranged ourselves in four rows for sleeping, two rows head to head down the centre of the tent, and one row at either side with heads to the wall. With a passion for information I counted the men in my row and calculated that there were at least 400 men in our marquee. The heat and stench were soon overpowering so our trio took the first opportunity to go outside and explore the compound.

In one corner of the compound there was an open trench with a forked two foot post at either end and these posts supported a pole the length of the trench. This was the latrine. In another corner was a wooden trough with water taps over it. I anxiously shouted to a guard outside the wire, asking him if it was *Trink-Wasser* (drinking water). When he said it was we drank our fill, telling each other how we would never take water for granted again after our lack of it on the march. Almost immediately we had our first roll-call as prisoners of war. Lining up in fives we were counted innumerable times by two German NCOs and a Private, who could never agree about the total. At last we were permitted to go into the marquees and prepare for sleep.

Hours later, in the dark, somebody shook me by the shoulder. It was Don. 'Listen to that!' he whispered and, faintly in the far distance, I could hear the sound of bombing and anti-aircraft guns. 'The air-raid warning went ten minutes ago', he whispered and by now we were all awake and silently listening. George spoke, loudly enough for all to hear, 'Our lads are probably bombing the Ruhr industrial area, which, I reckon, must be at least 50 miles from here!' I could sense the relief of the men who had recently been in the thick of action themselves. The raids were repeated every night we were at Bockholt although the guards always dismissed them with a laugh, saying that there was never more than one plane sent over and that merely for propaganda purposes. Nevertheless the sound of those planes was a great boost to our morale.

At morning roll-call next day each man was issued with a German mess tin and a rusty spoon. Then we were told to queue up for a food ration. We queued for eight hours, squatting in the sun, and at last we were rewarded with a good helping of thick noodle soup. After we had eaten our rations George, Don and I were returning to our marquee when we noticed a man, naked from the waist up, sitting in the sun carefully examining his shirt. 'What's he doing?' asked George. 'Good Lord', I said in disgust, 'he must be lousy!' Then the man, who must have overheard me, looked up and said, 'Excuse me, old man, but have you had a look at your own clothing since you arrived here?' When we said we had not, he tactfully suggested that we should and so the three of us sat down, not too near him, and followed his example. George found a small slow-moving insect, grey in colour, about the size of a large greenfly, which he showed to Don and me and then went over to the expert.

'Yes, that's one', agreed the expert.

'Well, what do I do now?' asked poor George and our new friend took the shirt and demonstrated how to crush the intruder between one's thumb-nails. Every man was infected and, in spite of all we could do, nothing seemed to reduce the plague. 'It's the straw', complained the expert, 'it's alive with 'em.'

We were at Bockholt for a week. The morning and evening roll-call, the hours spent in soup queue and the nightly air raid completed our daily routine. On one occasion the Germans attempted to make us do foot drill and PT, but so many men collapsed within the first few minutes that they were forced to abandon the idea.

One morning roll-call, our mess tins and spoons were taken from us and we were ordered to prepare to move. As we left the camp each man was given a loaf of rye bread and once more we climbed into closed cattle-trucks on the railway.

There were 55 men in our truck. It was still the height of the summer and as we were all suffering from an acute form of diarrhoea our journey was one of great discomfort. It was made worse for the doors of the wagons were locked, and the only ventilation was provided by a small window high up in one corner, which was about three feet long and six inches wide. This was covered on the outside with wire netting and barbed wire. The doors were not opened for three days and two nights, although the train did make frequent halts. Conditions soon became appalling, for there was not even enough room for us all to sit in reasonable comfort, let alone sleep. The men nearly went crazy and there were a number of fights as tempers began to fray.

We attempted to keep track of our position and by standing on tip-toe a tall man could see out of the window. We took it in turns to look out so we could mark when we passed through Berlin and later through Frankfurt-on-Oder. At school my German master had once explained that there were two Frankfurts in Germany, one in the east and another in the west. He had added that we need not worry about the one in the east, as it was too far away for any of us ever to visit. As we passed through it I remembered how bitterly I had regretted, sitting at my school desk, how I was never likely to travel!

The train made a stop at Posen of over an hour and it made us realise how far east we had come. We attempted to explain to some of the men where we were and the fact that the 'next country is Russia' seemed to impress them a great deal. To break the monotony we started singing patriotic songs at the tops of our voices although we were ordered immediately to stop, and there were crashes as rifle butts hit the wagon door. The train was shunted outside the main station of Posen and I managed to look out of the window by standing on my pack. At the top of a grass bank a main road ran parallel to the railway. A German policeman passed followed by a small ragged boy who waved to the train and started strutting along behind the German, rolling his eyes and drawing a finger across his throat. Two girls in attractive brown uniforms passed and a van sped by lettered *Volkische Beobachter* (the official Nazi Party newspaper). The train moved off slowly and we passed a fine modern factory where Maggi's soup was made. Gathering speed, we were soon in the open countryside again and George joined me at the window as we silently watched field after field of golden Polish grain pass by which was now all Nazi-owned.

Towards evening we halted once more and there was a clank of metal outside our truck and a rumble as the door began to slide open. Blinded with the light of the setting sun, but delighted to be out of the hell hole, we scrambled out. The station was named Schubin.

No. *M४ / P / 89*
(If replying, please quote above No.)

Army Form B. 104—88A.

.... Record Office,

[stamp: RECORD & PAY OFFICE 13 SEP 1940 ASHFORD]

..........................Station.

............................19

SIR ~~OR MADAM~~,—

I have to inform you that a report has been received from the War Office to the effect that (No.) *6846 484*.
(Rank) *Pte*. (Name) *GAYLER. Robert. John*
(Regiment) *1ot P.2 KR*. MIDDLESEX REGIMENT
is a Prisoner of War *Interned at STALAG-XXIB GERMANY*.

Should any other information be received concerning him, such information will be at once communicated to you.

Instructions as to the method of communicating with Prisoners of War can be obtained at any Post Office.

I am,
SIR ~~OR MADAM~~,—
Your obedient Servant,

[signature]
Officer in charge of Records.

IMPORTANT.—Any change of your address should be immediately notified to this Office. It should also be notified, if you receive information from the soldier above, that his address has been changed.

Wt.30241/1250 500M. 9/39. KJL/8818 Gp.698/3 Forms/B.104—83A/6

It was not until September 13 that the family received confirmation that he was still alive, and a PoW.

34

6

Schubin

The first thing we saw as we left the station was a 32-sheet German propaganda poster printed in Polish. It depicted a battlefield on which thousands of Polish soldiers were being slaughtered. In the foreground a desperate Pole with his arm in a sling, was appealing for help to Neville Chamberlain who, looking like the Devil in a top hat, was laughing as he refused.

We were lined up in sixes and marched off with a heavy escort of guards on either side of the column. Although the Germans had not been in this town for more than a few months, they had already given it a strong Nazi character. All the Civic buildings were newly decorated and had the huge German eagle in relief over their main entrances. Each eagle held a wreath of oak leaves in its claws within which was a swastika, which symbolised the Party. I was on the outside of the column and beside the man in front of me marched a guard with a rifle and fixed bayonet. All the civilians of the town were standing in their doorways to watch us pass, and as the guard was seen by a friend he was greeted with a *Heil Hitler!* At this the prisoner in front of me grunted to himself, 'Confound Hitler'. At once the guard tore his rifle from his shoulder and went to hit the Englishman with the butt, screeching, *'Was sagst du, du Schwein, du verflucht Lump?'* (What are you saying, you swine, you stupid lout?). The Englishman looked at him with a disarming smile and said mildly, 'I only said "Confound Hitler — Confound Hitler"', and the guard, apparently mollified, grunted, put his rifle back on his shoulder, and marched on in silence. Suddenly the guard turned to the prisoner again and said, in perfect English, 'Well, confound Churchill and confound you too!' and everybody within hearing roared with laughter. (Actually the word used in both cases was quite a bit stronger!)

On the outskirts of the town was Schubin Prison Camp, known as Stalag XXI B. It was surrounded with the inevitable barbed wire fences and guard posts, and as we marched slowly through the main gate, counted by excited Germans, the prisoners already resident in the camp gathered to greet us. There were many reunions between comrades although our trio saw nobody we knew. George called out to ask, 'What's it like here?' and most of the men gave the 'thumbs down' sign, while others shouted, 'Rotten!' and 'Bloody horrible!'

The new contingent was directed to one end of the camp where there were some half-built brick barrack-rooms. By now it was quite dark and, exhausted by the short march from the station, we quickly fell asleep on the bare floor boards of the incomplete building.

Next morning we explored the camp. Built on a sloping site it was about 750 yards long and some 500 yards wide. Unlike Bockholt it was not divided into compounds and there was evidence that until recently it had been part of a farm. Inside the main gate stood the farmhouse, a white building of three storeys, which now housed hundreds of Polish prisoners of war, all of whom were transferred to another camp shortly after our arrival. Outside the farmhouse stood a water pump at which there was a never-ending queue of prisoners. Our 'barracks' were at the north end of the camp and since the Nazis were still building them they had neither roofs nor windows. In each corner of the camp was a latrine trench 'à la Bockholt', and in the centre near the white house, there were some barns and outhouses which were in the middle of being demolished.

My first quest was for an eating utensil as my precious tin-can had been used for quite another purpose during the train journey! I had the good fortune to find a hollow brick in the rubble of the demolished outhouses and managed to chip the mortar from it with a stone. Then with an old razor-blade I carved myself a spoon from a piece of wood and was thus fully equipped to dine. Food was almost our sole preoccupation. I am sure a Puritan would have been most impressed by us, for we, the traditionally rude and licentious soldiery, never thought or spoke of women now except to talk about the food our girl-friends and mothers cooked. Our rations were one Polish army biscuit in the morning, a small ladle of soup and five small potatoes at midday. The soup was always 'interesting' and came up in a large container from which the British Warrant Officer in charge of each barrack-room issued the soup to the men. The pea soup, for example, was steaming clear, pale green water with eight or nine peapods on the bottom of the container. The potatoes were black right through and stank. We used to salvage any white pieces from the black mass and eat them.

After we had been in Stalag XXI B for a week the first copy of an English-language newspaper produced by the Nazis was given to us. This publication was entitled *The Camp: An Illustrated Weekly Newspaper for British Prisoners of War*. Even at this early stage the Germans realised that we were a potential source of hostile propaganda, and were attempting to neutralise us by making sure that our only news came from their own Ministry of Propaganda. The paper also seemed to have a second function, to try to develop hostility between prisoners of different nationalities. This first issue was particularly interesting. The editorial said that as prisoners of war we could no longer influence the war and so the sole purpose of the paper was to 'give British prisoners the news, good or bad,' and went on to assure us that from the British point of view it was *all* bad. A map showed a small white Britain engulfed by black German-occupied territory from the Arctic Circle to the Franco-Spanish frontier and had the caption, 'Who is blockaded now?' On the front page was a photograph of a British policeman on point duty directing a German Army officer. This was taken, said the caption, in the Channel Isles which were in German hands. We studied the photograph minutely and dismissed it as a fake, 'The shadows are all wrong,' 'The policeman's uniform is wrong,' 'The shop in the background is out of focus, but it looks like a German shop to me,' etc, etc, but even so there is not much doubt now that it was, in fact, a genuine photograph.

An article on an inside page was written by the Countess von Zeppelin, an English woman married to a German aristocrat. She wrote that 'My husband's friends are the men who will matter in the Europe of tomorrow'. She gave it as her opinion that it was for Churchill to decide if 'the fate of London shall be that of Warsaw or of Paris', that is, whether to fight on and be wiped out or to surrender and survive. There is no doubt that these articles were written by the Countess, and she immediately became the most hated woman in the world to all British prisoners.

One morning after roll-call Don commented that he thought we could now say that we were no longer hungry, we were starving. A man had died during the night in another barrack-room. More deaths, chiefly from dysentery and pneumonia, quickly followed, though the total will never be known as we were un-registered as prisoners at that time and no records were kept. The competition was keen to get on the grave-digging parties at the local cemetry, as Polish civilians often smuggled food to the men as they worked.

I did not find the deaths so unnerving as the occasional cases of madness caused by hunger. One of the men in my regiment made a little fire and danced round it naked until the guards took him away. In the end we remained on the floor of our barrack-room nearly the whole day, and whenever we stood up we would experience a 'black-out' for a few seconds before we could walk on. Gradually we found that our mental processes were being influenced by starvation. When a rumour circulated that the prisoners would be allowed to write home I spent the whole of one day in torture because I could not remember the number of my girlfriend, Dorothy's, house so I thought I would be unable to write to her.

In our roofless hut one of the men was discovered stealing another man's biscuit. He was forced to 'run the gauntlet' — each of us hitting him as hard as possible with the heels of our boots. Nobody thought for a moment of reporting him to the guards, for we had our own ways of dealing with offenders.

There was a roll-call every morning and evening although after a time the Germans had to allow us to sit down for them as we were too exhausted to stand. During this period I did not witness a single case of brutality by individual guards to prisoners. However, the fact that at this time food was plentiful in Poland makes the conduct of the men responsible for our condition criminal.

One blazing hot day during roll-call a huge louse slowly came into view on the collar of the man standing directly in front of me. I watched it with complete detachment as it crawled along the top of his collar, and nor did I feel any emotion when the man next to me lent forward, gently removed it between his forefinger and thumb and ate it.

Our trio was lucky for we were all non-smokers. Many of the men who died had the added torture of longing for tobacco as much as they longed for food. Indeed, often we would see men offering their biscuit or soup ration for a cigarette, yet it seemed strange that the heavy drinkers did not have nearly such powerful cravings for alcohol. When conditions were at their worst all the Irishmen in the camp were ordered by the Germans out on parade. Then they were all interviewed individually by a sleek and well-fed individual who claimed to be a representative of the Irish Free State government, but who was probably a member of the IRA. He offered the Irishmen their freedom if they would agree to 'take up arms in the defence of Ireland if necessary'. Not one of them accepted this offer, and they all rejoined us in the Stalag where they told us of the incident and where, in due course, some of them died.

It was at this period that I managed to pick up a German newspaper discarded by a guard. The news was all Nazi propaganda as in *The Camp*, although it was the financial news on the City pages which seriously depressed George and myself. The value of the pound on the international money markets had fallen so far that I said to George, 'Good God, the damned Yanks think Hitler is going to win this war!' Needless to say, we kept our find to ourselves, not even sharing it with Don.

Eventually a British Medical Officer was sent to Schubin from an Officers' camp. He had, of course, no medicines and no equipment, but he warned us that the drinking water from the pump was the probable source of our dysentery, as the sloping site of the camp was causing the latrine trenches to drain into the water supply. He also added, as an after-thought, that any man who ate the daily potato ration was certain to contract dysentery sooner or later. Another visitor to the camp was the representative of an American Bible Society. How the Nazis could be so foolish as to allow a national from an important neutral country to see us we could never understand. He was shocked by what he saw and, after he had handed out all the cigarettes he happened to have with him, he diffidently mentioned that he had some Bibles to distribute. He obviously feared a rebuff from his starving listeners, and was quite overcome by the immediate unanimous demand for copies. I don't doubt that he wrote a very moving account of the incident to his organisation, not realising that one of our minor privations was the complete lack of toilet paper at the latrine trenches. . .

The time came when we were officially registered as prisoners. The British Medical Officer took the opportunity to examine us as we lined up to report our rank, name and army number. George and Don were both suffering from scabies and although I slept between them, as the proud owner of the overcoat which was our only bedclothing, I was free of this scourge. We were issued with German identity discs with our prison number on them. My number was 7033, and I was glad that it came between George and Don's numbers because if we were ever split into groups by our numbers, I would be always left with one or other of them. The next day we were photographed for Nazi records, with our prison numbers chalked on a board hung round our necks. However, my intended grin of defiance looked like a very weak simper in the print, which I managed to see at a later date. The German photographer asked me my age, and commented to a guard that I looked more like a weary forty-two year-old than a young man of twenty-one.

The second issue of *The Camp* took us to task for 'the filthy condition of the British prisoners and their camps', as compared with the French and Poles; adding in parentheses that the Germans had always regarded the Poles as the 'filthiest of God's creatures'. The insulting editorial commented that many of us derived from the slums for which our country was infamous, and that we must try to cultivate some self-respect. No mention was made of facts that since falling into German hands we had had no soap, no change of clothes and no proper living quarters. Nor did they say that it was only since arriving in Germany that we had been introduced to lice for the first time in our lives, and that we were starving. It was an obvious attempt to lower our morale. We were so obsessed with thoughts of food that by now, in spite of our weakness, we found it difficult to sleep at night.

The day after this second issue of *The Camp*, a number of men returned to the Stalag from working on a nearby estate. An attempt had been made to employ them on filling trucks with sand while keeping them on the same rations as were issued in the camp. They had been sent back as useless after a few days. In spite of this they had been paid 'wages' of three marks for their work, (about 2/6 as far as we could judge). This payment was made in *Lager-geld*, which could only be spent inside a prison camp at canteens set up by the enemy. One of these institutions was set up in Schubin, in one of the old barns. Bread and artificial honey were put on sale, causing frantic longings among the starving inmates.

Two days later 100 men were named to leave camp next day, and it was with mixed feelings that our trio found our names were on the list.

We knew we were far too weak to work, but welcomed any chance to get away from Schubin. Then came one of the most dramatic moments of my life. Don produced an unopened tin of English tobacco which he had been secretly hoarding which could have made him one of the richest men in the camp had he kept it to himself. He gave this treasure to George to sell as he was the business man of our combine. A few of the men who had received wages clubbed together and paid five marks for it. Immediately we went to the German canteen and purchased five loaves of rye bread and three blocks of the substitute honey. The German who sold the food to us, warned us not to eat too much at once, as on the previous day a starving prisoner had died after gorging himself on three new loaves at one sitting; he had sold his boots and overcoat to buy them.

The men who had purchased Don's tobacco set up in business as cigarette makers. They bought some German cigarette papers at the canteen and made seventy-five 'fags', which they sold at ten pfennigs each. They made a profit of nearly fifty per cent on the deal. With their profit they purchased German tobacco and more cigarette papers, plus a supply of bread and ersatz honey for themselves. Strangely enough these profiteers were not at all resented by their needy comrades, indeed they were rather admired, and the cigarette-starved even looked on them as public benefactors.

The day we left Schubin some amazing bets were made concerning the duration of the war. One man bet another that Britain would win by Christmas 1940, that was within the next five months! If victory came within that period the loser was to pay the winner £100, but, if the war continued, the other man was to pay £1 for every week it lasted after Christmas. It was typical that no mention was made of the possibility of a German victory. I managed to have a few words with the man who backed his belief in 'Victory by Christmas', agreeing that we would win, but pointing out that it would take longer than a few weeks to achieve. He looked around to make sure that nobody could hear us and said, 'Look, I can't lose. If conditions remain like this, and the war is still going on at Christmas, the other chap will have starved to death and won't be able to collect his winnings anyway.' After a pause he added, 'But, if he is alive it's likely I won't be!' Later that day I met a rather more optimistic prisoner, a man in the Black Watch with some unfamiliar ribbon on his uniform where medal ribbons are usually worn. As they were obviously not medal ribbons, I asked him 'What are those, Jock?' He replied that they were the colours of the original Tank Corps in which his father had served in the 1914-18 war. Pointing to the brown, red and green ribbons in turn he explained 'Through the mud, through the blood, to the green fields beyond'.

7

Konin

The time for our departure arrived. We paraded with our few possessions and shuffled to the station where once more we got into some cattle trucks. This time there were only 30 men in each truck instead of the usual 50, so the conditions were not nearly as bad as during our previous journey, although the physical and mental state of each prisoner was far worse.

We went west to Posen and then south-east to Konin, where we arrived late that afternoon. As we stiffly climbed out of the trucks at the railway station I realised with a shock how ragged, thin and filthy we were compared with the civilians. It was a most humiliating experience. We were herded into a small field outside the town where a lorry transported 20 prisoners at a time to our unknown destination. The rest of us sat in the field and played with a little Dachshund puppy who ran excitedly among us. From where I sat I could read a gaudy cinema poster announcing a crime film, which bore the question 'How did the Polish woman get the German police revolver?' In small type at the bottom the poster carried the slogan 'Jews not admitted'. We watched the trains go in and out of the station, noticing that each had a single dilapidated coach on the end labelled 'For Poles'. Obviously Poles were regarded as a race of lower class beings by the Germans.

In the dusk the last 20 of us boarded the lorry with the remaining guards. It was quite dark before we reached our destination which was an isolated farmhouse in the middle of a bleak moor. During the journey we were depressed to notice that there was no attempt to black-out lights, clearly proving to us that the Germans in this area had no fear of air-raids. At the farm our guards were greeted by another German soldier, who beckoned Don, George, another man and myself to follow him, while the rest of the party moved off into the darkness. We were led into the farm kitchen which was poorly lit by a single oil lamp under which a man was standing. He was well over six feet tall, of athletic build, with great wide shoulders and a good-humoured grin. He wore a black peaked cap with a skull and crossbones on it as a badge, a black uniform, a khaki shirt, a black tie and top-boots that gleamed in the flickering lamp-light. He was armed with a revolver and on his left arm he wore a red band. This arm-band bore a white circle in which was a black swastika.

'Who d'you think he is?' whispered George to me.

'A member of the SS 'I replied, 'the brown shirts denote ordinary Party members, while khaki shirts, like this one, shows the wearer is a full-time Nazi and as such he has to be a perfect physical specimen. Hitler's personal bodyguard of SS men.' This SS man was only a Sturmmann, the lowest rank in the SS, but, such was the fear in which this organisation was held, that he was always treated with the respect due to an officer both by other German soldiers and by civilians alike. We observed a man and woman standing in the shadows on the other side of the room. 'I wonder who they are?' said Don.

'Poles I expect', answered George, a little uncertainly. The SS man turned to us, and said in English, 'Yes, yes, you are quite right, they are Poles and you must begin to understand the Polish question'. He beckoned the couple into the centre of the room under the light and said derisively, 'Look at these people! They are Poles, a race of murderers and whores.'

Outside we were given four bags of grain to carry to the prisoners' camp. Normally, we could each have easily carried a bag in either hand, but our debilitated condition made each man stagger as his load was hoisted onto his back. We started out over the moor in single file, a guard leading, and the SS man bringing up the rear. The night was black and absolutely silent. As we followed a narrow path down a steep slope it became progressively darker and mist swirled about us, until I could only just see the dim torch carried by the German in front of me. The ground became waterlogged and marsh gas bubbled up; it was the one of the most eerie experiences of my life. Suddenly, the guard in front of me took a false step and sank up to his knees in the bog. Don and I pulled him out and without a word we marched on.

At last the path began to climb steeply and we were forced to make frequent halts as we were becoming progressively weaker. As soon as we climbed above the mist a barbed wire fence loomed up in front of us and we knew we were 'home'. Nearby a voice hailed us in German and thankfully we dumped our bags in a hut just outside the fence. We lurched into the barbed wire compound following the SS man.

An Englishman came out of the darkness to greet us and said, 'This way, you chaps', and led us into a hut so dark that it made no difference whether one's eyes were opened or closed. One of the residents of the hut guided us to four unoccupied bunks. We dumped our kit on the bunks, which were merely bare wood bases with some loose straw sprinkled on them. Somebody shouted, 'Soup up!' We all rushed outside and lined up in single file in the dark. As we slowly moved towards a German field kitchen each man was given a mess tin and a rusty spoon. Two English cooks doled out a mass of steaming barley to each of us.

'What's it like here?' I asked.

'Better than Schubin, but still pretty ropey', replied one of the cooks. Our trio returned to our hut to eat our meal, which we supplemented with one of our two remaining loaves and a block of honey substitute. Then we collapsed on our bunks.

When we awoke next morning we could see that our hut was a ramshackle affair of wood, with an earthen floor. Looking through a hole in the roof and at others in the walls, George said to me sarcastically, 'This will be grand in the Polish winter, won't it?' As he spoke Don climbed out of his bunk below looking very serious. During the night his pack, containing our last loaf and block of honey, had been stolen. We talked it over and agreed that there was not the slightest reason to suspect any one man more than another. I jumped down from the bunk and shouted for attention. I told the rest of the men what had happened and warned them to guard their property, adding 'We don't know who did it, but there are three of us and if we find out, we will kill the man'. We were so angry that I think we would have done so, too. The only clue we found though was Don's pack lying empty at the bottom of the latrine trench.

The compound of this camp contained four huts and these housed about 200 prisoners of war. Outside the barbed wire was another hut, far superior to ours, in which our guards lived. The camp stood at the fork of a wide, deep, empty canal which a British company, McAlpines, had started to construct for the Polish government before the war. Now, ironically enough, the Germans were using British prisoners to continue the work. When we arrived at Konin there were already 100 men working long hours on it. They were delighted to see us, for we were to form a second shift of workers, working from 6 am to 2 pm while they worked from 2 pm to 10 in the evening. Our shift paraded at 5 am for roll-call, and breakfasted on a mess tin of porridge, in which there was a little dab of milk. Then we marched to work, our hunger returning almost at once, but we were given nothing more to eat until we had finished our shift.

Almost at once we discovered that the work could easily be shirked. The guards took the attitude that their job was to shoot any man who attempted to escape, and beyond that they took no interest in us. We worked in gangs under civilian foremen, who were nearly all Poles and thus hostile to the Germans. They were perfectly content to let us loaf around as long as they did not get into trouble. The gangs unfortunate enough to have a German foreman had to keep working steadily. However, even these men had a fairly easy time as it was obvious that they were starving and as weak as kittens, so they were not pushed too hard. Our chief problem during working hours was the SS man, but we soon found his Achilles heel; his vanity about his strength. If, for example, one of the trucks came off the rails six of us would strain to lift

43

it back on again, but if the SS man was nearby he would wave us aside and do the job alone and then swagger off, dusting his hands.

George and I usually managed to work with a tall quiet Pole whom we nick-named 'Paddy', because of his very Irish looks. Supposedly we were meant to cut peat from the bed of the water-logged canal and stack it in neat pyramids to dry. Actually we spent most of our time leaning on our spades talking. Don got an equally easy job 'loading sand', which really meant that he rode along the lines on the empty trucks, from one end of the rail system to the other. Although we were far better off than at Schubin, hunger still dominated our lives. In addition to the morning porridge we were given soup after our shift, which sometimes contained some very odd types of meat. One day I had a piece of bone in mine with two huge yellow teeth in it! At evening roll-call a loaf of black German bread was issued between five men, together with a minute fragment of sausage or margarine, and some ersatz coffee without milk or sugar. The result of this largely liquid diet was that throughout the night we had to keep getting up to pass water. Nine visits to the latrine trench was normal, 20 not unusual.

One day I got separated from George and worked with a young Polish civilian and another prisoner who was a Scot. Like many old soldiers the Scot had a great collection of regimental and other badges fixed to his belt. Suddenly the Pole, who was looking at them with interest, pointed excitedly at one and kept repeating something incomprehensible. The cause of the excitement was a Boy Scout badge and although I could not understand him I turned to the Scot and said, 'I think he wants to know if you were ever a Scout.' The prisoner shook his head, whereupon I suddenly had an inspiration. Giving the salute by which Scouts always recognise each other, I said slowly and distinctly 'Baden-Powell, Baden-Powell'. The young Pole gave a huge grin and we gave each other the left hand-shake of the Brotherhood. After that whenever he could he would smuggle pieces of bread or sausage to me and even, on one occasion a hard-boiled egg.

In the camp one night, two men on the other shift came to ask me if I had been at the Latymer school in Edmonton. We discovered that we had attended the school together for some years, but a difference in age and the passing of the years had prevented us from recognising each other.

We were at Konin for about eight weeks in all. Conditions were still hungry and lousy but gradually improved as time passed. Our trio made a new friend, Ralph, a studious looking youth with horn-rimmed spectacles and a cultured voice. When we first met him George thought he had him all summed up so asked, 'And in which bank did you work, Ralph?' Ralph laughed, replying, 'Good Lord, old man, I drove a lorry for the local council!' Before long the four of us were christened 'the Connor Club' (Connor being Army slang for food). We agreed to meet after the war ended and celebrate our own 'Stalag Day' in London. I forget the details, but we were to meet in a milk bar in the morning and eat all day. The programme included a picnic lunch of cold chicken in Hyde Park, and was to reach a climax with dinner, which included our girl friends, at Simpson's in the Strand. Our dreams were all a far cry from our present conditions. Once, when it was raining and we were huddled together under a truck for shelter, Ralph suddenly turned to me and said, 'I will always remember this moment, Bob' and, because he remarked upon it, I too have always remembered the incident.

During our first week at Konin the Nazis provided us with a supply of paper to use at the latrine trench. I found it grimly significant that it consisted of the leaves from an ancient book printed in Hebrew. On the second week we were paid 'wages' and a canteen was opened where we were each allowed to buy one loaf of German bread and a bag of boiled sweets every fortnight. The canteen was a great boon and the Germans were obviously impressed when we asked for tooth-brushes and shaving kits to be put on sale. This request encouraged the SS man to arrange for an issue of soap and shaving sticks to be made to us. The so-called toilet soap was very heavy and dark grey in colour and it seemed to be made of clay and sand for it was quite useless. However the shaving soap proved to be quite reasonable. Prisoners of war were supposed to be given a tablet of soap every month and a shaving stick every six months, but we were lucky to get that much in a year! Later on the canteen also put note-books and pencils on sale. I still have one of these note-books containing a collection of recipes I made at the time.

During August a great event occurred; we were allowed to write home. Each prisoner was given a letter-card inscribed *Kriegsgefangenenpost* (Prisoners of War Post) and although we doubted if they would ever get to England, we wrote with care. Before writing my friends calculated the number of words they could fit in the space allowed and then composed a suitable communication. Our letters were intended to sound cheerful, although we still asked for food and clothing so desperately needed. The whole camp hoped for food and clothing parcels from home. This optimism was the strength based on information given me by an uncle of mine, that he received such a parcel while a prisoner during the war of 1914-18. Theoretically we were allowed two letter-cards and two postcards a month throughout our captivity, but the issue was erratic and very infrequent. The fact that we had written a letter led us to hope for news from home, and hereafter a favourite subject for discussion was, 'Would you rather have a letter from home or an extra soup ration?' The camp was fairly evenly divided, some men arguing logically that it would be selfish to choose the letter, as that would only relieve the immediate and personal anxiety of the prisoner, while an extra soup ration would improve his chances of surviving to see his family again.

September 3. The anniversary of the Germans' entry into Poland and of Great Britain into the war. It was celebrated vigorously by our guards, who nearly all got drunk. At this time the Germans all confidently expected to win the war within a matter of weeks. Herr Ritz, the senior German foreman, went so far as to assert that Britain could not hold out until the end of October. The simple German peasants, with whom we worked, even talked of building a bridge over the English Channel for the invasion, 'It's narrow', they argued. 'It says in the newspaper that you can see the opposite coast and that people often swim across!' The Polish workmen were correspondingly depressed. Paddy asked me one day if it was true that France had fallen, this three months after the event, thus showing us his distrust in the German news service. He seemed even more depressed when I had to admit it was true but I pointed out that Britain could beat the Nazis by herself.

One night in the middle of September, I was making one of my nocturnal visits to the latrine when I found the camp to be a hive of activity. All the men on the other shift had been roused from their beds, and were carrying heavy burdens from two carts outside the compound, closely watched by the guards.

'Good Heavens' I said to a friend at the latrine trench, 'Have they started a night shift?'

'No,' he replied, 'It's food parcels! Bloody great boxes full of food from the Red Cross!' This news was just too incredible to be true so I returned to bed and thought no more about it. Yet, it was true for next day we were given one parcel between two men!

The Connor Club congregated on my bunk to open these wonderful gifts. Each weighed about ten pounds and was 12 inches long, six inches wide, four inches deep, and tied securely with string. Don silently opened the first and we saw a layer of wood shavings. Removing these we found the shining tops of a number of tins. I pulled out the first tin, which contained margarine. The rest of the contents quickly followed, a tin each of meat loaf, powdered milk, biscuits, peas, jam, fish and M&V (meat and vegetable stew). There was also two ounces of sugar, a two ounce packet of tea, a tin of cocoa, a bag of sweets, a box of cheese, some meat stock cubes and a tablet of soap. The whole hut went mad! George and I shared one parcel and although our cheese was bad and the bag of sugar had burst, everything else was intact. We set in on the milk powder with our spoons. A man with his mouth full of biscuit shouted above the din, 'Gawd! Look at the old Connor Boys! If you don't watch 'em they'll eat the mucking shavings!' I have never seen so many hysterical men in my life, and not for the first time did I hear a prisoner say, 'Thank God for the Red Cross!'

For all British prisoners who were in captivity more than a few months, there is no doubt that the regular arrival of Red Cross parcels were a life-saver. I often wonder if the people who contributed to the Red Cross Penny-a-week Fund for these parcels ever knew what they meant to us. Not only did the parcels keep us alive but they had great propaganda value. Soon every German knew that the British were able to send their men chocolate, cocoa, coffee and many other things that were unobtainable in Germany. This must have led some of them to speculate about the British standard of living, the equipment we could give our armed forces and the resources of the British Empire.

At the end of September another event occurred to boost our morale. A few letters arrived from England. Although only six men were lucky the spirits of the whole camp were high, as we had never expected any of our mail to get through to us. For the first time we dared to hope that the letters we had written might reach home. I could imagine my letter going to Schubin to be censored and then crossing Europe to Spain. I could even imagine it going by sea to England and being censored again in London. However, there my imagination (or was it my hope?) failed. I could not believe it possible, that the piece of paper I had so recently handled, could be carried by the postman through the streets I knew so well and pushed through the letter-box to fall on the mat of my home.

The issue of one food parcel between two men each week continued throughout our stay at Konin. Thus, we had some item of Red Cross food each day in addition to the normal German rations. So, although we were unable to cook the food ourselves we did add a tin of stew or vegetables to our soup or thickly spread our bread ration with jam or margarine.

One day panic set in when a rumour circulated that Japan had entered the war against us and so we were very relieved when I managed to get hold of a Nazi newspaper, thrown away by a guard. From it we learnt that Japan had only agreed to come in if any other great power (ie America) should attack the Axis powers.

The summer was now over and we had our first fall of snow on October 1. The cold became a serious problem, as we only had the clothes in which we had been captured in mid-summer, and these were now in rags. However, the food parcels prevented us from despairing. The soap tablet in these was a great boon, for we could not only wash ourselves, but also our verminous and tattered clothing (even if we did have to go naked in the cold while it dried).

The Red Cross parcels sent our morale up so much that one man, without consulting anybody else, attempted to escape one night. The guards seemed quite unmoved by this, saying that he had been shot dead two kilometres from the camp. This may or may not have been true, for though we never saw the body or heard a shot, the guards certainly knew that a prisoner had escaped and who the man was even before they held a special roll-call. Two nights later in the early hours of the morning there were shots fired just outside the barbed wire. Two guards had seen the SS man in the dark and had mistaken him for another escaper. Although it was at point-blank range they missed him, unfortunately. Our opinion of German marksmanship went down a number of points.

In such a community as ours there were naturally men of all types.

One day a few of us were discussing literature, when I mentioned a series of works by an ex-convict which had been widely read just before war broke out. A man, who would not normally have been interested in our conversation, suddenly looked up from his bunk and shouted over to me, 'He never wrote those books with his name on 'em'. I turned round in surprise and the man added, 'He was supposed to have written 'em in prison. Well, he told the stories to a con man, who had the job of prison librarian at the time. It was the con man who wrote it down for him and made books out of 'em!'

'How do you know?' I asked curiously. The man jumped down from his bunk and walked towards the door. As he passed me he said quietly, 'I was in the next cell to him in Chelmsford Jail at the time'.

As the daylight hours grew shorter our work grew shorter, until each shift was only doing three hours work each day. This was too good to be true, so we were not surprised when one Sunday morning we were paraded, and the guards and German foremen began to pick out 100 of the worst workers for return to Schubin. Ever since we had arrived at Konin George and I had preached that any man who worked for the enemy harder than he was forced to was a traitor, so we were quite proud when we were both in the first five selected. In fact all the Connor Club were in 'the chosen hundred'.

At this parade a sensation was caused by the SS man who wore a civilian suit for the first time since we had been at the camp. He got a great cheer and asked us in stilted English what we thought of his garb. We never lost any opportunity to criticise German workmanship and materials, so the comments he received on his suit were far from complimentary. His grin grew wider and wider as he listened to us. At last he broke into laughter and said, 'It's an English suit, boys, I bought it in Manchester!'

Next day we left the camp and, with typical inefficiency, the Germans forgot to collect our messtins and spoons from us. Early on that October morning we marched into Schubin Stalag once more after an uneventful journey from Konin by cattle-truck.

8

Spitzwald

Schubin had changed considerably during the two months we had been away. It was now divided into two compounds, one for the French and one for the British. The lower one, containing the now-completed barracks, in which we had previously lived, was now being inhabited by French officers. The upper compound still had no buildings and although there was snow on the ground, we were housed in huge tents. Our bedding consisted of damp straw strewn on the bare earth although we were each given a tattered German army blanket.

The British compound was full of men who had returned from working parties and we were soon exchanging experiences. On one work party two men had attempted to escape but had been caught. Having been returned to their camp they had been told to prepare to return to Schubin for punishment, and had left the working party with a German NCO as escort. Within five minutes the guard had returned smiling to his camp to report that both prisoners had tried to escape again, and he had shot them both dead. Later on the two bodies were dragged into the camp and left near the latrine trench for a fortnight, as a warning to the other men.

Another would-be escaper told his story. When he had been recaptured the German in charge had paraded the prisoners and told them that because they had not informed him of the planned escape, they would receive no food for two days. Then he called the escaper from the ranks and repeatedly slashed him across the face with a stick in an hysterical fury, while the guards faced the other prisoners with loaded rifles, with orders to shoot the first man who moved. When the escaper had twice fallen to the ground and his face was a gory mess the exhausted German turned to the senior British NCO and ordered him to continue the punishment. The Englishman, with a rifle still aimed at his stomach, refused and demanded an interview with a German officer. This sobered the NCO somewhat and he dismissed the parade. One of the German guards, a Private, later went into the prisoners' sleeping quarters and confessed that he was ashamed by what had happened and would report the matter to the German company headquarters. Two days later the German NCO was replaced.

Some other men had been on a large work party near a Polish prisoner camp. When they arrived, the Poles saw what a bad state they were in, and started to throw packs of cigarettes and slices of bread over the barbed wire to them. To get these gifts over successfully they had wrapped the gifts up in newspaper weighed with a stone or piece of brick. The Nazi local paper had reported this under the headline 'Polish prisoners stone British'. One day the men on the same working party were paraded and all those needing underclothes were told to raise their right hands. As soon as they did so they were photographed and the picture was published with the caption, 'British prisoners learn to "Heil Hitler"!'

On arriving at the camp we had received a half-parcel issue and we found that the French officers, who had seemed very well-off in most respects, were very anxious to exchange bread and other things for tins of Red Cross food. The exchange was done in the latrine block (for the trenches had now been replaced by a brick building, one end for the British and the other end for the French). This rendezvous was nick-named the 'Stock Exchange', and a great deal of bartering went on over the partition which divided the block half. During these exchanges some Englishmen carefully removed the labels from their tins of peas and replaced them with meat loaf labels, and sold them as such to the French. These gentlemen were quite hurt when George warned the French of the swindle and advised them to inspect the contents of each tin before accepting it.

In the afternoon of our arrival the enemy issued clothing to us, our first since capture. I received a cotton vest and pants, two *Füsslapen* (or foot rags, which were standard peasants' garb in Poland) with which to wrap my feet and a huge pair of wooden clogs. In addition to these I was given an ornate Polish postman's hat!

After a miserable cold night in the tent, 15 names were called out at morning roll-call for a working party. The last two names called out were George and myself. We were sorry to be parted from Ralph but to lose Don, with whom we had been through so much, was a tragedy. We were not granted much time for farwells and, after a hasty agreement to get together again whenever possible and to meet 'soon' in London, we left the Stalag.

The journey from Schubin was a great novelty as we travelled in third-class compartments of an ordinary passenger train (our party consisting of only 15 prisoners and three guards). Although the seats were only of varnished white-wood, it seemed luxurious after our recent mode of travel in the cattle trucks. Our only regret was that the guards would allow no civilians in our compartment, for we had looked forward to infecting them with their own German lice!

The snow had cleared that day and so the Polish countryside looked flat and uninteresting. Throughout the journey the guards were quite worried for they had strict instructions from their NCO, nicknamed 'Dicker' (or 'Fatty' in English), to bring an English interpreter back from the Stalag. The authorities at Schubin had laughed at the request, saying that German-speaking Englishmen were far too rare to be squandered on working parties of only 100 men. I was so amused by this that I determined to continue in my concealment of my ability to speak their language.

At last after a long slow journey we arrived at a station named Orlaho, a wayside halt in open country from where we marched ten kilometres to our destination, the village of Spitzwald. We arrived there at midnight and were met by a fat German NCO. Questioning the guards he started to curse them for not having brought an interpreter back with them. He regarded us with great disfavour and jerked his thumb to direct us to go into a large building in the main street of the village. The building had a barbed wire fence round it about four feet from its walls. In fact, it had been the church hall and in the darkness it seemed to be crammed full of British prisoners. There were some 85 prisoners in the hall and they all crowded about us seeking friends. As soon as it was discovered that we had no tobacco, packets of Polish cigarettes were handed round to those who wanted a smoke. The British cooks had known that we were expected and had waited up to have some German soup ready for us, which was very welcome indeed. Suddenly, a man pushed through the crowd and asked 'Who is the chap from Enfield?' I made myself known and asked where he lived.

'D'you know Ladysmith Road?' he asked and when I said I lived at 119 he gasped, 'Good Heavens, I live at number 115!' It seemed that his wife had moved there since I had joined the army, and as he had only been there on leave, we had never actually met before. 'My name's MacKenzie', he told me, 'and there's another Enfield man here as well. Eddie Fox who lives in Willow Road.'

The prisoners started going back to bed now the excitement was over. Some of them slept in other small rooms in the building but most of them lived and slept in the main hall itself. In the darkness we managed to discern that along one side of the hall two huge wooden 'shelves' had been erected. Some 20 prisoners slept on the first shelf, and we were directed to get up a rickety ladder to the upper one. Palliasses filled with straw were all ready for us and there were three quite good blankets on each. Thinking that things could be far worse we quickly fell asleep, but we were not allowed to sleep for long. Suddenly I woke up as the shelf started to collapse. The men near the ladder scrambled down as quickly as possible while George and I remained where we were to throw down the palliasses, personal kit and blankets. We all finished the night sleeping on the floor. Thankfully the next day two Polish carpenters reinforced the shelves so we had no more trouble.

When daylight finally came we took our bearings. At one end of the hall there was a platform while in the body of the hall were four trestle tables and forms as well as a cast-iron stove. This stove had a long flue that ran the length of the hall and disappeared through a hole in the wall. There was an apparently unlimited supply of coal and during the recent cold spell the stove had been kept alight day and night, so the bored prisoners had conducted experiments to see how much of the iron chimney could be made red hot.

Within the hall the men were organised into groups of five, each group sharing a loaf of bread each day. As newcomers we were absorbed into the community as groups 18, 19 and 20, and were told that we could share the use of table number four with the existing groups 16 and 17. The initial supply of Red Cross parcels for this work party had been exhausted the week before, and the men were very disappointed that none had been sent from Schubin with us. However, the fact that there were parcels at the Stalag was reassuring, so we all hoped for a delivery in the near future. As usual the men had been regularly paid for their work, at the standard rate of 70 pfennigs a day although they were not able to buy anything with their money except Polish cigarettes, and these only at rare intervals.

On our first morning at Spitzwald we were sent out to work. The church hall in which we lived stood next to a farm yard beyond which was the house of the Nazi Bürgermeister of the village, who was a drinking companion of 'Dicker' (the German NCO in charge of our party). Coming out of the barbed wire gate we stepped into the main street of the village, facing a large house in which our guards lived. Turning left down the street we marched passed a huge Catholic church standing at the village crossroads. It was a fine modern building and in sharp contrast to the hovels in which the villagers lived. It certainly symbolised to us the position of the church in pre-war Poland. Continuing our march to work we passed a row of dilapidated terrace houses and then some cottages. Whenever we passed a pretty Polish girl always came to the window of one of these cottages to smile to us, although she dared not wave. Passing a small schnapps factory which smelt continually of rotten potatoes, we found ourselves outside the village and turned left over a field towards the river. This was the river Orlah. Our task was to build up great banks of earth on either side to prevent it from flooding when the winter snow began to thaw.

The weather had now much improved, with dry crisp days and long hours of autumn sunshine. We worked with Polish labourers under the direction of the sensitive-looking Polish foreman, but with our German guards in constant attendance. I quickly established friendly relations with the Poles, who all spoke German, and I protested to the foreman that far too much work was being done to help the Nazis. He agreed that the prisoners should do as little as possible, but assured me that the work was useless anyway as any banks we built would be swept away within five minutes of the spring thaw setting in.

The British prisoners worked in pairs, one man filling a wheel barrow with sand and another pushing it up a series of planks to the top of the bank. To enliven the task each pair of men would change places every hour and we became expert at delaying tactics. After MacKenzie had filled a barrow, we stood talking for an hour before he gave me the spade. Then we stood by the full barrow for another hour before we changed places again and I at last pushed the barrow up the planks. Thus, one barrowload would take us three hours to fill, wheel up the bank and empty!

One of the most interesting men on the party was nicknamed 'The Pterodactyl'. A bank clerk in civilian life, he had an appalling taste for sensational science fiction. This was coupled with such an amazingly retentive memory that he could recall every character and incident in all the books he had ever read. As we worked he would tell us these epics in the first person. Usually they were about life at the centre of the earth, on another planet or in the distant past or future. A pterodactyl, or other dinosaurs, always seemed to be featured in these stories, hence his nick-name. One day a man, who was not in our clique, said to me naively, 'Ere, your blokes don't believe all those stories old Carter tells you about having been to the moon, do you?'

After a time I got quite friendly with two of the Poles, Jan and Albin. They told me the terrible story of 'Blood Sunday' in the nearby town of Bromberg which had occurred soon after the German army had occupied the place. The German minority had shown the Nazis round the town and had denounced thousands of their Polish neighbours to the Nazis. At least 10,000 people had been shot out of hand, two thousand of whom had been murdered en masse outside the cathedral. Naturally Jan spoke bitterly about the incident and swore 'When the day comes we will know what to do'.

There was a law in Nazi Poland that whenever a Pole passed a German soldier, whatever the latter's rank, the Pole must step off the path and remove his hat. On one occasion our foreman failed to comply with this law. The following Sunday, when everybody was coming out of church, 20 German soliders were posted at intervals along the main street of the village and he had to walk up and down 30 times taking off his hat to each of them. 'Christ' said the Pterodactyl when I translated this news to him, 'If the Nazis ever got to England I suppose that could happen to our fathers, Bob.' On another day I commented to Albin that he spoke very good German and he told me that before the First World War he had been a German citizen and had served with the German army on the Western Front. When I said that he could have been facing my father, he replied that I must tell my father when I got home that he, and thousands of Poles like him, had never fired accurately at any target when ordered to shoot at the Allied trenches.

At Spitzwald we quickly got to know our German guards very well. They were dominated by their NCO, who was surprisingly popular with us. He was an old soldier with medal ribbons from the First World

War and he treated his own men with contempt. He made no attempt to disguise the fact that he overcharged us for the cigarettes he sold us. Ingenuously, he explained how his army pay did not nearly cover the cost of his schnapps, so he had to supplement his income somehow. Undoubtedly he was a rogue, but at least he was a good humoured one and we knew where we were with him. He was vastly more popular with us than the German NCO who was in charge at Konin. He had been a dark introspective sadist who, when drunk, had shot dead his pet dog.

Another guard who was very popular as a figure of fun for us was nick-named 'Stupid' (which, we told him, was the English word meaning 'soliderly'). Whenever a new guard was sent to Spitzwald Stupid would ask him how long he had been in the army and, if the new man said that he had served three weeks, Stupid would beam at him and say smugly, 'I've been in seven', and be as proud as Punch for the rest of the day. He always called me Robert because he thought I should be proud of having a 'real German name', and having found out that I came from London he told me that he and his wife would be going there on holiday next summer, after Hitler had won the war. They planned to go with the Nazi *Kraft durch Freude* (Strength through Joy) organisation, but he wondered if it would be 'worthwhile' as London had been reduced to a heap of ashes by the German air raids.

The guard we liked least of all was called 'Schubiner', for he was always telling us that he would have any man he did not like sent back to Schubin for punishment. He took a particular dislike to George, who had given him his nick-name, but it was so suitable that soon all the other guards were using it too, including Dicker. Dicker also shared the secret of the real meaning of Stupid's name, and delighted in using it and seeing the little man glow with pride.

One day in November a German Medical Officer paid us a visit. He marked nine men as unfit to work and said that we must all be sent to Schubin for delousing, for the necessary equipment had now been installed there. He also gave the men who were still passing water 20 times a night some pills to take, but warned them to use as few as possible. This man spoke enough English to make himself understood but kept introducing French and Polish words into his conversation under the impression, I assume, that non-Germans could understand all non-German languages!

On November 10 we marched to the station for our delousing trip to Schubin. Dicker warned us to take all our kit with us as the building was to be fumigated while we were away. Schubiner was the joyous bringer of bad news as told George that he was to be left behind at the Stalag with the sick men because he was such a bad worker, while little Stupid went nearly mad with pride at being seen in public in charge of prisoners. We arrived at Schubin on the 11th and as we entered we were amazed to see a man wearing a Flanders Poppy in his hat. He must have had it since the Armistice Day in England the year before. We were marched directly to the delouser, where our clothing and belongings were 'baked', and where we had the luxury of hot water showers. When we had finished we were joined by ten new men, who were to return with us to replace George and the nine sick men who were to remain at Schubin. One of these new men, named Jefferies, was an official interpreter. It so happened that one of the sick men had a friend with us who let it be known that he would rather face the hardships of life at Schubin and remain with his 'mucker' than return to the working party with us. Immediately George arranged to change places with this man at the very moment we were marched out of the Stalag. It was at the station that Schubiner suddenly saw George getting into our cattle-truck. At once he ran yelling to Dicker that *Der Fauler* (The Lazy One) was still in the party. Dicker took no interest whatever in the matter. It was obvious that his only concern in life was to get himself, his guards and his prisoners out of Schubin and the sight of his superiors as quickly as possible. Schubiner foolishly persisted in trying to arouse the interest of the Unteroffizier by shouting excitedly at him. Finally Dicker lost his temper and shouted such personal insults at the guard that he was promptly reduced to a shaking and silent heap!

On our return to Spitzwald we were delighted to find that all the lice in the hall had been efficiently exterminated, and we were at last free of those degrading parasites. Not only this, but we learnt that two hundred Red Cross parcels had arrived for us at the station. This meant there would be enough for a half parcel per week for each man until the middle of December. At once Dicker offered to hire a horse and cart from a Pole to transport all the parcels from the station for us. It would only cost 50 marks. Dicker had a decided twinkle in his eye when he made this offer, and we knew that most of the money would go down his throat in the form of schnapps, but we accepted his price without hesitation.

Our life at Spitzwald continued without much change. The first letters from England began to arrive in twos and threes, but all the Connor Club were unlucky. One man, Stephenson of the King's Royal Rifle Corps, was the recipient of over half the letters that arrived. It soon became widely known that his girl friend's name was Winnie, and every time any letters arrived the new interpreter who distributed them would repeatedly shout 'Steve from Winnie!' After he had received about 20 letters, and the rest of us had not had any, feelings began to run so high that I really think Stephenson would rather not have had any mail at all. The German censors often wrote personal comments on the bottom of these early letters, 'She sounds a nice girl', or 'You are a lucky young man', or more cynically, 'Do not believe all that a woman writes'. One man's brother stupidly gave detailed war news and George and I were seriously depressed until we saw that the German censor had let it all through untouched, only writing at the bottom, 'What a lot of idiotic lies!' Later we were told that most of the letters that arrived at Schubin at this period did not have our prisoner-of-war numbers on them. Without these numbers it was almost impossible for the Stalag authorities to locate us on our various working parties and, as a result, hundreds of thousands of letters were burnt at Schubin. Fortunately for Stephenson his friend was employed in dealing with the mail and had taken the trouble to find out that Steve was at Spitzwald and so sorted out his letters for delivery.

One morning we awoke to find deep snow everywhere. We paraded for work as usual and it was so cold somebody commented, 'Christ! Even the Connor Club will have to do a bit of work to stop freezing to death today!' When we arrived on the job we had only just started our labours when one man broke his pick on the frozen earth, so we started to work with such fury that within a few minutes the guards and workmen were surrounded with prisoners holding damaged tools for their inspection. As the guards themselves were as reluctant as we were to stand about in the cold Polish winter they grasped the opportunity to march us back to camp. We entered the hall, sat down and looked at each other. What would happen now? Dicker soon came in and told us, through Jefferies, that he had received telephone instructions that we were not to be sent out to work until he considered we could do so without breaking our tools. This was greeted with a huge cheer and we settled down to one of the strangest periods of captivity.

Imagine 100 men, hungry and badly clothed, locked up in the church hall of a remote Polish village with very few books, no newspapers, radio, games or any other method of recreation for 13 weeks. The first thing we did was to go to bed for, although the stove was kept roaring day and night, it was far too small to heat the hall completely. It was definitely warmer in bed and so during the first week we got up only for the morning and evening roll-calls, and our midday soup.

The reading matter in the hall was limited, to say the least. One Roman Catholic Missal and a complete file to date of *The Camp* was our complete library. I borrowed the Missal and read it through twice. When I returned it to its owner he looked expectant but I pointedly made no comment, apart from thanking him. George and I studied the file of the Nazi propaganda sheet with interest, having seen only the first two issues. The progress of the Italians in North Africa was a leading topic in the early numbers but, we noted with satisfaction, that it had been dropped in the later issues. The air-raids on Britain replaced the Italian news as the leading front-page story each week. We learnt that 'Reichsmarschal Goering himself is directing operations against London from Northern France', and that 'Our bombers visit the capital of the British Empire with the monotonous regularity of an air mail service'. The German propaganda was rather too evident to us but, on the whole, it was very reasonable too. We were told that 'The German people have nothing but admiration for the gallant young men of the

56

Royal Air Force, who so fruitlessly attempt to defend their country against overwhelming odds, but we deeply regret that such valuable Nordic blood should be spilt in the service of Jewish International Finance'. There were many photographs of Blitz damage to London but we dismissed them as fakes. Pictures which looked genuine some men claimed to recognise: 'Why, the *Daily Express* published that picture years ago when there was a big fire in Stratford!' In fact, not one man on the working party believed in the Blitz at this period, and our deep conviction even caused some of the guards to become doubtful about what they read. As George said while reading of a German fighter strafing a convoy of lorries near Norwich, 'It stands to reason that it can't be true'.

I am rather reluctant to report that there was a series of humorous short stories in these early numbers of *The Camp* attributed by that periodical to 'Pee Gee Wodehouse'. Now Mr Wodehouse, as he was then, was a civilian internee in German hands and had, we knew, been broadcasting to America on behalf of the enemy. So British prisoners assumed that he had also written these stories, all of which had anti-Jewish incidents in them. They also assumed that he had adopted this unusual form of his name so that he could easily deny authorship if Britain should eventually win the war. I must admit that a small minority of my friends, who were devotees of the Master, hotly protested that Wodehouse could not be anti-Semitic. I have to say that I was with the majority, the plots, style and characterisation of these stories seemed pure Wodehouse to me.

By the middle of December our stock of food parcels had been exhausted, so now we had to continue to keep in bed in order not to use up too much energy and thus make ourselves more hungry. It was at this stage that the Pterodactyl came into his own. He started us composing crossword puzzles on any scrap of paper we could find. I remember causing some bad feeling, because in one of my clues I gave 'Big Ben?' for the three-letter combination HUR. Later, however, he really saved our sanity by producing a home-made set of Monopoly. He found a piece of plywood of suitable size for the board, made the various cards from pieces of Red Cross parcel boxes and the 'money' from Polish cigarette cartons. He made the whole set from memory without any help and later, when we could check it, we found there were only two minor errors in the whole set! Six men could play this game at a time, and the demand was so great that a strict rota was kept. As time meant nothing to us the game was in use 24 hours a day, and we all grew to be real experts. On average a game took three hours to play, and if it ended, say, at three o'clock in the morning the 'school' would break up and call in the next six men on the list before retiring to bed. These six new men would probably finish their session by morning roll-call, and would return to bed as the next six men took over. We could, therefore, hope for a game of Monopoly every three days. As we did not have enough material for another set of Monopoly a game called 'L'Attaque' was made from odds and ends, but only two men at a time could play this and it lasted for only about an hour.

Christmas came and went without much comment or fuss. George and I had hoarded a table jelly from our last parcel and ate it after our German soup for our Christmas dinner dessert. We spoke very little during this festive occasion, as everybody was thinking of home and of Christmasses past. The week after Christmas some Red Cross food arrived in the form of a supply of 'Bulk food' from the Swiss Red Cross (as the British Red Cross parcels had not got through). The chief items in these parcels were huge tins of quince jam and packets of 'Ovosport', little solid blocks of Ovaltine. The arrival of this unexpected food transformed us, and we arranged our first concert to celebrate the New Year, 1941. The concert was a great success. Having a stage at the end of the hall was a wonderful help and having little else to do we put all our ingenuity into the show. One of the small rooms off the main hall called itself the 'Loony Room', and produced a male voice choir of surprising excellence. We had short plays, soloists and George and I sang duets. The only bad moment was when the interpreter was giving his celebrated impersonation of Hitler addressing a Party rally and Dicker suddenly walked on the stage. However, to our relief he was quite drunk and only informed us that he hated the British Army, the German Army and, in fact, all armies and he hoped we would all be civilians by the end of the coming year. The whole affair concluded with MacKenzie on the stage leading the singing of 'Auld Lang Syne' at midnight.

Living under such conditions we all got to know each other very well, far too well in some cases and inevitably there were a number of quarrels and fights. In spite of being individualistic there was a corporate spirit that helped to sustain our morale and on the whole tempers were very even. Jefferies, for example, the interpreter, was an interesting fellow. Physically he was immensely strong, was highly intelligent and had a dynamic personality. Later on he managed to escape and worked with the underground movement in Poland. After a while he married a Polish girl and flew to England on numerous occasions, returning each time to Poland to carry on his mission.

One of the men, Richard, was quite a spinner of tales. When he discovered that I was a librarian in civilian life he casually remarked that his own small personal library contained some 23,000 books. He qualified this by explaining that if ever he happened to say that he knew very little about a subject to his step-father, this benevolent gentleman would make no comment, but would order the ten best books on the topic. Thus, in this way he acquired his collection. His story to another man, who was a keen swimmer, was that his girl friend was the British Empire Champion for the breast stroke, modestly adding that he was not *so* good himself as he was *only* Southern Counties Junior Champion in free style. After he had told somebody else that his cat had 320 kittens in ten years, Jefferies sacrificed his only notebook to collect Richard's yarns under the title, 'The Cat Bag'. This work was classified under such headings as 'His Family' ('My father was British Cement, old man, my step-father is British Steel'), 'His Travels' ('I once sailed a small boat from China to Australia single-handed for a bet'), and 'His Hobbies' ('They had to knock down one side of our house to take out the light aeroplane I had built in my bedroom'). I found that a few minutes in the presence of his massive ego was quite a tonic!

One morning early in January the cry 'Mail up' was heard but I remained sitting at the table in the Loony Room, not wishing to be disappointed yet again. Suddenly somebody put his hand on the back of my head and pushed it down until my nose touched the table. I struggled up with a curse, to face Dicker who had a great grin on his face. 'Get in the hall, Gayler', he said in German, 'there are two for you!' I stared at him and then rushed madly into the hall, just as Jefferies was shouting out, 'Gayler from. . .' (turning over the letters to see the sender's name, as was his custom) 'Miss D. M. Dewsall'. I grabbed the two letters and took them to my bed to read. Dorothy had seen my father in the street, so he was alive and well as she was too. She had been to the cinema, so it 'stood to reason' that the air-raids could not be really serious. She had been to a dance, and had danced with a Free French Naval Officer. I stared unseeing to the hall below my bunk-shelf. I must escape. Dorothy was very good at French! Mentally I examined my kit. Nothing could be done about my jacket or trousers which were in rags. My overcoat was still in quite good condition, but it was my footwear that gave me most cause for worry. I had no socks although I had managed fairly well with the German 'foot rags' up to now but even these were showing signs of wear. My boots, which were fairly new when captured, were in a poor state by now and I knew that I dare not wear them much more. I would have to start wearing my wooden clogs lined with straw so as to save my boots and foot rags for escape.

For two days I actually went off my food, the first time I had not felt hungry since June. Now I had something more important to think about. At this point Jefferies called a public meeting on the subject of escape. Everybody attended and during the meeting many interesting and practical ideas were presented. It was generally agreed that any attempt to pass as a German was impossible — we were too haggard, had no papers, no civilian clothes, no money (apart from the *Lager-Geld* in which we were paid), and no outside contacts. To hike by night seemed to be the best bet, but this limited the escaping season to the summer months when the weather was good, the crops high enough to hide in and when one could live off the land. To steal a bicycle was suggested as a better form of locomotion but limited one to travel by road. Polish railwaymen were suggested as possible contacts for getting to Russia, if one could hide under the coal on their engines. The meeting was not really a very profitable one, but at least it started everybody thinking about escape and we all promised to co-operate in outwitting the enemy. Ultimately, however, the meeting depressed me, for now I realised that it would be three months before I could make any attempt at escape.

Dorothy's letters were in reply to the one I had written her from Konin in August. She had previously sent over 20 letters, none of which had ever arrived, but from this time on mail came through at irregular intervals. Dorothy was very concerned because she couldn't send the food for which I had asked, but she hoped that we were getting Red Cross supplies. She added that we would be sent clothing parcels as soon as the Red Cross could arrange it.

Life dragged on. One night Schubiner came into the hall drunk and fired a shot through the roof. On another occasion it was Dicker's turn to get intoxicated. He got the idea into his head that somebody had escaped and ordered a roll-call to be held in the middle of the night and during a snow storm. The shivering guards, as scared as we were, were instructed to 'shoot to kill' if anybody moved, and Dicker proceeded to stagger along the line counting us and arriving at impossible totals. Then he imagined that someone in the ranks was laughing at him (the last thing that any of us felt like doing), and he burst into tears.

'Don't laugh at me, boys', he sobbed, 'I'm not like this collection of fools behind me' (pointing to his guards). 'I'm a front-line soldier like you. Look at my medal ribbons. I fought your brave fathers in the last war.' And, crying like a baby, he wandered off through the snow down the deserted village street. On roll-call next morning he joked uncomfortably about his lapse of conduct and said, 'I bet I had some of you worried last night, if I did half the things Stupid tells me I did!'

In the middle of January we were taken out to clear a deep snow-drift on the Spitzwald-Orlaho road. We were amazed to find a village so deep in snow. It emphasized to me that escape in such weather was obviously out of the question. While we were clearing the snow an ancient horse-drawn cab came along the road. As it passed I peered inside and saw an old priest sitting well back in his seat with one hand raised and his lips moving. He was blessing us. Later a young Pole passed on his bicycle, and grinned at us but unfortunately he ignored Schubiner who shouted to another guard to stop the boy. Schubiner ran up to the boy shouting, 'Why didn't you take you hat off to me, you Polish swine. I'll teach you to respect the German uniform!' He tore the rifle from his shoulder as if to strike the lad but all we prisoners let out a roar of protest and held our spades as if they were rifles with bayonets fixed. We must have looked as if we were going to charge for Schubiner quickly turned on his heel and hurried away. We returned to our snow clearing muttering together about German bullies.

Later that same week another guard had a difference of opinion with

George and myself and for our punishment we found ourselves locked in the cellar beneath the German billets for twelve hours. It was a stark stone place and bitterly cold in the middle of the Polish winter. There was a little straw on the floor and only a small grating near the ceiling to light our cell. We found that this grating was at pavement level and, by standing on tip toe with our heads on one side, we could see out into the village street. We had not been in the place more than ten minutes when there was a slight noise at the grating and a medicine bottle full of warm milk was passed through! The news had reached the Poles that two Englishmen were being punished and all day long cigarettes, food and milk were smuggled to us. The Polish schoolboys made a house-to-house collection for us round the village. Only those who have lived in German-occupied Poland can fully appreciate the risk these boys took in passing their gifts to us under the noses of the Nazi soldiers, and how ill their parents could afford the goods they sent. Our great problem, of course, was how to get the items we could not immediately consume to our friends. In the end, I kicked on the door of the cellar until the guard came and I asked him to let us have a blanket each, which was surprisingly granted. That night when we were released we were able to smuggle out masses of things in our blankets. Our booty amazed our friends who had imagined we would be starving and had got up to heat up some soup they have saved for us from their midday rations. After our success the competition was keen to be put in the cellar. However, Dicker was intelligent enough to catch on quickly to this scam and for future punishment he made offenders empty the latrine trench, a really terrible job.

In February some personal parcels arrived, most of which contained books. Stephenson's disgust on receiving a prayer book was quite comical. 'It's not as if I had any tobacco and could use the paper for making fags!' The hero of the tall stories featured in the 'Cat-Bag' was sent a pack of playing cards with a picture of a horse on the back. 'Because my uncle is the most famous of Irish horse breeders', he explained to us, but we forgave him his lies as his cards were such an asset to our recreation. Some men had notices from the German authorities of the Stalag saying that parcels of Penguin books had arrived for them but had been destroyed because, 'This communist firm had printed disrespectful drawings of the Führer'.

One day I received a personal clothing parcel from home. Our families were permitted to send one parcel to us every three months and they contained chocolate, toilet kit and clothing in specified limited quantities. One bar of chocolate I could not resist sharing impetuously with George, but the rest I put firmly aside for use in my escape attempt. I was aware that any prisoner with a large supply of food would soon come under suspicion if the Nazis ever made a search, so I distributed my hoard among my friends. It says a lot for the loyalty of these friends that not one bar was eaten. The underclothing from the

61

parcel was a real blessing and greatly increased my comfort (as well as my chances of a successful escape), the most valued item being two pairs of socks. I allowed myself the luxury of wearing one pair with my wooden clogs but reserved the other pair for use with my boots when I made my break.

Since Jefferies had arrived I had taken less care in concealing my knowledge of German. So, when he and the senior British NCO paid a visit to Schubin (under guard) to arrange for a clothing issue for our work party, another NCO took charge and I became his interpreter. Dicker had us both over to the German billets and explained to the NCO, through me, that he had got into serious trouble because he had not reduced our rations when we stopped working. He said that he must do so now unless we would be willing to do jobs about the village, and thus qualify to remain on our present issue of food. By now the men were in the mood to do anything in order to get out of the hall for a few hours a day, especially if it meant that their food would not be reduced, so we went back to work. As the weather still made it impossible for us to be employed on the river bank, we were sent out in small parties to do some street cleaning. When we got onto the main road outside the village we were astounded by what we saw. The foreman had been right. The banks we had built so labouriously had been swept away by the river at the first thaw, and the whole countryside was flooded from horizon to horizon. Spitzwald was an island linked only by the slightly-raised main road. We were delighted at the damage wrought on our embanking.

While in the village I managed to have a few words with Jan and Albin, who were worried about the future of their children. It seemed that the enemy had replaced all the Polish schoolteachers with Nazis. The first thing these people had done was to give their new pupils a German language test, since in future all instruction was to be given in that language. Many children near the frontier understood German and so were allowed to remain at school, but those who failed the test were expelled from school at once and had to go out to work. Jan said that Polish children of seven years old were working in the fields, and they would never receive any education at all. They were destined to grow up as illiterate members of a race of slaves, while those who remained at school would be trained as little Nazis and to hate everything Polish, including their own parents.

Already I had managed to pick up a few odd words of Polish. Now, with the incentive to escape, I attempted to learn more, but found it a most difficult language. The one sentence I did learn parrot-fashion from Albin sounded like, 'Ya yest-um angelski yae-ne-atz', or, 'I am an English prisoner'. I reasoned that this would be the most useful sentence to an escaping prisoner, as it implied that one was a friend, and needed help. However, in spite of my discreet questions Jan and Albin were unable to tell me much about the present division of Poland. The river Bug was, they thought, the frontier between the Russian and German parts of the country, but how heavily it was guarded they had no idea. West of the Bug the Nazis intended to incorporate part of Poland into the German Reich, and were treating the Poles in this area as a hostile minority. The remainder of German-occupied Poland was known as the General Government area and was thought to be considered a conquered foreign country. Jan had been told that the frontier between these two areas was very heavily guarded.

A few days later I managed to speak to Jan again and found him in a state of panic. During the night the Poles living in a row of the best houses in the village had been woken up by the Nazi Bürgermeister and some fully armed SS men. The families were ordered to dress and to be outside their houses within five minutes. When this was done the men were ordered to harness their horses to their carts and the women to prepare enough food for one meal. This had been completed under the supervision of the SS so escape was impossible. The bewildered Poles were ordered into their carts, told that they were being sent to the General Government area and driven off under SS escort. Early next morning German peasant families from Romania moved into the deserted houses which naturally they found completely furnished for them, even to the clothes hanging in the wardrobes and crockery on the dressers. Jan knew that it was only a matter of time before he suffered the same fate.

As spring came the flood water began to recede and Dicker told us that we would soon be returning to our river-bank job. The day before we were due to start work I was called over to our guards billet-room to see a German Sergeant-Major (he was in charge of a number of British Prisoner of War working parties in the district and paid occasional visits to us). He grinned when I walked in and said, 'Well, Gayler, I've got some very good news for you. You are going to hate it.'

'What is it?' I asked suspiciously.

His grin grew even wider. 'I'm sending you to another working party as an interpreter!' he announced.

Before I could protest he held up his hand and continued, 'I know you will not wish to be parted from your comrades, but at the other working party they have two medical orderlies and no interpreter. Here there are two interpreters and no medical orderly, so, for the good of all prisoners I have arranged your transfer. It will be an easy time for you as interpreters do no work. You will go tomorrow morning with a guard who will exchange you for the medical orderly.'

Stunned, I returned to the hall to tell my friends the news. The thought of being parted from George was beyond comprehension and a real fear of the unknown future, which I must face alone in a community of strangers, swept over me. Practical matters had to be attended to, however, so I collected up my chocolate from my friends, and the Connor Club had quite a feast (as I was sure to be searched as I left next day, and such a quantity of food would obviously indicate that I was planning an escape).

Next morning all my friends went off to work and I was left alone in the empty hall. George and I had said very little as we parted and, without much hope, had promised to try to contact each other as soon as possible. At 11 o'clock, with all my belongings in my treasured cowhide pack I left Spitzwald with a guard. Near the church we met MacKenzie and another German returning to our billets. Mac had the German's bayonet prodding him from behind as he strolled along in a most carefree manner, although the guard was spluttering with rage. 'I'll teach this *verflüchte Engländer* who is master here!' the guard shouted to us. Of this Mac understood only one word, '*Engländer*'. He turned round and shouted in the guard's face '*Engländer* nix mate, I'm a *Schottlander*, bloody *Schottlander*, and don't forget it!' Then he smiled happily at me and said 'Don't take any notice of him, Bob, I'll be seeing you in Enfield soon!'

Above *The author's PoW identity card.*

Below *One of the vital Red Cross food parcels.*

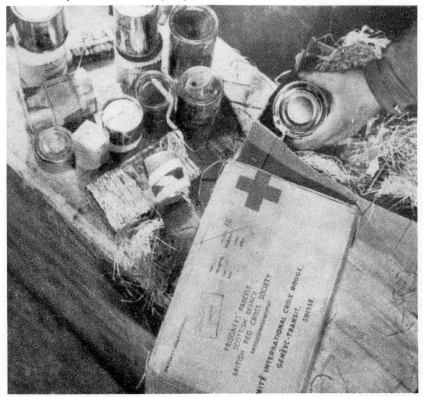

Dear Everybody,   18th August 1940

My usual good luck has seen me through a number of tight corners without even the traditional scratch. I'm unhurt, fit, with friends, and in good spirits, so please don't worry any more. I'm rather scared that worry may have upset you, so write quickly with all the news. We may receive unlimited letters and parcels, both are urgently required; the Red Cross will tell you what may & may not be sent in parcels, but I need the following badly: thick long winter underclothes, socks, soap in metal container, towel & sweater. Also any form of food, suggest chocolate, (Plain "Motoring" best, can't have too much of it), blocks of Velveeta, slab toffee, cake. Tins are opened, so please only send one of meat per parcel. Sorry to sound so greedy, but A/C Fryer will make excuses for me. I think about you all a lot & wonder how you are, is Eve in the GPO yet? I'm just longing for your first letter. I may write twice a month; please pass this letter on to Dorothy and tell her I'll write my next one to her. Again, don't worry, conditions are much better than I expected, & what Mr Dewsall calls "Bobs lough" is quite well-known in this part of the world. Love and best wishes to you all, and I'll be seeing you soon.   Bob

Robert Gayler's first letter home after capture.

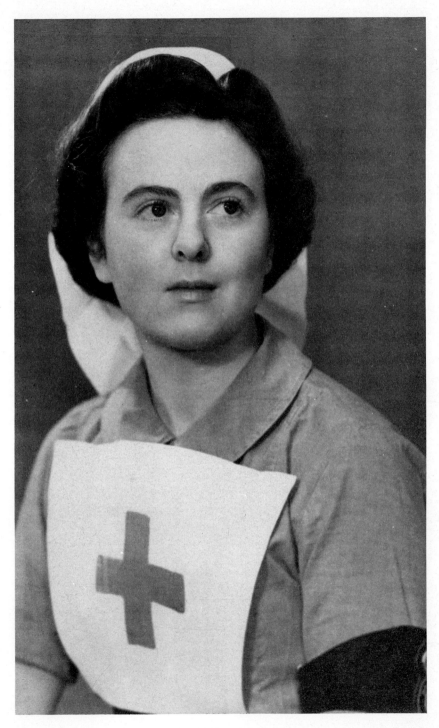

The author's later wife, Dorothy, in her wartime nurse's uniform.

Stalag roll call. Three well-known characters drawn by Len Stoppani in Lamsdorf.

9

Görschen

From Orlaho station we travelled in the third-class compartment of a
local train. I noted with satisfaction that we travelled due east for about
20 miles; 20 miles nearer Russia! Miles that I would not have to walk.
Our destination was a small town named Görschen in an agricultural
area. The guard and I descended from the train and marched down a
cobbled street and out of the town to an isolated hall, surrounded by the
too-familiar barbed wire fence. There was quite a large compound
within the wire but the sentry box outside was an unwelcome sight for
it indicated that, as at Konin and Spitzwald, there would be a guard on
duty all night. We entered the hall and reported to the guardroom that
was just inside. Adjoining the guardroom was a larger one in which the
guards lived, while the prisoners slept in the hall itself. Living in the
same building with one's guards does not appeal to a potential escaper.

In the prisoner's quarters a hundred Britons slept on loose straw
littered about the floor and as soon as I entered I was greeted by
Sergeant Jack Black, a quiet young Scot, who was the leader of the
prisoners. He had what I considered as the correct attitude about
working for the enemy, and out of his hundred men he kept ten
employed on 'non-productive' duties in the camp. I quickly established
myself with this party, holding a key post, and was soon able to sort out
many misunderstandings between the prisoners and the guards. These
men had been together since their capture for they had been wounded
and had been together in the same hospital when it fell into German
hands. The only unwounded man among them was the medical orderly,
Frank Sturrock. He was very popular with the men for he had
volunteered to remain behind with the wounded when the rest of the
hospital staff had been evacuated, just before it was taken by the
Germans. As soon as the men were convalescent they had been sent by
the Nazis to a special punishment camp high in the Alps, near the
German-Swiss frontier at Heiberg. It had been bitterly cold, the rations
atrocious and the prisoners had died like flies. One day a few men had
been talking together round a bonfire when an irresponsible guard had
thrown a hand grenade among them, killing the whole group. At

Christmas 1940 a rumour had circulated that a special meal had been prepared and Sturrock admitted to me that although he was unwounded he had nearly cried when the usual half pint of coloured water had been issued, humourously called 'soup' by the Germans. He said he had never imagined men could possibly exist in such terrible conditions. During the whole of this period the prisoners had been forced to work, many collapsing and dying while the others continued labouring.

In January the whole party had been transferred to a camp on the outskirts of Strasbourg, where conditions were the exact opposite. For a month they had good billets, much improved food and no work. The Germans let it be known that they had been sent to Heiberg 'in error'; an error that had cost many British lives. Now these men had reached Poland and were employed on road-mending and on the whole the conditions were fairly good. The week I joined them a large supply of Red Cross parcels was delivered and we enjoyed the luxury of a whole parcel each. The parcels made us almost independent of German rations, especially those of us who were not road-mending. However, for the first time the enemy insisted on each parcel being opened under their supervision and each tin of food was punctured. I suppose they feared illegal material might be sent in the tins or that food might be hoarded for escape purposes.

I quickly made some good friends on this work party. One was a Corporal in the Royal West Kents named Alexander Constantine Mineeff. This curious name had come about because his mother was Scottish and his father was an exiled Russian aristocrat. He was also cousin to the famous Rugby player Prince Obilansky. Alex was highly intelligent and the most enthusiastic soldier I have ever encountered in the British army. The military life was in his blood, his ancestors having held high ranking position in the Tsar's bodyguard for many generations. He was the youngest NCO in his regiment and probably the most efficient solider the Royal West Kents had ever known. Frank Sturrock, an insurance broker and amateur violinist of professional standard, was another companion in distress, while another new friend was Sergeant Robbins of the Cameronians, a middle-aged PT expert. The Sergeant spent many hours teaching me to box and I became quite useful with my fists, developing a degree of skill which quite surprised me. Fortunately, I have only had to use my knowledge on rare occasions but I have found it a great boost to my self-confidence.

The German guards at Görschen were quite an interesting collection. Before long I came to realise that the German soldiers given the job of guarding British prisoners of war were either physically unfit, or politically unreliable from the Nazi point of view. On one occasion I was talking politics with a guard when he asserted that we had no political liberty in Britain. He had once gone to England on holiday, but before he could land Scotland Yard men had boarded the ship with the Customs officials to tell him that he could not enter the country. I said that was quite possible, as Britain could not afford to have Nazi agents in the country with a war about to break out. He replied that this happened years ago, before Hitler had ever come to power, but, he explained innocently, 'I was Berlin staff photographer for the English newspaper *Daily Worker* (the British Communist newspaper) at the time!'

To me the most interesting German was the one who joined the party about a week after I did. His name was Walter, and he was an extreme anti-Nazi. He told me that he looked on the British democratic soldiers as his real comrades rather than his fellow guards for they were either avid Nazis or secret communists. He had been a Berlin shop-keeper before the war and, immediately upon arrival, he organised a first-class canteen for us where we could buy bread, watery beer, toilet goods and other items. Walter also had a Polish fiancée, a thing strictly forbidden under the Nazi racial laws. He told me the story of his girl-friend's father, a farmer who had fought in the Polish army during the Nazi invasion and who had returned home to his farm under the German victory. All went well for some months, and although a Nazi Bürgermeister was installed in the village, life went on normally enough. Then one day the Pole was summoned to the Nazi's office for an interview. The first thing he was asked was, 'When did you buy your farm and how much did you pay for it?' The Pole replied promptly that he had purchased it in 1927 and named the price. The Bürgermeister replied, 'How strange, you are a Pole, yet you tell the truth! You are quite right, I have all the legal records of the transaction here.' Then he held out his hand and said '10,000 marks please'. The Pole looked puzzled so the Nazi explained 'All this territory has been captured by the German armed forces and is now the property of the National-Socialist government. However, we are decent people, a thing you would not understand, and we are giving you the chance of buying the farm you occupy, so I want 10,000 marks please.' When the Pole started to protest that he had invested all he had in the farm the German waved him to silence, remarking that he knew quite well that he would be unable to pay. He instructed the farmer to move his family into one room of a house, in which the Jewish village doctor had formerly lived, and added that a German family would take over the farm that afternoon. He warned the Pole that if the new owners found as much as a single stick missing or damaged his whole family would be sent to a concentration camp. In turn I was able to tell Walter of the fate of the families in Spitzwald who had been sent to the General Government area at a moment's notice and was surprised that he did not know of this Nazi operation. He promised he would warn as many Poles as possible, so they could prepare themselves by hiding their valuables, in case the same outrage was continued by the SS in their district.

Some days later Walter came charging into our quarters livid with rage. 'D'you people call yourselves soldiers?' he shouted. I ran up to see

71

what was happening. 'For God's sake, Bob', he yelled. 'Do you know what your people have done now? They have lost Crete! Now what will Turkey do? Good Heavens! You English will let Hitler win the war, and then what will happen to us all?' Walter was a known democrat, for he declared that Communism would be as bad as National Socialism, but also felt that the British democracy, which tolerated slums and three million unemployed, was also open to criticism. I suggested that a Labour Government in Britain would show the world the way.

On another occasion Walter told me in great excitement that Rudolf Hess, Hitler's deputy, had flown to England. 'If only I was in Berlin now', he said, 'I have friends there who would be able to tell me what it all means.' After we had got to know each other well Walter asked me if I had ever thought of escaping. I replied with caution that I supposed that every prisoner had thought about it, and asked why he wanted to know. He said that if I would be prepared to put myself in his hands he would do all he could to get us both over the frontier. 'While we are inside Germany I'll be in charge and get us both through,' he said, 'but once we are in Russia it will be up to you to look after me!' Trusting him I told him to go ahead, for this was an offer I had not dreamed of even in my wildest moments. However, a week later he told me that escape to Russia was impossible. 'There is going to be trouble between Germany and Russia very soon,' he told me. 'I have found out for certain from anti-Nazi friends in the Army that there are masses of men and material on the Russian-German frontier and it is now a military area, out of bounds to all civilians. Even a mouse could not cross without being seen. Go ahead if you want to, Bob, but there is going to be war on the Russian Front before the summer is over, and I do not propose to go walking into the middle of it.'

This was bad news indeed, although at first I only half believed it. Perhaps Walter was a subtle Nazi agent sent to prevent us escaping by circulating depressing rumours. However, on thinking this over I realised that the Germans would not waste such an obviously intelligent man as Walter (if he was a Nazi) on an obscure working party of low-ranking prisoners and I concluded that he must be telling me the truth.

The weeks dragged by, and we started to break up the monotony of our routine by organising concerts, mock trials and plays in the evenings when the men returned from their work. Every morning, those of us employed in the hall cleaned, tidied, helped to prepare the German soup and patched the men's worn and ragged clothing. One morning during one of these domestic periods Walter came in and quietly said to me, 'You are to be moved west into Germany to a place called Wallstein just over the frontier in two days time, Bob. I think there is to be a movement of all British prisoners in Poland, and my guess is that this is because my "beloved Führer" is about to stab his good friend Stalin in the back.' He told me that he had had the news of our move from an anti-Nazi friend at Regimental Headquarters and that none of the other guards knew about it yet. He added that, if I still wanted to try to get to Russia, now was the time, but he seriously advised me against it. I wandered outside into our compound to think things over on my own, and soon came to the conclusion that Walter was right and that escape to the east at this juncture would be suicidal. Looking through the barbed wire I watched boys of the Hitler Youth being drilled in the next field. Their slogan was 'Youth shall be led by youth', and the sight of lads of 13 screaming abuse and orders at 12 year-olds was pretty sickening to me, so I turned away. That evening I told the other men of Walter's news so next morning at roll-call there was a feeling of anticlimax when nothing was said and the men went off to their road-mending as usual. During the day four of us were taken by a guard to the village school, to move some desks and other equipment for the pretty young school mistress. I was interested to see that in every classroom there was a picture of Hitler on the wall. In the infants' room he was bending down smiling as he was given a bunch of flowers by some small children while in another room, which I presume housed boys of about ten, he was depicted examining a model aeroplane shown to him by some youngsters. I had a quick look at a map of Europe on the wall. If the Russian frontier was out of the question I had better look to the west to Switzerland, Spain or unoccupied France. This being so, our move into Germany would be in the right direction for me so I would be wiser to wait and escape after the move.

On the following morning the Nazi NCO announced dramatically that we were to move that same day. We were, of course, quite prepared for the news, so the fellow's opinion of phlegmatic Englishmen was abundantly confirmed. He was impressed by the speed with which we got ready to depart, and within three-quarters of an hour we were at the local station and climbing into the inevitable cattle trucks. On this occasion, however, each man was carrying a bundle of belongings which he had received in parcels from home, or bought at Walter's canteen. The journey was reasonably comfortable by prisoners of war standards. The weather was wonderful and we were allowed to have the truck doors open though an armed guard was placed in each truck to prevent escapes. As we passed the German girls in the fields stopped working to wave to us, presumably thinking we were their troops, but we hoped that some of them were Poles who would recognise us as British. After travelling all day we reached Wallstein, where we were marched into a squalid and dilapidated building which had been a factory. This was our 'new' prison.

10

Wallstein

The first news to greet us on our arrival was that an Englishman had just been shot dead by a guard, for no apparent reason. The senior British Warrant Officer had demanded an interview with the German commandant to protest. After the interpreter had translated his objections the commandant had pointed to the telephone on his desk and said, 'If that phone should ring and I was ordered to have one Englishman in three shot I would carry out that order without a moment's hesitation. You are dismissed.' Next day the guard who had committed the murder was on duty as usual, although closely accompanied by two armed bodyguards.

There were hundreds of British prisoners already in this camp and there was no doubt that there was a general move of prisoners of war from Poland to the west, just as Walter had predicted. Our party was marched into an empty barn which had a cement floor on which we had to sleep with only a single tattered blanket each. Next morning we were called out on parade and after a sketchy search we were marched out of the camp with an escort of guards. We were not sorry to leave. Carrying all our wordly wealth, we passed through the dusty streets of Wallstein with the sun blazing down on us from a cloudless sky. There were pictures of Hitler and Nazi slogans everywhere, but only a few people about who took scant notice of us. I imagine that prisoners were no novelty in this district. We soon left the town behind and marched throughout the day, becoming increasingly weary and thirsty. The countryside became more heavily wooded and reminded me of Epping Forest, though few of us had much energy to admire the beauties of nature as we became more and more exhausted. To lighten their load some of the men began to throw away their less valued possessions; and still we marched on. Eventually we turned off the road down a cart track overhung by trees on either side and soon reached a group of buildings in a clearing. This was the hamlet of Rustungsmühle which was nothing more than a few cottages dominated by a water-mill. We limped into a small barbed wire compound which contained two huts and despite our weariness a mad scramble began to reserve the best bunks. Almost at once Sergeant Black and I were summoned by the German NCO in charge. He was an elderly man with twinkling eyes, and soon he had our cooks preparing a meal for us.

After we had eaten, a guard asked me to take our medical orderly to see an old woman who was ill. Frank Sturrock and I were directed to a house outside our compound. The patient turned out to be an old Polish peasant who was suffering from very high blood pressure. Frank told her, through me, to avoid starchy foods as far as possible, such as potatoes and bread, and to try and eat white meat, such as chicken, rather than red. The old lady smiled sadly and confessed that she had to live on potatoes for there was nothing else for Poles to eat, and it was impossible for her to get any medical attention since the Nazis had taken over her country. During this interview her attractive young grand-daughter of 17 had been standing quietly by her. Suddenly she interrupted our conversation in broken German to tell us fervently that every night she prayed for the victory of the British soldiers. Frank gave the old lady some Prontazil tablets and we returned in silence to our compound depressed by what we had seen.

At dusk we discovered the 'Plague of Rustungsmühle' — mosquitoes! They swarmed in a black cloud biting wherever there was a piece of exposed skin. In the sweltering summer heat we got onto our wooden three-decker bunks and covered ourselves with blankets and greatcoats, anything to avoid the little beasts. Fortunately we were only at Rustungsmühle for a week, and in spite of the mosquitoes it had its compensations. The men had a very easy job clearing the banks of a small stream from forest undergrowth, and while they worked Frank Sturrock and I sat nearby brewing tea from our Red Cross parcels and arguing politics with our guards. I remarked to one of the Germans that I understood that before the war Poland had had a very large Jewish minority, about one fifth of the entire population, yet I had not seen a single one of them during my stay there. He laughed and went through the motions of firing his rifle at a nearby tree, and seemed quite non-plussed at my look of horror at his calm assumption that the whole community had been murdered.

Near the compound was a large lake (presumably where the mosquitoes bred), and every evening after work our guards took us there for a swim, which was certainly greatly appreciated. It always puzzled me that the majority of our guards were such decent people, yet they would carry out the most barbaric orders and approve of the most outrageous Nazi policies without a thought.

After a few days it became quite clear that the German NCO was having an affair with the wife of the mill owner, for neither of them took any trouble to conceal it. I found out that the miller was half Polish, and was only keeping his property because he was married to a German woman. One word from the NCO to the local Nazi authorities and the miller would have been expelled from his property and possibly would have been thrown into a concentration camp. Such domestic tragedies must have been multiplied thousands of times in Nazi-occupied Europe.

A week later we made the return march to Wallstein, in weather that had turned much cooler. We found that thousands more prisoners had been pouring into the camp during our absence, and that rumours were circulating about Russia's entry into the war. I managed to get hold of a copy of the previous day's *Angriff*, the newspaper of the Ministry of Propaganda but the only mention of Russia was at the bottom of an inside page, where it was reported that a new section of the Metro, Moscow's underground railway, had been opened.

Our party had established itself in a filthy barrack-room when suddenly I received a huge thump on the back and wheeled round to find George grinning at me! All the party from Spitzwald were in the next room and from then on our two parties merged into a single unit of some 200 men. Next morning thousands of us were marched to the local railway siding, where we were ordered into the usual cattle trucks. On the way to the station somebody managed to get hold of a newspaper and I read the news aloud; Russia was at war with Germany! The Nazis claimed huge advances and asserted that overnight the whole of Europe was united in a common struggle against Communism, with volunteers coming forward from every country. The war was presented as a crusade to preserve Christian Europe from godless Asiatic barbarism.

We were elated by the news and secretly I hoped for speedy liberation by the Red Army, but George, whose shrewd and well-informed comments I had learnt to respect, doubted if the Russians could resist the experienced might of the German armed forces. He did admit that it would be a great asset to have the USSR on our side, and it would at least take the pressure off Britain for now a great deal of the Luftwaffe's energies would be transferred to the Eastern Front.

We travelled south all day in our locked cattle trucks, passing through Breslau during the night. Early the next morning we stopped and the doors of the trucks were opened. We scrambled out to find ourselves at a little country station called Lamsdorf. We formed up in a column of five abreast (after a lot of excited screaming from our guards) and eventually we marched off. The march was only a short one and we soon reached a huge barbed wire fence with a heavily guarded gate, over which hung a limp and tattered Nazi flag. This was Stalag VIIIB, Lamsdorf.

11

Gleiwitz

As we marched into the Stalag, loudspeakers were blaring out propaganda in English claiming still further advances against the 'Bolsheviks', but we took no notice as we looked curiously about us. This camp, unlike any other I had lived in, had been specially constructed as a prisoner of war camp. I found out later that it had originally been built to house French prisoners in the Napoleonic Wars, had been used again in the First World War, and was now in use for the third time. The compound was about half a mile long, a quarter of a mile wide and was divided into three main sections, the whole thing being surrounded by a giant barbed wire fence. The prisoners of war area, which was by far the largest of the three, was sub-divided into further compounds. The German administration section occupied the far compound, while the middle area between was open, presumably for parade and recreation. Lamsdorf Camp has been referred to as 'A Zoo in Silesia', which describes it rather accurately.

In each compound in the prisoners' area there were four long single-storeyed buildings in which we lived. Each of these was divided into two large barrack-rooms by a wash-house in the middle. As one entered a barrack-room there were tables and forms to the right, and a solid mass of three-decker beds to the left. Two hundred men lived in each room while the camp itself held over 12,000 when full to capacity.

The combined Spitzwald and Görschen party occupied one of these huge rooms, and I impressed on everybody that I no longer wished to be an interpreter, as I had seen others lose touch with their own people by mixing too much with the enemy. In the next compound to us there were some Yugoslav prisoners and I bought a mess tin and an army belt from one of them for five marks, throwing the money over the high barbed wire fence which separated us. Talking through the wire he gave me a graphic account of events in his country during recent months. He was a professional soldier and told me how the local radio station had broadcast news of a German invasion. The broadcaster had ordered the armed forces of the country to resist the enemy at all costs. His commanding officer had called the men on parade and told them that he had received no orders or official news about the situation, but he thought that a few political revolutionaries had taken over the radio station, and were broadcasting false news. As he spoke German planes had suddenly screamed down on the parade, machine-gunning the ranks. 90 per cent of the men, including the commanding officer, were killed or wounded. A short time later a Nazi armoured column had taken over and the remnants of the regiment had been taken prisoner without any fighting.

We had been in the Stalag for only a day when a party of 200 men were detailed for a working party. Eighty Spitzwald men, 80 Görschen and the remainder from various other groups made up the work party. All my particular friends were with me on this work party, for which I was very thankful. To have been separated from George again having just been so unexpectedly reunited, would have been cruel luck. We had an English Sergeant in charge of us, whom we had never seen before, and a Scot as interpreter, who had every qualification for the job, except a knowledge of the German language!

We had travelled by train for ten hours when we reached a large industrial town named Gleiwitz. I was aware that it was on the Upper Silesian coalfield, and feared that we were to work in the mines, but the sight of railway sidings around the station cheered me up. Hundreds of goods and passenger trains must leave here every day for all parts of Germany, and it promised to be an excellent place from which to attempt my escape.

Lorries met us at the station and my heart sank to my boots as we reached our working party for it would be about the most difficult place from which to escape in wartime Germany. It was part of a military aerodrome. Our first reaction was to refuse to do any work whatever at this place, for it was illegal under the Geneva Convention of the International Red Cross to employ prisoners of war on military tasks. Somebody said as much to one of our guards as we entered the working party compound but we merely received the reply that none of the planes operating from this aerodrome were used against Britain, 'Only against the Bolsheviks'. They obviously assumed that we would be pleased to co-operate. However, it turned out that we were never employed on any task even remotely connected with the aerodrome, but only on general labouring jobs well away from the main hub of activity so we could not object.

Our billets at Gleiwitz were by far the best any of us had had since capture. We were housed in Luftwaffe barracks, with only ten men in each room and slept in double-decker beds in place of the usual prisoner of war three-deckers. We even had showers and a cookhouse, in which we could prepare our Red Cross food. After the last 12 months this seemed paradise. The room in which George and I got beds contained men of kindred spirit, and we all felt that things had taken a distinct change for the better. Our first day at the camp was a Sunday and on parade our British sergeant said that we must have a democratically elected *Vertraumsmann* (Prisoner's Representative) to support him in his dealings with the enemy. This post of Prisoner's Representative was often a difficult one and the method of election was crude. Names were shouted out and the man named stepped forward, his supporters falling in behind him. Mine was the third name called and instantly all the Görschen and Spitzwald men lined up behind me. The other two candidates, seeing 160 men in my column out of 200, gave a cheer and led their supporters on to the end of my line! The Germans, who had watched this in surly silence, looked at me with contempt and one said, 'He looks a proper English democrat', and he spat on the ground in disgust.

The work at Gleiwitz was not heavy or difficult. I was with a small gang putting down drains in the main street of the town, judging it to be the best job from which to attempt my escape. Following our usual practice we did as little work as possible and I spent all of one day sitting on a pile of rubbish chipping cement from a single brick, or at least pretending to do so. It was very interesting to be in the centre of Gleiwitz, for it was a fascinating mixture of eastern and western Europe. There was a large Woolworth's store in the city which closely resembled the ones in Britain. Many of the women who went into it wore peasant dress — long black skirts which reached the ground and scarves tied securely over their hair. We were nearer normal life than we had been since capture, for we saw mothers take their children to school and going shopping, and business people hurrying back to their offices after lunch. Close by us a squad of young men from the *Arbeit Dienst* (Labour Service) were working digging a trench. At intervals throughout the day their leader would blow a whistle and they would all scramble out of their trench and form up.

Their leader would then shout out, 'Who gives you your daily bread?' and the squad would bawl out in reply, 'Adolf Hitler!' This would be followed by two or three more questions, all of which were answered with the same, 'Adolf Hitler!' The leader would then shout '*Arbeit!*' (work) and they would all jump back in the trench and, one assumed, renew their labours with greater effort after their bout of political indoctrination.

We soon discovered that these boys were, in fact, less enthusiastic about their duties than we imagined. During our first morning the most burly of them made his way unobtrusively over to us and asked for a German speaker. When I was introduced he said, in a very belligerent manner, 'If you don't stop work as soon as it rains we will come over and beat you up'. I replied that we were English front-line soldiers and that if there was any beating up to be done, we would do it. This, it seemed, was not the correct attitude for a foreign prisoner to take when addressing one of the Master Race, and a long silence followed. Then the young man explained, in a more concillatory manner, that if prisoners of war worked in bad weather the *Arbeit Dienst* were expected to continue their tasks too, but as soon as we stopped they could stop. I was able to assure him that at the first spot of rain every Englishman would disappear as if by magic. This was exactly what he wanted to hear, and so we parted with expressions of mutual esteem.

Our guard had made arrangements for us to use a WC in a block of flats near our job. One day when I was coming out of the WC a middle-aged woman opened the door of one of the apartments, looked furtively about her, and asked if I would care for a drink of milk. When I said I would she handed me a full glass and watched me drink it down. When I thanked her she cut me short, and asked if I was a Catholic and when I answered I was not she replied, 'Never mind, we are all against Hitler, aren't we?'

Our guard on the work party was an eccentric fellow. As we left the camp in the morning he would count us in German, '1, 2, 3, 4, 5, 6'. As we marched to work he would count us again, '7, 8, 9, 10, 11, 12'. When we got to the job it would be, '13, 14, 15, 16, 17, 18,' and so on throughout the day. When we arrived back at the camp at night he would finally count us, the numbers being in the region of '3,887, 3,888,' and so on. He would then produce a stub of pencil and divide his final total by six, a process which took him some little time, and if the sum worked out exactly we would disperse with a cheer. If he had made a mistake, however, he would shout out in great excitement, 'Five men have escaped!' and would then count us, '1, 2, 3, 4, 5, 6' and we would be dismissed in silence.

By this time I was aware of a great feeling of frustration for I was learning nothing new. One day I looked up and saw a horse nearby so I said to George, (who had once been an apprentice to his uncle, a New-market trainer) 'Teach me all about horses, George. Tell me about that white horse over there'. George glanced up. 'That white horse is a grey mare, old boy,' he said and I realised that the subject was too esoteric for me! On another occasion I exchanged a tin of Red Cross cocoa for two loaves of bread with a Polish workman. George's comment was, 'My pal is a magician, he taps a Pole with a tin of cocoa and it changes into a couple of loaves!'

At the end of our first week's work I was sent on a lorry with a guard to collect some bricks from a nearby brick works, and was startled to find the heavy labouring work at the place being done almost entirely by German girls. In Nazi Germany there were very few women in the armed forces so one would find a burly soldier inexpertly using a typewriter in an army office while, round the corner, slightly-built women would struggle to do heavy manual work. The British system of using women in the ATS and leaving males in the essential civilian labouring jobs, seemed to me to be far more effective. At the brick field an elderly man came running up as soon as he heard that a British prisoner was on the premises. That morning he had been informed that his son had been taken prisoner and was in England. He showed me a printed form telling him the news and pointed to an address in Piccadilly, to which he could send letters for the boy. I told him what I could of the conditions of German prisoners in England and explained that the address was that of a sorting office, and that there was no question of there being any prison camps in the West End of London. He was very grateful to me, not so much for the specific information I suspect, as for the realisation that Englishmen were not barbarians but fairly normal human beings.

Throughout this area and, indeed, throughout Germany the Nazis carried out a bitter anti-Polish campaign. So, wherever one went there were posters of an intimidating nature declaring 'He who speaks Polish is our enemy!' Some member of my work party managed to alter some of these to read, 'He who speaks Polish is our comrade for freedom and victory!'

On our first Sunday morning the German NCO in charge of the party ordered an elborate kit inspection on the parade ground. He made disparaging comments about each prisoner and his kit and took over two hours to carry out his tirade against our slovenly ways. When he had finished he announced, through the Scottish interpreter, that as we had not worked hard enough during the week there would be no issue of Red Cross parcels. A murmur ran through the parade and I stepped out of the ranks and over to where the Nazi was standing.

'Who is this fellow?' he demanded. I asked the Scot to remind him that I was the elected representative of the prisoners and requested him to reconsider his decision. The German's reply was to sneer at me and order me back in the ranks. He was rather startled when I remained where I was and explained in my best German that the parcels were our personal property and not wages paid by the Germans for work done. I added that under the Geneva Convention, which Adolf Hitler had signed, we were entitled to the parcels even if we were not working at all. The NCO came up to me and thrust his face to within an inch from mine. He screamed at the top of his voice that he had fought Englishmen for four years in the First World War, and that now he had the sons of those Englishmen under his control he would give the orders, and we would obey them. I controlled my temper and replied that I would be forced to report the matter to the British and German authorities at Lamsdorf, and if necessary, take it as far as the International Red Cross Organisation. At this point I thought he would break a blood vessel and we stood, toe to toe, shouting abuse at each other while the silent guards and prisoners looked on. He roared that he would have me sent to a concentration camp. I shouted in reply, 'It's all the ... ... same to me what you do!' It must have been the first time in his life that he had been sworn at on parade by a Private soldier. Suddenly he seemed to realise that the situation had got out of hand and walked stiffly away, barking over his shoulder to the guards, 'Dismiss the parade!'

After our dismissal all 200 prisoners tried to crowd into our room. Everybody was talking at once and various wild suggestions were made. There was talk of a physical revolt if I was beaten up by the guards or a mass escape should I be punished in any way. I tried to calm down everybody for I realised that a serious situation could arise if either the Germans or the prisoners lost their heads. A stony-faced guard pushed his way into the room. In the sudden silence he informed me that I was to return to Lamsdorf next day. Then he broke into a huge grin to add that the NCO had been told on the telephone to 'Issue your damned parcels at once!' This brought forth a great cheer. The fact that the Stalag authorities had ordered the parcels to be issued at once showed that we were in the right and suggested that I would receive only a nominal punishment. The actual issue of the parcels was rather comic, as it was supervised by the German NCO and myself standing side by side, neither of us speaking or even looking at the other. As each man took his parcel he said, 'Thanks, Bob'.

12

Straff Kompanie

Before I went to bed that night I packed all my belongings, for I had been informed that a guard would rouse me at three o'clock in the morning to catch the first train for Lamsdorf. When he tip-toed into my room I was quickly awake and dressed with speed. All my companions continued to sleep so I crept over to George's bed to look at him as he slept. It seemed a pity to disturb him, for sleep is the only way a prisoner can escape his confinement for a few hours, and I suddenly thought it would be too selfish to recall George to imprisonment, just to wish him goodbye (even though I realised that the chances of being reunited with him for a second time were very remote).

I stepped out into the chilly air of the early morning and made my way across to the guard's quarters, where my escort had some hot coffee substitute and black bread ready for our breakfast. As I sat down he produced a large liver sausage and handed it to me saying, 'This is from the guards for swearing at You-Know-Who!' In turn I produced a bar of Red Cross chocolate from my pack and gave him half, but instead of eating it he thanked me and carefully stowed it away in his pocket. I asked him what he intended to do with it and he explained he would save it for his little daughter. At once I produced my other bar and gave it to him for the little girl, on condition that he ate the half bar himself there and then. He was very grateful and obviously felt uncomfortable as we left for according to the rules he had to demonstrate to me that his rifle was fully loaded. 'You know what that's for, don't you?' I nodded, it was to shoot me if I attempted to escape during our journey.

We set off in the dawn by passenger train and soon reached Oppeln, where we had to change. On the platform I was very annoyed by some children who were obviously learning English at school and who kept pointing at me and chanting, 'English ape, English monkey!' over and over again. At last I said repressively in German, 'Quiet, children. Englishmen are also men and I am a front-line soldier.' They looked very sheepish and walked away, and some nearby adults, who had been smirking had the grace to look embarrassed.

We reached the Stalag in the late evening and I was marched to *Straff*

Kompanie (Punishment Company) at once. This was a special compound at the far end of the camp and was really a prison within a prison. It had its own guards, who were on duty day and night, its own machine-gun tower and extra barbed wire round it. When I arrived everybody was asleep so I quickly settled down on an empty bed and was soon asleep myself.

In the morning I took stock of the situation and found that nearly all my fellow-inmates were escapers who had been recaptured and that as a mutineer I was something of a novelty. On the whole these were the most intelligent and enterprising men in captivity and the British Sergeant Major in charge of the compound was never tired of telling everybody that although it was a disgrace to be in a British military prison it was a great honour to be in a Nazi one. Life in *Straff Kompanie* was reasonably comfortable and I soon found out that one was usually there for a week before being interviewed by a German officer who would either sentence one to a period of solitary confinement or, for more serious offences, send one for court martial. If the latter came to pass a death sentence could be imposed, or confinement in a German army prison, although it was considered that any sentence of over six months in one of those places amounted to a death sentence anyway.

In due course I was summoned for my interview and was amazed when my armed German guard remained outside the office when I marched in. The officer was a middle-aged, educated man and as I entered he was reading a document, which I quickly realised was an account of my conduct from the Gleiwitz German NCO. In the corner of the room behind me a German girl was busily writing at a desk. The officer was quite good-humoured and observed that I *had* been getting myself into trouble, hadn't I? He asked me a few random questions as he read the report in front of him. Suddenly he sat up and became more interested.

'What did you say when the Unteroffizier threatened to have you punished?' he asked, curious.

'I said "It's all the same to me".' I replied.

'Is that all you said?' he asked, looking at me sternly.

'I'm afraid I was foolish enough to use some strong language,' I confessed. With a half-suppressed smile he insisted on my telling him the exact words I had used. Acutely conscious that the girl clerk had stopped work and was listening intently, I leaned forward and whispered hoarsely, 'I said, "It's all the ... ... same to me what you do!"'

The girl gave a little gasp and, covering her ears with her hands, dashed from the room, while the officer leaned back in his chair, slapped his thigh and howled with laughter. When he recovered his breath finally he wiped his eyes and said, 'All right, Gayler, two weeks' solitary confinement'.

Back in *Straff Kompanie* I reported to the British Warrant Officer. He consulted a notebook and told me that it would be about six weeks

Right *Robert Gayler's 'employers' at Lamsdorf.*

Below *Herr Neumann (note Party badge) and Frau Neumann with their two staff. The two guards are wearing the carpet slippers which were Christmas presents from the Neumanns.*

85

Above *Unloading sugar beet at the Neumanns.*

Below *Christmas at the Neumann's. The author is fifth from left in the back row.*

Reprinted from Interlude, *the story of British PoWs in Stammlager VIIIA at Gorlitz.*

The *identity card Robert Gayler received on his release from captivity.*

IDENTITY CARD

FOR

EX-PRISONER OF WAR

This Identity Card MUST be retained until collected at the Reception Camp in the United Kingdom

Service No. 6846484 NATIONALITY Br
Serial No.

Surname } Gayler
Last Name

Initials R J

Rank Pte

Regiment, Squadron, Ship } Kensington Regt
or Organization

Holder's Signature R.J. Gayler.

Signature of
P.W. Camp Contact Officer

Issued at   on   194

18. April

STALAG XI B

88

before I could be punished by the enemy, as there were only 20 cells in the Stalag jail and a very long waiting list. He consoled me by pointing out that the 'Escaping Season' would still have at least two months to run after I came out. I was not surprised by the casual assumption that I intended to escape for it would certainly apply to 90 per cent of the select company in the Punishment Compound.

It was very convenient to have all the escapers together for, by pooling experiences, we could avoid mistakes in the future. My contribution to the happy band was to teach my celebrated course, 'Complete Polish for Escapers in Four Words,' to anybody interested. ('Ya yest-um Angel-ski yae-ne-ats,' with thanks to Jan and Albin of Spitzwald.) Among other things was advised that cycling was by far the best means of transport. I was told of three men who had stolen bicycles and had travelled right across Germany to the Swiss frontier without being challenged, in broad daylight, and in British Army uniform. However, the German-Swiss frontier had proved impossible to cross as it had been so heavily guarded. The general consensus was that the best plan was to make for occupied Holland or Belgium and make oneself known to a policeman on duty. It was estimated that half of these men were anti-Nazi enough to put an escaping prisoner into touch with the Underground Movement, while of the others, very few would actually report one to the Germans. On no account should one go to a police station, as there was reputed to be a German informer stationed in each one.

Opportunities for escape from a working party was usually difficult but if it could be planned with care then your chances of escape were fairly good. Travel across wartime Germany was not impossible, even in British uniform, but the vast majority of escapers were recaptured between their working party and the frontier. To try to pass as a German was useless. It was impossible for even a genuine native soldier or civilian to make a journey without a mass of documents which we were totally incapable of faking. Shabby British battledress passed well enough, as there were a multitude of foreign forced-labourers in the country wearing nondescript uniforms. The 'golden rule' was to avoid contact with the public by keeping out of towns. In the country districts, even if an Englishman was recognised as an escaped prisoner, civilians would usually keep well away from him, fearing that he was armed and desperate. Escape was recognised by the International Red Cross as a prisoner's duty and therefore punishment under the Geneva Convention could not be severe. On the other hand, if a civilian crime was committed, stealing a car for example, the escaper risked a savage sentence of as much as 20 years in a military prison, or even death, if the car was a military vehicle.

The day before I was sent to the cells I officially reported my intention to escape to our Warrant Officer. He issued me with two pieces of toilet paper on which a small scale map of Germany had been traced and he took charge of the bulk of my personal belongings. When a man escaped he was unable to take more than the bare essentials with him, while to leave them on the working party was to lose them completely. At least by leaving them at the *Straff Kompanie* 'Left Luggage Office' he could reclaim them if he had the misfortune to be recaptured (for escapers were always sent there for punishment). If the kit was unclaimed for six months, it was disposed of, for it was assumed that the owner had either been killed or had reached England. It was estimated that only one per cent of escapers were successful, five per cent killed and the rest ignominiously recaptured.

At seven o'clock next morning I was marched down to the cells in the German administration section of the Stalag with an armed escort. I took the minimum amount of kit with me and was subjected to a thorough search, but my map, which I had hidden in the lining of my cow-hide pack, was undiscovered. The prison was a long low building with a corridor running the length of it and the cells opening off on either side. All was silence as I was marched down to cell No 23 which had a notice in German on the door giving the occupant's name, crime, sentence and date of admission and date on which he was due for release, including the exact hour of that happy event. The existing notice was removed and one with my particulars substituted. The massive metal door was swung open and a bearded Englishman strolled out giving me a huge grin. Prisoners were not allowed to shave during their stay in the cells as it was thought that they might commit suicide with their razors or use them to attack their guards. I entered at a curt word of command, the door was slammed behind me, and I settled down to my first experience of solitary confinement.

Standing with my arms raised sideways I found I could touch one wall with the tips of my fingers and the other one with the elbow of the other arm, while by lying on the floor with my arms above my head I could put my heels against the door and touch the external wall of the cell with my clenched fists. Thus I measured my new 'home'. On one side of my domain was a kind of wooden platform which, with one blanket, was my bed. At the foot of this was a metal radiator which was cold since it was midsummer. In the external wall was a small heavily barred window covered with frosted glass to prevent one from looking out, while in the corner of the cell was a metal jug full of water. I sat on the bed to think things over.

Suddenly, I became aware that somebody was looking at me through a peephole in the door. I regarded the unblinking blue eye for some seconds but it disappeared as I went to investigate. I found that in the middle of the door was a round spyhole about the size of an old penny that was covered with glass, so that nothing could be passed through it to the prisoner. This hole was covered on the outside with a metal flap and by pushing this aside the guard could get a full view of the interior of the cell. Closer examination revealed that there was a pinhole in the centre of the metal flap and that by putting his eye close to this the warder could observe the prisoner without the latter being aware of it. The guards often came along the corridor in their stockinged feet to spy on us, so it was impossible to know if one was under observation any moment of the day or night.

When I found myself alone for the first time since capture a great feeling of relief and liberation swept over me. I was able to relax completely and spent most of the first three days' solitary in sleep. I soon fell into the simple daily routine of the cells. We were awakened at 6 am and allowed to go to the latrine. Then we drew a bucket of water with which we had to swab out our cell and the section of the corridor outside. We washed in a tin bowl of cold water in our cells while the warders patrolled up and down the corridor in front of our open door. It was strictly forbidden for prisoners to speak to each other, but we always managed to grunt a message to a neighbour out of the corners of our mouths, in true convict fashion. At 6:30 am we were again locked in our cells until 10 am when we had one hour's exercise. This was in the form of a German punishment drill in an open space behind the prison. We ran round the parade ground in single file and flung ourselves to the ground whenever the guard shouted '*Hinlegen!*' Then, we jumped to our feet and ran on again at the order, '*Raus!*' If any of us was slow to obey the guard when he shouted '*Hinlegen!*' he would walk over, put his foot on the offender's back and press him into the dust. We could not complain at this degrading form of punishment as it was universal in the German army, and at Görschen I had seen it used by the Hitler Youth.

After an hour's drill we returned to our cells and remained there until 4 pm when we had another spell of exercise. After our second drill we would find our food for the day on the plank bed in our cell, one third of a loaf of bread. If there was a decent warder on duty he would allow us to pass round his knife to hack our bread into slices as we, of course, were not allowed to have knives. During the morning and after both drill periods we were permitted to fill the water jug in the corner of our cells. We always told our friends that food in the cells was unlimited, the bread ration might be small but you could have as much water as you wanted! Although, it was unwise to drink too much as visits to the latrine were limited.

On my third day in the cells I remembered how I had read once that messages could be sent by tapping on hot water pipes and so I took off my boot and tried it, but failed to get any response. Tapping on the walls was equally unsuccessful and while I was doing this the observation flap in the door suddenly moved and an eye surveyed me. The eye rolled upwards in a rather comic manner and there was a sound of scraping above the door where, high up near the ceiling, a brick had been left out for ventilation. In this opening a round tin appeared and when I reached up and carefully got it down I found it was full of quite good stew which I ate ravenously, still watched by 'the Eye'. I discovered later that the stew had come from one of the prisoners who was employed by our guards as their orderly. Part of his duties was to go to the German cookhouse to collect their rations for them but, before delivering them, he would help himself to a liberal portion and smuggle as much as he dared to the men in the cells. Then he would add hot water to the remainder to make it up to the original bulk.

For the next few days I followed the routine and must confess that I found myself completely impervious to the famed horrors of solitary confinement. I passed the time by calculating exactly how many postage stamps it would take to paper the walls, ceiling and floor of the cell, making due allowance for the door, windows and ventilator. I recited to myself all the poems I knew and then surprised myself by remembering quite long passages of *Macbeth* and *Paradise Lost*. I concluded that solitary confinement held no horrors if one had clear conscience and mental resources to draw upon.

On the seventh day I was delighted when, after some soup had been smuggled to me, a book was pushed through the ventilator. It was a cheap edition of *Riders of the Purple Sage* by Zane Grey, from which the cover had been torn off. I not only read this work avidly, but afterwards tried translating it mentally into German only to realise how sketchy my knowledge of the language really was. One day while we were out at exercise our cells were searched and the book, which I had hidden under the blanket on my plank bed, was found. It lay face down in the middle of the floor when I returned to the cell, but nothing was said to me, so I can only conclude that a sympathetic guard had turned a blind eye to it.

At last, after 14 days, the door of the cell swung open and I, a bearded figure, strolled out grinning and gave the 'thumbs up' sign to the unfortunate who was about to take up residence. While serving solitary confinement prisoners were not allowed to receive their Red Cross parcels so as soon as I left the cells a guard escorted me to the Stalag Parcel Store to collect my overdue issue. The tough little British Sergeant Major in charge grinned at me as I walked in and rapped out in the traditional manner of Warrant Officers, 'Take that man's name and number, Corporal, he needs a haircut and shave!' Then, suddenly serious, he asked me if I would mind accepting a parcel that had come open in transit. He explained that the contents were intact but if such parcels were issued in the normal way the dishonest were often tempted to claim that something was missing and caused a lot of trouble. I agreed and with my precious parcel under my arm, was marched by my guard to the Working Compound.

When a working party closed down the men were sometimes sent back to Lamsdorf and housed in this compound for a few days, before being re-allocated to another party. Some individuals, by devious means, managed to stay there for a considerable period without being sent out to work. However, I found that this was not possible for those who had passed through the *Straff Kompanie*. We were branded as the extreme nonconformists of prison life and rightly considered to be a potential source of trouble. So, both the British and German authorities of the Working Compound knew, from bitter experience, that the sooner they could be rid of us the better. I reported to the compound office, in which all the furniture was made from Red Cross packing cases and I was informed that I would be off to a working party next morning.

I dumped my Red Cross parcel and the few possessions I had not left in the *Straff Kompanie* on an empty bunk. Suddenly feeling very much alone I climbed up onto the bunk and examined the parcel, only to find that the chocolate, tea and condensed milk were all missing. Immediately I tried to get to the Red Cross Store to complain, but discovered that the gate of the Working Compound was locked and guarded. The little Sergeant Major knew he was quite safe from unwelcome visits by the men he swindled. In a thoroughly bad temper I asked the man sitting on the next bed if he knew anything about the working party to which I was to be sent. He led me to a corner of the barrack room where the wall was covered with writing. It was a directory of working parties in numerical order, written up by men who had been to them, and it gave pithy details of location and conditions. My heart sank as I found mine described as 'Horrible — hard work and bad food and rotten for take-off (ie, escape). They take away your boots and trousers at night.' Very depressed by this information I wandered out of the barrack room lost in thought, when suddenly I saw an amazing sight; an old lady in Edwardian dress came running down the main road of the compound, chased by young men in civilian clothes of the same period. We were all stunned for a moment, and then hooted with laughter and cheered, for the last man had a placard on his back advertising the first night of *Charley's Aunt* at the Stalag Theatre that night. The Working Compound was always given a special allocation of theatre tickets for men who were leaving for working parties the next day, so I was given one. The 'Theatre' was a barrack room fitted up with a pitifully small stage, but where first-class productions were put on. Among the prisoners were a number of professional actors, artists and tailors, and in spite of the handicaps under which they worked, they produced shows of West End standard.

During the afternoon of this eventful day I was sent to the Stalag Clothing Store for a complete new British Army uniform. We had been prisoners for over a year now and so our clothing was very much the worse for wear. It gave me a wonderful feeling of well-being to be decently dressed once more but I was haunted by the brief note in the Working Party Directory, 'They take away your boots and trousers at night'; so, at the clothing store I managed to buy a second pair of old trousers for 50 cigarettes, although it was impossible to buy an extra pair of boots at any price. I should explain that an issue of English cigarettes was made to each man weekly with his Red Cross parcel and they rapidly became the accepted form of currency in the prison camps. As a non-smoker I was automatically one of the Stalag Middle Class, having, in effect, a weekly unearned income, which I did not consume.

That evening I went to the theatre worried about the lack of a second pair of boots and apprehensive about the 'Hard work and bad food and rotten take-off', to which I was to be introduced next day. It says a great deal for the Stalag Theatre that the moment the curtain went up, *Charley's Aunt* captured my attention to the exclusion of all else. Never has that famous farce been presented to a more appreciative audience. For me at least, it was a really memorable evening.

13

Escape

Next morning 15 of us were assembled and marched to Lamsdorf railway station by three guards, who went through the usual routine of demonstrating that their rifles *were* loaded before we set off. I did not know any of the other men, but judged that none of them were potential escapers as they were carrying all their possessions with them, while I had only the contents of my cow-hide pack. It soon became clear that four of them were together and that the rest were five pairs of friends, making me the odd man out. Around this time, rumours had been circulating that the Germans were introducing their own English-speaking spies into the Stalag and its working parties, to help them discover escape and sabotage plans. From the outset of our trip I could sense a certain coolness towards me, which I did my best to ignore.

The journey was quite a pleasant one by third-class passenger train. We travelled south-east, which was the opposite direction to where I wanted to go, for it was away from the railway sidings of Gleiwitz. Yet the weather was that of a Continental summer and as such was ideal for escape. The only immediate discomfort I suffered was from the heat as I was now wearing both my pairs of thick uniform trousers, for, if it had been discovered that I had a second pair of trousers when I had been searched at Lamsdorf, the extra pair would have been confiscated.

During the journey two of the men became very suspicious of me. Where did I live in England? Why was I in the Kensington Regiment, (of which they had never heard) if I didn't live in Kensington? Why was I in the Highland Division if I was in a London regiment? What was my civilian job? Why did nobody in the Working Compound know me? It became very clear to me that they suspected me of being a spy, especially as I answered all their questions truthfully and had also admitted that I spoke German. They said grimly that they hoped some-body at our new party knew me, apart from the guards of course. When I said hotly that I would know none of the guards they immediately pounced on me and asked how I could be so sure unless I had been told what guards were on the party? They made almost no attempt to hide the fact that they considered it their duty to arrange a fatal accident for me if I could not prove my innocence.

We arrived at the working party in the late evening. It consisted of the usual barbed-wire compound with single-storeyed prisoners' quarters (which had heavy bars at all the windows) along one side, the guards' billet and stores along another side, and a prisoners' latrine along the third side. I sized up the situation and judged that there would be enough space between this 'Comfort station' and the barbed wire for a man to hide. Once more we went through the degrading routine of being searched, this time under the contemptuous gaze of the fat Unteroffizier in charge of the party. Luckily the man who searched me was as inexpert and inefficient as his peer at Lamsdorf as once again it was not discovered that I was wearing two pairs of trousers.

At last we were permitted to go into our new quarters, where I removed my best pair of trousers, when nobody was looking, and hid them in the straw-filled palliasse on my new bunk. Dorothy had, at my request, sent me a photograph of herself so I stuck it on the underside of the bunk above mine (I was on the lowest bunk of a three-decker) and, stretching myself out on my bed, I looked at the portrait and mentally promised her that I would be with her soon.

When the men came in from their day's work I was alarmed to find that there was not one familiar face among the 200 men that I had ever seen before. My two questioners observed this and I feared that they would take some action against me after we had been locked up for the night. During the evening the British Sergeant in charge gave me some very searching looks and I was convinced that their suspicions had been reported to him, but nothing was said and I was left in peace. During the evening the whole party ate a meal of German rations and Red Cross food and I began to take careful stock of my situation. One man impressed me very much. He was the natural leader of the four friends who had come with me from Lamsdorf that day, very well spoken and a man of obvious intelligence. I was particularly interested when he got into an animated conversation on Rugby football with some of his new acquaintances and said that his brother at one time played for the Coventry City team. Of course one of the men asked, 'What's your name, chum?' and he replied after a slight pause, 'Er — Roberts.' The other man got up from the table at which they were sitting and said, 'I'm a Coventry supporter, buddy, and nobody named Roberts ever played for them.' I was surprised to see Roberts look very sheepish as the man walked away in the ensuing silence. I had not thought he would be a liar, nor that he would allow himself to be called one but, after a few moments, general conversation was resumed and the incident was closed, though not forgotten.

That evening at roll-call all 200 prisoners paraded bare footed and in their shirt tails. After being counted, we filed into the clothing store past a guard and left our boots and trousers there. Another guard checked us as we came out. The one good feature of this nightly occurrence from an escaper's point of view was that the enemy felt so confident that they did not bother to keep a guard outside the wire all night, but slept peacefully in their beds.

After roll-call next morning we collected our clothing once more and, after a hurried breakfast of German bread and coffee substitute, marched to our work. On the way we passed under a railway bridge and I noticed with some excitement that an anti-Nazi slogan had been written on one of the walls with white paint, although it had been subsequently obliterated. This suggested that there was some form of opposition to the Nazis in the district and I began to wonder if I could get any outside help in attempting to escape.

Our work was very heavy. At the top of high banks were railway trucks full of logs, each log being about the size of a man. I assumed that these logs were pit-props for the local mining industry. The trucks were large ones and the logs were so cleverly stacked that each truck contained far more than they normally would. Six prisoners were allocated to each wagon and the new men were told that our wagon had to be empty by midday. At first the task looked reasonably easy, as all we had to do was to tip the logs over the side, when they rolled to the bottom of the bank. By the end of the morning, however, we were having to man-handle each log from the floor of the truck so that we were all sweating and totally exhausted by the time our task was completed. I hated working for the Nazis like this, but to slack resulted in one's companions having to work harder, for the Germans had told us that unless the wagon was empty by lunch-time we would have to work on until it was completed. They added that the afternoon work would also have to be completed on time, or they would keep us there all night if need be. One guard grinned as he told us that we need never eat or sleep again, unless we really wished to!

Our midday meal was a poor thin soup, although we supplemented it with our own Red Cross food. The afternoon work consisted of loading the logs we had thrown to the bottom of the bank that morning on to small trucks on a miniature railway and pushing them to a huge pile where we had to unload and stack them neatly. This was not such back-breaking work as the morning job and at least we worked as individuals, but by the end of the day I was almost unable to make the march back to our camp.

When at last I was resting on my bed I felt most depressed. It was Saturday and I was determined to escape the following night after the normal day off on Sunday, when the British Sergeant came in and called for silence.

'Sorry, lads', he said, 'but Jerry says 25 men must work all day tomorrow on a special job.' Groans and cat-calls greeted this news and the Sergeant continued, 'It's the turn of Platoon Six to do overtime and the 15 new men from the Stalag will join them to make up the 25'.

In a flash my plans were changed. If a man did not even rest on the

Sabbath in this place, there was nothing to keep me. I would escape that night. Watching for my chance, and with all my exhaustion suddenly gone, I strolled over to the clothing store. I was amazed to find a number of pairs of boots there, each labelled with a prisoner's name and number. These were spare pairs which the lucky owners had to keep in the store. I realised that there would be nothing easier for me to do than to borrow one of these pairs for a few hours and to hand them in that night in place of my own. I strolled back to my quarters as nonchalantly as possible, with a borrowed pair of boots in my hand and quickly changed into them. My own boots joined my best trousers in my straw-filled mattress. With boots safely stowed, I paid a visit to the latrine to plan a hiding place for my boots, trousers and pack before the evening roll-call. I planned to conceal myself there as well once roll-call was over. I satisfied myself that there was ample room between the WC and the barbed wire for this purpose and was cheered to discover that the fence was only about 12 feet high. Moreover, if I climbed over near one of the posts it would support me better and, with reasonable luck, I could get away more quickly. Knowing that luck entered far too much in my calculations, I went on to explore other possibilities. Back in the barrack room I examined the bars on the window near my bed and discovered with surprise that, although the bars themselves were stout enough, they were welded at either end to a metal frame which was only attached to the wall by a single bolt at each corner. I judged that, if a number of men seized the bars and gave one concerted heave, the whole thing could be pulled away from the window with ease. I had just reached this conclusion when the man named Roberts casually strolled over to me and said very quietly, 'Don't examine those bars too closely, or people will get the idea that you are planning to go through them.'

Without stopping to think I replied, 'I am.'

'Oh my God, when?' he asked, startled.

'Tonight.' I replied, now regretting my impulsiveness.

'Come to my bed and have a chat', invited Roberts.

Without hesitation he told me that he and his three friends were also escaping that night. 'One day in this dump is a day too long, so as we are going sooner or later, there's no point in waiting. One of them, a tough little Midlander, observed.

So, yet again, my plans were changed. The 'Big Four', as I called them, had discovered that every night the guard who locked the prisoners in would then proceed to search the compound thoroughly including behind the latrine, so I was sure to be found. This was a major setback but then Roberts produced a huge pair of wire-cutters, the type used by Post Office wiremen. With these he proposed to cut the heads off the bolts that held the window bars in place and afterwards cut the barbed wire. As they had the essential tools for the job I agreed to help them get away at midnight, while I would follow an hour later.

Roberts confided to me that he was, in fact, an RAF pilot and as such was not allowed by the Germans to leave the Stalag with the work parties in case he should steal a German aeroplane during an attempted escape. For this reason he had exchanged identities with a Private soldier named Roberts, who did not like having to work for the enemy. So the Private was walking around the Stalag in an Air Force uniform, enjoying the privileges his status as an RAF pilot could offer, while my new friend, the pseudo-Roberts, was given the opportunity to escape. This explained, as 'Roberts' pointed out with a grin, why nobody of that name had ever played rugger for Coventry!

The five of us had a meal together and then went out for the roll-call, each man with his boots and trousers in his hands. I was highly elated by the recent turn of events and the knowledge that my own boots and best pair of trousers were in my mattress. On parade the British Sergeant called for silence.

'I have an important announcement to make. There is a dirty bloody thief in the camp who has stolen a pair of boots from the clothing store!' A deep-throated roar of anger went up from the prisoners. With the missing boots in my hand I roared with the rest, my mind racing. The Sergeant continued, 'I mean it from the bottom of my heart when I say, 'God help that man', because this is a tough camp and we will know how to deal with him when the parade is over. I have a pretty good idea who it is already and after lights out there will be a special private investigation just to make sure.'

I had been in some tough spots, but nothing like this. I knew the punishment for theft — I had even threatened to kill a thief myself when our bread had been stolen at Konin. If the NCO asked the Germans to allow the owner of the boots to walk along the ranks, I would be spotted immediately. I realised with horror that I not only faced the possibility of serious injury, or even death, but the news that I had suffered at the hands of my fellow prisoners as a thief, would slowly circulate to my friends in other camps in Germany and after the war might even reach my family in England.

My relief can be imagined when I left the borrowed boots with my trousers in the clothing store and emerged empty-handed and safe. I returned to my bed immediately so my looks should not betray me. Almost at once the Sergeant came into the room and announced that the owner of the missing boots had reported that they had reappeared in the store. The Sergeant commented that 'He was a wise man who returned them!'

Roberts came over to my bed and looked at me. 'What's wrong with you suddenly?' he asked with contempt in his voice, 'Feeling scared?' I told him about the affair of the boots and thought he would kill himself with laughter. 'Golly, you'll be in England within 24 four hours for you must have the luck of the Devil to get away with that without being lynched!' Then he told me the Big Four were not going to sleep, but he advised me to get some rest as they would wake me at midnight. Thankful enough to relax after the exertions of the day and the crisis of the evening, I slept like one of the dead until the Midlander woke me at the appointed hour.

In the dark and silence of the prisoners' dormitory Roberts attacked the bolts on the window bars with his gigantic wire-cutters. They gave him no trouble whatever so we were soon lifting the frame and bars to the floor. By the time we had done this every man in the room was awake and silently watching from his bed. In turn I shook hands with each one of the Big Four as they climbed out of the window. They landed silently outside on their stockinged feet, their boots, the laces tied together, dangling round their necks. I handed out their kit and then retired from the window in case a sleepless guard should chance to look that way and have his suspicions aroused by seeing movement at the window.

Roberts had described carefully where he would cut the wire, exactly opposite the latrine, and I waited in silence on my bed for the full hour. If I followed them immediately and was caught, the Big Four would still be in the vicinity and would be quickly recaptured as well. So I watched the moon from my bed and determined not to leave until it had reached the corner of the window. When at last it did I got out of bed, extracted my boots and trousers, made ready my pack. Requiring help I went over to the bed of a man from Ponders End, which was near my home, and asked him to help me through the window. In a few moments I was standing in the compound with my pack in my hands and my boots round my neck.

I crept across the compound to the barbed wire and located the hole cut by the Big Four. Expecting to find a small slit I was amazed to find it was big enough for me to walk through upright! I stepped through and stood still. A few yards away the guards were sleeping with all their windows wide open in the heat of the summer's night. If one had awoken I would have been seen at once, yet I had such a feeling of unreality, that I could not bring myself to move. 'So, this is one of the great moments of my life' I thought. 'Well, standing here in the dark is doing no good. I had better pull myself together before somebody starts to take a few pot shots at me!' I put on my boots and strode forward across a field into the darkness. However exhausted I might have been earlier on I must put as much distance as possible between myself and the working party before the escape was discovered. I was on my way to Gleiwitz where I could jump a train for Holland or Belgium. I was on my way home!

14

Free In Nazi Germany

Behind me was the camp, to my right was a block of flats and I wondered what the sleeping inhabitants would do if they saw an escaping prisoner. Before me was open country and overhead the starry night sky which was to be my compass. Before I left the camp I had picked out the Great Bear and from it the North Star, giving thanks that I had been a Wolf Cub! My direction was confirmed when I came to a road and examined a signpost. I realised that the map I had been given in *Straff Kompanie* was of little use at the moment as obviously it had been taken from a map of the German railway system, the type displayed in passenger compartments of trains for instance. As such it was a diagram rather than a map, but it would be invaluable once I had caught my train at Gleiwitz.

I was aware that German railway trucks had many documents attached to their sides and, although I had never been able to examine one, it was reasonable to assume that their destination was included among the other information. Also, apart from having read W.H. Davis' great book *Autobiography of a Super-Tramp*, I knew nothing of the technique of riding the rods. However I was confident that I would be able to clamber aboard safely and make myself comfortable.

When I judged myself to be about five miles from the camp and with dawn imminent I hid in a small wood where I could rest during the long hours of daylight. I boldy pushed into the undergrowth and immediately found myself up to my knees in water. My path was effectively blocked by a large lake. I turned about and walked back along my own tracks for about a quarter of a mile to a large tree. I took off my pack and threw it as far as I could at right angles to my present route and then climbed the tree. I worked my way along a bough, and dropped to the ground beside my pack. Thus, I hoped that if the dogs had been put on my trail, the Germans would track me from the camp to the tree at the edge of the lake and assume that I had drowned and call off the search.

Having completed my little subterfuge I made for a small wood in the distance, my feet squelching in my boots and my wet trousers flapping round my legs. Exhausted, but in high spirits, I searched for a place to

101

sleep during the coming daylight hours. Only those who have done it can appreciate how incredibly difficult it is to choose a place to sleep in a wood by night which will provide adequate cover once daylight comes. I pushed through the undergrowth for a short way and then wriggled under a thick bush. With the last of my strength I managed to remove my wet boots, socks and trousers and, although I had an adequate supply of Red Cross food, I was too tired to eat and, anyway, I wish to conserve my food supply for the unknown future. I settled down to sleep with my pack as a pillow.

I awoke to blazing sunlight and judged from the position of the sun that it must be mid-afternoon. I ate half a tin of corned-beef and a bar of chocolate and then slept again. I awoke for the second time in the late evening and found, to my delight, that my clothing was perfectly dry. I reviewed my situation with care and realised how incredibly difficult it was going to be for me to reach England, and yet I was infinitely nearer success than those men still imprisoned behind the barbed wire. I also derived a great deal of satisfaction from the thought that I was once more on active service, causing the Nazis the expend a great deal of time and trouble in securing my recapture. When it was completely dark I resumed my 'March on Gleiwitz' which, I calculated, would take me about five days.

The following days and nights were strangely uneventful. By night, I would tramp over open country, checking my progress and distance by signposts whenever I came to a cross-road. By day, I slept in the undergrowth of a suitable wood, but I soon discovered that I had a 'flair' for choosing bad places to hide. On the second night of my escape I thought I was safely in the middle of a wood but I was aroused in full daylight by the sound of children's voices and discovered that my 'hiding place' was a single bush next to a woodland path. I observed the children at close quarters and, as they all had books with them, they were presumably on their way to school. Next night I found a delight-fully soft patch of ground, well hidden, but only when it was too light to move did I realise that the whole area was uncomfortably damp and mossy. As my uniform gradually became sodden I grimly pondered that when I was 70, and a victim of rheumatism, I would inevitably think back to this incident. This train of thought led me to gloomy specula-tion about the chances of anybody in my present hazardous situation ever surviving to such an age.

Worries about food did not trouble me at all for a man could live comfortably for a week on one food parcel and I had saved the equiva-lent of two and a half over the past four weeks. I rarely got hungry and felt it likely that the starvation in the early days of captivity had caused my digestive system to adjust itself to an inadequate diet. Also, it was quite probable that the privations of those days had given me quite a different standard of physical discomfort. I learnt a great deal during the long nights of marching, chiefly about astronomy. Few 20th century townsmen spend much time alone in open country at night and the starry sky fascinated me. Every quarter of an hour I would check my direction by the Pole Star and, every time I did so, the whole aspect of the heavens seemed to have changed. The discovery that the planets moved across the sky, each in its own path, just as the sun does by day, made it difficult for me to keep my mind on my own petty earth-bound affairs.

The fifth night of my escape found me approaching Gleiwitz. Crossing a field I climbed a steep bank to a major road which ran along the top, and looked cautiously in either direction. Seeing the road was empty I crossed. On the other side I stood transfixed, for, looking down the bank in the pitch darkness, I had the illusion of standing on a cliff-edge, looking out over a black smooth sea. There was also a pier with lights along its length which jutted out from the coastline below me. As my eyes adjusted themselves I saw that I was quite mistaken but that there had, in fact, been a road accident and a single-decker bus had crashed down the slope and was on its side in the field below, with its lights blazing. By the worst possible luck I had chosen this particular spot at which to cross the road. I wondered why I had not seen the lights before I crossed the road, but realised that they were in fact quite dim and would certainly have been hidden by the embankment.

At first I thought the bus was deserted but a voice shouted out in German, 'Hands up or we will all shoot!' A little man was standing alone at the front of the bus looking up at me and pointing something in my direction. It was obvious, even in the dark, it was not a revolver. I was about to make off into the night when there was a sound on the road to my left and I found myself looking at a very real revolver. It was held by a young Luftwaffe pilot who had come up silently on his bicycle and when he said 'Hands up!', I obeyed promptly. He demanded to know if I was armed and the little man from the bus took this cue to scramble up the bank and search me in a very inexpert manner. The Luftwaffe pilot then ordered me to march along the road with my hands on my head, while he followed me pushing his bicycle with his revolver prodding me in the back. Apart from his first curt command my captor remained silent but fired a sudden single shot into the field on our right to demonstrate that his revolver was loaded.

We soon reached a small village where my captor banged on the door of a substantial house and shouted for admittance. After a few minutes the door opened and we entered the living room of the village Bürgermeister. Knowing that such an official had to be a keen Nazi I was very relieved to see that one corner of the room was devoted to religious statues and pictures. Taking heart from this evidence of Christianity I said 'Gruss Gott' to the middle-aged owner, who looked a little startled, but then roared with laughter and said to the Luftwaffe pilot, 'Well, that beats everything! An English gangster comes to murder us in our beds and then says "Gruss Gott" '. Then he pulled on his boots and coat and took us to the house of the village policeman. Obviously this worthy had been in bed for he came hurrying to the door in his night-shirt. By this time the Luftwaffe pilot and the Bürgermeister thought it was a great joke to pass on the responsibility for an escaped prisoner to somebody else. Once more I was searched, this time by the policeman although inexplicably he missed my pack. Then he put on his uniform belt over his nightshirt and lifted the flap of his holster to display the re-volver inside. The Bürgermeister and my Luftwaffe captor now left, first shaking hands with me and consoling me on my hard luck and wishing me better luck next time. The policeman looked at me and said kindly, 'I suppose you are hungry?' and produced some bread, cheese and two bottles of beer which we shared at his kitchen table. Then he put on his jackboots and, still in his nightshirt, a comic figure to anybody but an escaped prisoner, took me down the deserted village street, and put me in to the local lock-up. This was a stinking hole, which probably had had nobody in it for the last 50 years except, per-haps, the village drunkard. After wishing me goodnight and locking me in the policeman left, but still hungry even after my snack, I gorged my-self on Red Cross food from my pack after which I quickly went to sleep on the bare and sagging springs of the metal bunk bed.

Next morning the policeman woke me up and said, grinning, 'Now for a spot of work!' I asked if I could first be allowed to clean out the lock-up and wash and shave myself. He was obviously surprised by my request but he readily agreed. Having made myself more respectable, I was taken to a local farm and set to work helping some French prisoners and German peasants gathering in the harvest. These people were all very interested in me, and one old woman pointed to a Frenchman in a nearby field who was driving a combine harvester and asked, 'Why don't you work well like him and be well treated, instead of running away and being punished?'

'Because he is working for Adolf Hitler and I am fighting against him for my country!' I replied stoutly. I had always found that an attitude of extreme patriotism was the correct tack to take when talking to the vast majority of Germans for, as a result of years of National-Socialist indoc-trination, they would respond to me immediately. All the Germans present immediately understood my sentiments although none of the Frenchmen ever spoke and studiously avoided me.

I worked at the farm for two days, saying little, but learning with interest of the hard and simple life of the mid-European peasant. Since even the old women worked bare-footed in the fields with the men I did my best to ferment a little class warfare by commenting on the Nazi Paradise where the workers had no shoes while the Party Members who owned the land wore shining leather boots and leggings. The workers were talking of the RAF's heavy night bombing of North and West Germany and, when they looked questioningly at me, I could assure them that we had hardly started to bomb their cities and that when the winter came they would really see what the RAF could do. I further informed them that we could return to the Continent whenever we wished but for the moment we were quite content to sit and watch the Nazis and Communists slaughter each other, (which, I thought, was quite a good propaganda line, even if not strictly true!).

Back in my lock-up that evening I heard some scuffling outside and managed to drag the iron bedstead to the barred window so I could look out. All the village children were there to see *der Engländer* and, as soon as I looked out, a small girl asked in very precise English, 'Do you speak English?' I smiled and said in German, 'Yes, I am an English soldier and I speak English'. This information caused great excitement and I was told that they were learning English at school and knew an English song. I replied that I would like to hear it and, standing in a line, they solemnly sang:

> *'London's burning, London's burning,*
> *Fetch the engines, Fetch the engines,*
> *Fire! Fire! Fire! Fire!*
> *But we have no water.'*

I applauded their singing and told them seriously that Berlin was also burning and that maybe Gleiwitz would be one day. Then I told them to go home and go to bed so they would grow up big and strong and be able to fight against war, for, I continued, war and killing people were wicked so they must help put a stop to it when they grew up. I hoped that the novelty of talking to me would help them remember these sentiments and that it would do something to counteract the propaganda to which they were subjected at their Hitler Youth meetings.

On the following day there was no work for me for, when the door of the lock-up was opened by the policeman, there was an armed grim-looking Unteroffizier with him. This was obviously my escort back to Lamsdorf and I felt quite gratified that, in the opinion of the Stalag authorities, I warranted a senior NCO to guard me instead of the usual Private or Gefreiter. When we were leaving I turned to the policeman, who had not spoken to me in front of the Unteroffizier, and said a polite 'Thank you'.

At once my guard snarled at me, 'What are you thanking him for?'

The policeman looked relieved when I replied primly that it was 'Because he has treated me as a soldier and not as a criminal!'

I marched along the road to Gleiwitz in silence, with the surly Nazi walking behind me. I was quite annoyed by having to walk as I felt that although it was a pleasure to go on foot when escaping, when returning to a prison camp I could at least expect transport!

Although I had not had any breakfast it was not hunger but thirst that troubled me as we proceeded along the dusty road in the heat of the mid-summer. In the middle of the morning my companion called a halt outside a beer-garden in a small village and called for a glass of beer.

The publican's wife asked if she could give me a glass of water but my guard snapped at her, 'Certainly not! He is one of the enemy!'

A small group of villagers had now collected and seeing I had an audience for British propaganda and not wanting to allow the Nazi even a small victory over me I proceeded. 'Yes, I am one of the enemies of National Socialism and so are millions of others to the west, to the south and to the east, and just you wait a little for the Americans are coming to join us too!' This last observation was greeted with incredulous laughter and rather than look at my unpleasant escort guzzling his beer I walked over to the edge of the road opposite to examine the *Stürmer-Kasten*. (A Stürmer-Kasten was a notice board on which pages from Julius Streicher's semi-pornographic anti-Jewish newspaper *Der Stürmer* were displayed for propaganda purposes.) One of the group by the beer-garden commented with satisfaction that, 'Now the *verfluchter Engländer* (damned Englishman) will learn something about the racial question from reading *Der Stürmer*.'

I turned round and grinned, saying, 'Yes, and I believe every word in it, but when Streicher writes the word "Jew" I always read the word "Nazi"'! Then I demonstrated my method for them by reading aloud, 'The Nazis are curse of our country!' and 'He who knows the Nazis knows the Devil'. At this my delightful companion brandished his rifle with a roar and ordered me to stop talking and start marching.

It seemed, however, that the beer had failed to quench his thirst for, after a few miles, we came to a pump by the roadside and he called another halt. He nodded towards it and went through the motions of pumping. 'You first!' I said, using the second person singular form 'Du', which is restricted for use to inferiors but he must have been nearly as thirsty as I was for he ignored my insult and started to pump for me! I took off my shirt and not only drank my fill but also had a thorough wash. Eventually we changed places and at last continued on our way considerably refreshed.

Marching on in complete silence we passed four English prisoners with their attendant guard on the outskirts of Gleiwitz. As we passed they looked at us with keen interest and I realised that to see a single Private soldier with an Unteroffizier as his escort would be something of a novelty. As we passed one man politely bid me, 'Good afternoon'.

'Good afternoon' I replied. 'Wonderful weather we are having!'

'Indeed it is' he answered, and, the social conventions completed we parted without further conversation.

Near Gleiwitz my companion took the opportunity of visiting his Company headquarters, handing me over to another NCO while he paid a visit to the office. No sooner he had left when a Feldwebel (a Company Sergeant Major) passed by with a group of junior officers. Seeing me he stopped and demanded to know who I was, and asked if I spoke German. I admitted I spoke a little and he sneered 'Yes, words like "Bread" and "Sleep", and so on, I do not doubt. You would not understand "Work" or anything like that I am sure!' I sprang smartly to attention and replied promptly 'I am a front-line soldier', (a reference to the fact that he had a safe job behind the lines) 'but I do understand six words in German: *Heil England Sieg in diesem Krieg!*' (Hail England's victory in this war!) Then I stood at ease while he stormed abuse at me and I could see that some of the young officers were hard put to it to suppress a grin. When my guard returned we continued our progress to Gleiwitz without further incident.

In Gleiwitz we went directly to the railway station where my guard discovered that there would be no train for some hours so he took me to a German Red Cross canteen. A very pretty Red Cross girl brought him a meal for which he signed and she said, 'I'm sorry that I cannot give the Frenchman any food, it is against the rules'.

Before he could answer I interrupted. 'Excuse me, I can manage without a meal, but I am not a Frenchman, I am an Englishman!'

She looked at me with interest and asked where I was going and on learning that I was on my way to the Stalag *Straff Kompanie* for punishment she queried why I had tried to escape as 'We treat our prisoners well'.

Following my usual policy I replied that it had been, 'To help my country'.

She gave me a dazzling smile and nodded 'That's why our brave boys in England all escape!' She left us and got a German soldier, who was drinking a cup of coffee, to sign for a complete meal for me and thus I was soon enjoying a bowl of thick soup and a ration of rye bread and sausage.

Back on the station platform I took the opportunity to extend my knowledge of the sidings and of the rolling stock. It had taken me quite a lot of time and trouble to get to Gleiwitz on this first attempt and I still had high hopes of escaping in the future so any increase in knowledge would be helpful to me. It was now early evening and the station's loudspeakers announced that our train would not be leaving until 11 pm so my guard marched me to the second class waiting room where an officious military policeman tried to order us out. 'Third class only for prisoners of war', he bellowed. My guard protested that as an Unteroffizier he was entitled to second class travel and I backed him up by saying that, in spite of my uniform, I was a British officer of field rank and as such should be in the first class waiting room in accordance with the provisions of the Geneva Convention. This was, of course, a complete fabrication but one which my companion immediately confirmed and which convinced the policeman who left us in peace thereafter. Eventually the policeman left and my guard and I grinned at each other, for once in alliance. Military Police are the common enemy of all fighting soldiers whatever their nationality and mutual dislike of this man was probably the only thing that the Unteroffizier and I had in common.

After a time I said that I needed to 'relieve nature', partly in the hope that this would afford me with an opportunity to escape, but my NCO insisted on keeping me in full view throughout this operation, with his rifle dramatically aimed at me all the time, to the intense interest of the other men using the same facility at the time. When we returned to the waiting room my companion became conscious of a similar need and handed his rifle over to a fellow Unteroffizier, who was also waiting for a train. Before he left my guard added some remarks about me, which I took as compliments, but which made my new guard look quite concerned. The fellow sat directly opposite me and stared unblinking at me the whole time. I was startled when he suddenly started to hum 'Home sweet home'. I commented that it was an English song and he told me that he had studied English at school for three years but apart from that one English song had forgotten every word. I commiserated with him but assured him that when the British eventually won the war he would be surprised how quickly his knowledge of the language would return!

At last our train came into the station and since there were very few passengers at that hour we had a compartment to ourselves. I stretched myself out on one of the seats and composed myself for sleep, teasingly informing my surly companion that the moment he closed his eyes I would be out of the window taking his rifle with me!

The train must have been a very slow one for we did not reach Lamsdorf until it was full daylight. On reaching the camp I was marched directly to the gate of *Straff Kompanie* where the Unteroffizier at last broke his silence to bid me farewell, saying smugly, 'Now you will find out how we treat people like you in Greater Germany'.

15

Neumann's

The first people to greet me in the Punishment Compound were the Big Four! They had been recaptured within two hours of escaping by blundering on to a Luftwaffe aerodrome in the dark where they had been halted by a sentry. When questioned in the guardroom of the airfield they had quite correctly refused to give any information except their ranks, names and prisoner of war numbers. They had resolutely refused to admit that they came from the local working party for they did not want my escape hindered. The Germans could see, however, that they had not come far and in the early hours of the morning telephoned the working party to enquire if any prisoners were missing. Their captors were told that it was thought that a fifth man had been in the party who had escaped, but Roberts denied this, not wanting the area searched too soon in case I was still close at hand. Suddenly there had been a lot of shouting outside and shots were fired and a German soldier came dashing in shouting 'We have just killed the fifth man!'

'Good God! Poor old Gayler!' Roberts had whispered, appalled. The guard commander shouted in triumph, 'Ah! You fell for that trick didn't you? There *is* a fifth man after all — continue the search!' Later they were told soberly that I had indeed been killed but that I would be buried with full military honours. Thus, when I entered *Straff Kompanie* they had thought they were seeing a ghost and they were very apologetic for they had been telling everybody I was dead!

Later on I was able to piece together the events at the Stalag on the night of our escape. Men who had been there and later returned sick to Lamsdorf told me that there had been an emergency roll-call in the middle of the night, presumably as soon as the telephone call had come through from the aerodrome. The prisoners were expecting this and had already fixed the bars back at the window and continued to cause as much confusion as possible in the darkness. When they were counted at roll-call five men at the beginning of the line managed to creep along the back row to the other end of the parade and be re-counted. The guards had been so happy to find that they still had their full muster of 200 prisoners that they didn't even bother to examine the barbed wire and so didn't discover the huge hole. They sent the men back to bed and the hated Stalag Unteroffizier presumably rang up the airfield and reported, with relief and pride, that the captured Englishmen were not from his work party.

When the dawn came, one may imagine the consternation of the enemy ranks when it was discovered that five prisoners *were* missing. Every prisoner savoured to the full the mental picture of the Unteroffizier once more 'phoning up the aerodrome to say humbly, 'Please, those prisoners were mine after all'. That same day he was replaced by a much more mild character and the whole working party sincerely hoped that his predecessor would be sent to the Russian front for the rest of the war.

The *Straff Kompanie* had fewer inmates than on my last visit but they were as intelligent and as high spirited as the other lot so in the company of Roberts and the rest of the Big Four I settled down to quite a happy period of waiting for my turn in the cells. The routine of the place had altered little during my absence, although a new commandant of the Stalag had issued an order that *Straff Kompanie* was a misnomer as the men there were not undergoing punishment but only awaiting it. The new Nazi Unteroffizier now in charge of the compound was known as 'Ukrainian Joe'. He was very unpopular and the story circulated that although he was from the Ukraine and so one of the German racial minorities he had endeared himself to the Nazis by murdering a Ukraine commissar for them. For this he had been rewarded with the rank of Unteroffizier in the German Army and given the safe job guarding prisoners of war. How true this tale was I do not know but life became far more comfortable for us when he was transferred to take charge of the RAF compound and was replaced by a milder type of man.

At the end of the war I heard how 'Ukrainian Joe' was taken prisoner by the British. He was spotted by an ex-inmate of the RAF compound while road-mending outside the Oval Cricket Ground in London. He was reported to the British Authorities by the RAF Sergeant and punished for his conduct in Lamsdorf.

As the Punishment Compound was isolated from the rest of the Stalag we suffered from an acute fuel shortage and were unable to cook our Red Cross food or make tea. One day I was brooding over this important matter with some others when one of the men looked out of the window and said thoughtfully, 'The 40 Seater would burn'. The Lamsdorf latrines, or 40 Seaters as they were usually called, deserve a chapter to themselves in the history of sanitation. All the other latrines in the Stalag were brick-built bungalows, but those of *Straff Kompanie* were of wood (presumably to symbolise the disfavour in which we were held by the Nazis). These bungalows had no partitions inside them, just a low bench along the length of the two longer walls. Each bench had ten holes in it, while an 'island' bench running down the middle had another 20 holes on either side. A urinal across either end of the building completed the furnishings. Under each latrine block was a huge cellar into which the night earth fell. These were pumped out at monthly intervals and the contents removed by the 'Soup Cart' which was a familiar sight in the Stalag and drawn by a magnificent pair of Belgian horses.

Our plans for attaining an adequate fuel supply thus got underway. Measurements were secretly taken of the *Straff Kompanie* 40 seater and a new industry was started by the inmates of the compound — removing the tops and bottoms of Red Cross food tins, opening them down the seams to make a small sheet of flat metal, and then joining these to make a metal strip as long as a plank. When opportunity offered one of the planks was removed from the latrine and our metal substitue inserted. For months the Punishment Compound never lacked fuel and eventually became the proud possessor of the only all-metal latrine in Greater Germany!

After a long wait in *Straff Kompanie* I was taken to the German section of the camp and marched into the now familiar office, while my guard, as previously, remained outside. The same officer as before was sitting at his desk and the same secretary was sitting in the corner at her typewriter. As I entered the officer was saying to his Secretary 'You will remember Mister Gayler, Gnädige Frau (dear lady). He is in the way of becoming one of our most frequent visitors.' I clicked my heels and gave the woman a short bow, as German good manners demanded. She acknowledged this by inclining her head and giving me a broad grin. The officer then turned to me and said, 'Mutiny last time and now escape, you do have an eventful life, Gayler!' Then, as before he started to read a typed report about my escape, and suddenly commented 'Like your friends, I see you solved the problem of the boots and trousers. It will, of course, be a waste of time to ask how you managed that as I do not doubt you will have unaccountably forgotten.'

Without batting an eyelid I agreed with him and it dawned on me that I never had found out how the 'Big Four' had solved that little problem. He continued to read, suddenly remarking 'You had three boxes of matches in your pack'. He looked at me over the tops of his glasses and said with mock severity, 'and not one of them in a waterproof container!' After completing his reading he said 'Very poor, Gayler. You averaged only just over ten kilometers a night. In future you must do far better than that!' His words took me back into the past when almost exactly the same sentiments were expressed by my form master, the redoubtable J. A. Morris, during a distressing interview at Latymers a few years earlier.

I was sentenced to three weeks in the cells and, as I left the office, the officer called after me, 'Try to do more than one day's work before you visit us next time, Gayler, that's all you did last time you know'.

Back in *Straff Kompanie* I reported my sentence to the Sergeant

Major. Having been an inmate once already I found that I was considered to be a member of the inner sanctum. As such I was entrusted by the senior British Warrant Officer in charge with organising a voluntary collection of Marmite cubes from our food parcels for the prisoners from Crete who had recently arrived in Lamsdorf and who were suffering from beri-beri (vitamin B deficiency). When I handed in the proceeds of the collection the Sergeant Major had a long chat with me and strongly advised me to keep out of trouble with the Germans until the following spring. He pointed out that a third spell in the cells would ear-mark me as a trouble maker and then the Stalag Authorities might be tempted to pretend that I had committed some civilian crime and have me sent to a concentration camp, secure in the knowledge that I would never survive to return to trouble them again.

The day before I was due to go to the cells we were issued with one of our weekly parcels and although I ate as much as I could at one sitting I had quite a lot left over. This I gave to a small RAF Sergeant who seemed to be always on his own and he thanked me very civilly for it. Shortly after I had done this an acquaintance informed me that the fellow was probably the least deserving case in the whole compound as he had been caught by a German guard stealing another prisoner's food. Thus, he was the only man in *Straff Kompanie* who was considered a criminal by British and Germans alike.

On this occasion solitary confinement was no longer a novelty to me and so I soon settled down in my cell. Gradually I found myself day-dreaming far more than on the previous occasion, imagining myself free and in various circumstances all of which gave me great pleasure. Becoming aware of this tendency I experimented with the technique of first inducing a mental state of happiness by day-dreaming and then consciously abandoning the imagined circumstances but retaining the emotion of intense pleasure. However, after a time I abruptly abandoned this exercise for it suddenly seemed to be dishonest and dangerous, but years later I was interested to discover in my reading that St Bonaventura had given a discipline closely resembling my 'day-dreaming' to the nuns of the Clarisse order as a spiritual exercise.

Having abandoned mental exercises I suddenly became obsessed with the need to keep myself fit while in the cells, so I began to practice a form of an Indian physical culture called 'Surya Mamaskars' which requires no apparatus and can be performed in a limited space and is therefore ideal for performance in a cell. Regretfully I had to abandon this too after fainting (for the first time in my life) during the German punishment drill one day. An excessive physical culture performed on a bread and water diet was obviously not to be recommended.

When my three weeks' sentence was over I was once again escorted by a guard to the Red Cross Store to collect the two parcels which I had missed while in the cells. Once more the cheerful Sergeant Major made his little joke about the fact that I needed a haircut and shave, and once more he suddenly became serious and asked me to accept a parcel which had 'come open in transit'. He was quite startled when I thrust my bearded face to within half an inch of his and snarled that I wanted parcels that had not been opened by him or anybody else. I was served quickly and silently and as I left the store I turned to the now worried looking Warrant Officer and said, 'You have done this once too often Sergeant Major so beware, some of the other characters in *Straff Kompanie* are not as easy-going as I am!'

In the working compound I was again amused by the speed with which I was allocated to a party of men who were leaving the Stalag next day. On the morning of November 3 1941 (the anniversary of my mother's death), we had the first snow fall of the winter as I left Lamsdorf with 14 companions and two guards for an unknown destination.

The new *Arbeitskommando* (Working Party) was a very small one, consisting only of the 15 prisoners from Lamsdorf Stalag. We were employed in helping to collect in the sugar beet harvest, a task which involved a huge number of British prisoners. Most of the British prisoners were employed on farms throughout the agricultural region of Upper Silesia, lifting the beet and loading it onto horsedrawn carts. Our small party was stationed in a café near a railway halt where the loaded carts were weighed, unloaded by us into railway wagons and then taken to a central factory, where yet more British prisoners of war were engaged in unloading them.

One of my friends was sent with a work party to labour in a sugar-beet factory. When they arrived there the German NCO in charge read out a long official screed saying that if any sugar was stolen, however small the quantity, the whole group would be severely punished. Then, he folded up the notice and said, 'Every Friday afternoon you will be searched on your return from work. God help any man who has not enough sugar on him to help keep the guards and myself supplied for the coming week! For the rest of the time you will not be searched at all, so any soldier who goes short of sugar will be a very foolish man indeed!'

The small group of men with whom I worked were a good crowd and our two guards were very friendly. We hated Herr Neumann, our employer, on sight because of his well-displayed Nazi Party membership badge. Yet, he treated us well and gave us better rations than we had ever had before as prisoners. He seemed quite prepared to make life comfortable for us as long as we worked well for him (which we were forced to do, for we were employed in the open fields in the middle of the bleak Polish winter, so it was work or freeze!) The small farmers, whose wagons we were unloading, were very anxious to get the job done as quickly as possible, and the word soon circulated among them that a few marks on the side in civilian money had a magical effect

113

on the speed with which the Englishmen would empty a wagon. Of course, this was strictly illegal, as we could then use the civilian money for bribery, but the farmers were willing to take the risk and even our guards were sufficiently corrupt to turn a blind eye to our activities in exchange for a few items of Red Cross food or some cigarettes.

Our working party was so small and we all got on so well together that we started to pool all our food parcels. Our leader, Corporal Bill Mitchell, had complete charge of the 'pool' and would make surprise issues of a small ration of chocolate or a mug of tea at odd intervals throughout the day.

Undoubtedly the most interesting man on the party was 'Dodger' Green who, in civilian life, was a baker employed by the Co-operative Society of Blackpool. He had been captured at Dunkirk after being wounded in the arm. During the march he had realised that he must get medical attention quickly or lose his arm or maybe even his life. He successfully escaped from the column of prisoners and had made his way to Brussels. There he had wandered round the streets in his British Army uniform, with his arm in a sling, but had attracted no attention — such was the confused state of Belgium immediately after the German occupation. At last he had seen a Salvation Army headquarters and, as a member of that movement in Britain, he went in and introduced himself to an English-speaking Salvationist. At this moment a German officer entered hard on his heels but quickly explained that he had been a member of the Salvation Army in Germany before it had been banned by Hitler and, seeing Dodger outside, he had come to see if he could be of any help 'during these difficult times'. He greeted Dodger in English and said, 'You are an English soldier and wounded. You are wise to come to the Army of Christ when in need for the brothers and sisters help men of all nations. Good luck to you!'

Events moved quickly and soon Dodger was whisked away to the home of a loyal Salvationist where he was nursed until his wound was quite healed. Then, as the Belgian Underground became more organised he was passed from one safe place to another. At one time he lived with a communist whose wife was a washerwoman and so poor Dodger spent most of his time turning the mangle for her. On another occasion he lived with a high ranking Roman Catholic priest and enjoyed a better standard of living than he had ever known in his life before. He had many stories to tell us of life in Nazi-occupied Europe. For instance, he told us how, in the early days of occupation of Belgium, as soon as a German entered a café every Belgian present immediately rose and walked out. This infuriated the Nazis so much that they issued a proclamation saying that nobody was to leave for 15 minutes after the entry of a German. The result was that as soon as a German came into a café everybody stopped talking, took out their watches, propped them against their glasses and sat and stared at them for 15 minutes. As soon as the stated time was up they all pocketed their watches, got up and trooped out.

On another occasion the Nazis had ordered that Jews were not permitted to possess radio sets and must all report to the Nazi headquarters to hand them in. When the appointed day arrived a long queue of people formed all carrying radios of every type and size, some so huge that they were in wheelbarrows. Just before the doors of the Nazi office were due to open a fleet of cars swept into the street, pulled up and out jumped a crowd of university students, each with a hopeless old wireless set. The students approached the Jews and said something to the effect of: 'Excuse me, Sir, I will give you 1,000 francs for your radio-gramophone and this old set to hand in to the Germans'. A few moments later the enraged Germans were taking delivery of the most worthless collection of radio rubbish to be found in Europe. However, Dodger continued, the last grim laugh was with the Nazis, for soon afterwards they had started shipping Jewish families off to an unknown destination in Eastern Europe so most of the men in that queue must, by now, be in concentration camps, along with their wives and children.

At one time Dodger had been on the staff of an underground newspaper, *La Libre Belgique*, which was printed secretly at the same plant where a Nazi propaganda paper was produced . Dodger had been on the distribution staff and told us that whenever a newspaper seller sold a German-sponsored paper his customers could help themselves to a free illegal newspaper from the sack at his feet.

When Dodger was dressed in Nazi uniform and given a small moustache apparently he looked remarkably like Hitler. One day his illegal paper had printed a photograph of Dodger with the caption, 'One of our staff in Brussels'. Most of the readers thought it was just a joke to suggest that Hitler was working for the underground, although a small circle were aware that the caption was in fact perfectly true!

In Holland as their Queen's birthday drew near the Germans refused to permit the usual celebrations as 'that treacherous woman has deserted her country and gone to England'. Dodger told us that when the birthday arrived every Dutchman 'just happened' to wash his country's flag and hang it out to dry! The whole country was a mass of flags, which naturally enraged the impotent Germans.

Eventually Dodger had been betrayed by an unknown informer and arrested by the SS in the early hours of the morning. He was unusually reticent about his life in the SS prison, although we had heard tell of how hostages were daily shot in the courtyard. Once, when I commented that Neumann's soup was a little monotonous, Dodger said he thought it was definitely better than that served by the SS, adding wryly that 'I found a used contraceptive in mine one day!'

Dodger gave me information that caused me to change my plans for escape. He explained that, although the underground movements had methods of getting escaped prisoners back to Britain, RAF flying crews always had priority as they were so important to the Allied war effort.

He assured me that a Private soldier only stood a very slim chance of being helped by the underground. Therefore, my only chance was to reach a neutral country where there was a British Embassy and where I could openly be repatriated or employed in some useful capacity. Turkey and Spain were too far away, while Switzerland was heavily guarded, so I decided that Sweden was probably my best bet. Although it would involve getting across the Baltic Sea I hoped that it would be easier to smuggle myself onto a Swedish ship in a German harbour rather than attempting to cross a land frontier crawling with troops.

We had little to grumble about at Neumann's for our billets were really very reasonable. They consisted of one small storeroom, in which we all slept and a second room of equal size, where we ate our meals by day and in which two buckets were put at night for our use. At the beginning of December Herr Neumann found that he needed the second room for storage purposes and so that night the two stinking latrine buckets were put in our sleeping quarters, where we were locked in at night. We protested in no uncertain terms at this and next morning refused to work when, as the most fluent in German, I found myself the spokesman for the work party. Since striking was illegal under Nazi law our action caused a great deal of excitement. One of our hitherto amiable guards worked himself up into such a fury that he aimed his rifle at me and screamed that if I did not start work right away he would fire. He was almost insane with rage! His face went a bright red, his pig-like eyes were flashing and he was spluttering with emotion as he looked along his rifle barrel at me. I knew that only one name could bring him to his senses so I stated clearly that 'Adolf Hitler will hear about my death for the British will hang ten Nazi Party prisoners if I am shot!' Slowly he cooled down, lowered his rifle and walked away while we were locked in our small room to speculate about our future.

At midday we saw the arrival of a middle-aged German Army officer from our window. He had obviously come to investigate the trouble. He had a long talk with Neumann and the guards before coming to see us for himself. I stated our case as forcefully as I was able, demonstrating how small our sleeping quarters were, and ended rather foolishly by saying, 'These men deserve good treatment, Sir. There has never been any trouble on this work party, nor has there been a single escape or act of sabotage.'

The fatherly old man seemed to have some difficulty in speaking but, in turn, stunned me by addressing me by name, 'You must be Herr Gayler', he said. 'You were at Gleiwitz for only one week before you were sent to *Straff Kompanie* for mutiny. Then, you were out of the cells for only three days when you attempted to escape. Now you have been here for three weeks and expect special treatment because you have organised a strike!' His eyes raked my companions and he demanded, 'Who is Herr Green?' When Dodger was pointed out the officer commented that he was surprised that he had not been shot as a spy and, when I translated this into English for Dodger, he modestly agreed that he too was a little puzzled. Eventually the officer settled the dispute and said that, although Herr Neumann must be free to use the second room for storage, he must also leave enough space clear to accommodate the latrine buckets. He went further and said that we were to eat our meals in the kitchen of the Neumann café in future. Naturally we readily agreed to this and in the end the Germans seemed to respect our refusal to tolerate any degrading sanitary arrangements.

A few days later a peasant told us furtively of a local man, a guard on long distance trains, who had been telling local people of the heavy air-raids on North Germany. As a result of spreading 'subversive rumours' he had been sent to a concentration camp. However, soon after, the facts were so generally known that the national radio stations and South German press started to report fully on the news over the radio. The railway guard was not, however, released from the camp.

There was an aerodrome near the Neumann's and I would often talk with the Luftwaffe men in order to learn as much as I could from them about the war. They told me how fanatically the Russians were fighting outside Leningrad, even the badly wounded continuing to use their weapons long after one would have thought it humanly possible to do so. One day, on December 8 1941, a Luftwaffe pilot with whom I got on well came over and asked, 'Well, what do you know?'

I replied with my usual quip that, 'Hess is not the only madman in the German government!' and, as usual my questioner just laughed and walked away.

On the following day I managed to get hold of a Nazi newspaper and belatedly I read of the Japanese attack on Pearl Harbor and how the USA and Japan were now in the war. Immediately I spread the word and realised that victory must come much sooner than we had dared hope. That night we had a spiritualist experiment, writing an alphabet round the edge of our table and taking it in turn to place our fingers lightly on the top of an inverted tumbler. For Dodger the tumbler spelt out the message, 'England next year, June' and, in the light of our recent news, it did not seem too impossible to us in December 1941.

Christmas Day came and the Neumanns had us all into their house for a glass of schnapps. When we returned to our quarters we had quite a surprise for they had fitted up a Christmas tree complete with decorations for us, and as we had already spent some of our illegal tips on a large quantity of cakes to be baked by the wife of a local farmer, we had a far better Christmas than one might imagine possible for prisoners of National-Socialist Germany in 1941. However things did not remain so pleasant for long as one morning in mid-January 1942 we were abruptly told that the sugar-beet harvest was now completed and that same day we were to be moved to another working party.

16

Friedenshütte

With the skill of long practice I packed my worldly belongings into my cowhide pack and two Red Cross food boxes and we left Neumann's by train through a landscape white with snow. Our spirits sank lower and lower as the area through which we travelled became more and more industrialised and we saw the typical pit-head gear of a mining district. However, our small group was not destined for the mines but for a grim, filthy, forbidding steel works called Friedenshütte. Friedenshütte was a nightmare growth from the Industrial Revolution. Ugly brick blast-furnaces, gigantic iron structures, blackened buildings and pollution surrounded us. Even the very air we breathed was laden with filth. Here we joined an existing party of British prisoners, bringing their numbers up to 300. We lived in fairly good German Army billets, but the food was meagre and of poor quality and, as the supply of Red Cross parcels had failed, we again knew hunger (although it was not the near-starvation of 1940).

The prisoners of this work party were employed in three shifts of eight hours each, from 6 am to 2 pm, 2 pm to 10 pm, and 10 pm to 6 am. Our job was to load small trucks with scrap metal and push them to the foot of a blast furnace. There they were carried to the top by machinery and tipped into the furnace. Once piece of Nazi humour, which we did not appreciate, was the provision of special air-raid shelters for British prisoners. These shelters were flimsy little huts at the foot of the furnaces. It was obvious to us that in the case of an air-raid the furnaces would be an attractive target and if a bomb exploded near one, it would crack open pouring molten metal over our little shelters and kill everybody inside.

I have never known more reluctant or inefficient workers than we were at this place, especially as some of us suspected that such a huge devil's kitchen as this could not exist in a country at war without producing munitions. I said as much to one of our guards and pointed out that it was against the Geneva Convention to employ us on such work. The German violently denied that the plant produced munitions and the next night he took me on a conducted tour to demonstrate the truth of what he had said.

We started our tour at the railway sidings where we saw the coal and iron ore arriving. Here, I was struck dumb, for I was confronted with one of the most unexpected and beautiful sights I have ever seen. The train containing the iron ore went to Sweden! I realised that once the weather became mild enough for me to travel I could escape by clinging to a railway wagon. Here was my route to a neutral country, and what's more the very one I had already chosen. With my head in a whirl I had to force myself from staring at the train and so arouse his suspicions. Pulling myself together we continued our tour. Next we visited a huge scrap metal heap where a gigantic metal ball was lifted by an electric magnet and dropped on the metal below to crush it. The we saw the various blast furnaces with the molten metal running from them into sand castings. From the castings the red hot ingots were carried by overhead cranes to the huge rolling mills where the metal was reduced to long strips. Dramatically the guard pointed at these and said, 'Railway lines, Herr Gayler. The same railway lines on which you will all travel home. Tell your comrades about this!' When I asked him if I could explore on my own he laughed and said that he had had a great deal of trouble to get permission to take me on a *conducted* tour and the last thing he would dream of doing was to let me loose on my own for even five minutes, which I took as a great compliment.

From this time on I spent a lot of my time thinking of my departure from Friedenshütte. There were thousands of potential hiding places and I planned to select a lair where I could build up a store of food and equipment to take with me. When my escape was discovered every exit from the works would be heavily guarded and all departing Swedish trains carefully searched for many days afterwards. Thus I planned to hide within the plant for at least a week and only then board a train. I selected my hiding place carefully and made sure that I could approach it from our working area by climbing over piles of scrap metal for, since these piles were constantly changing, no dog would ever find my scent over them. Once aboard the train, it was obvious that it would be searched at intervals throughout its journey to Sweden, although this could only be done while it was stationary. Therefore my technique must be to travel in as much comfort as possible while the train was in motion but to disembark and hide nearby every time it halted. However, I knew very little about ships and therefore could make no plans for my journey across the Baltic, but this did not worry me unduly as I realised that I could not plan ahead for everything. One thing I did hope for was that the trucks would be transported across the sea in a rail ferry so I could board simply by keeping on the train. However, if they were hoisted aboard by crane I would have to risk smuggling myself on ship for I would risk being seen while in mid-air, or of falling if I had to cling to the underside of the wagon. It was these thoughts that helped to keep up my morale during those grim winter days at Friedenshütte.

As well as my British friends I made a number of contacts with Polish workers at the plant. One of these was a youth of 15 who bitterly resented having to attend evening classes to study the German language, for, in this Polish area, the Nazis had made it illegal to speak any language but German in all public places. As my young friend's mother spoke only Polish she could no longer do the family shopping as nobody would serve her and if she did go out she ran the risk of being arrested for not speaking German. His father was the best blacksmith in Friedenshütte and, shortly after the Germans occupied the area, he had been called to the main office where he found three Brownshirts waiting for him. Without a word they had attacked him with rubber truncheons and had beaten him until he was unconscious. When he recovered they had said, 'That is to show you who is master now.'

Another of my Polish friends warned me to take care in what I said to any Pole, even himself, for my remarks might be reported to the Nazis. When I said I found it difficult to believe that any Pole would work for the Nazis, he gently explained how such things were 'arranged' in German-occupied territory. For instance any Pole could receive a letter instructing him to report to the local police station, and with fear in his heart, he would know that he must obey or, that night, the SS would come for him. When the Pole arrived at the police station the policeman on duty would, with strange politeness, show him into a back room where a plain clothes Gestapo man would greet him with a smile, shake his hand and invite him to sit down. Such unexpected treatment would completely bewilder the Pole and put him off balance. The Gestapo man would then inform him that he had been selected to become a member of the Nazi Party Secret Information Service, at which the unfortunate man would protest that he was a Pole and could not undertake such a post. His protests would be waved aside and the German would explain his duties to him. 'During the next 24 hours many Poles will criticise Hitler, the German people and Nazi Party to you. You will send me a complete list of these people and what they say. One of these people is already in our service and will speak to you under our orders. If his name is not on the list you submit to me, your wife and children will be sent to a special heavy labour camp inside Germany, your mother and father, being too old to be useful, will be shot, while you will be sent to a concentration camp where death is slow and very painful. On the other hand, if you send in a complete and genuine list you will continue life here for 18 months, acting as our agent in secret, and so we will know that you are not a Pole but a *Volks Deutsch* and sympathetic to our cause.' (*Volks Deutsch*, the Nazi term for a member of the pre-war German racial minority in Poland). 'As such you will be moved to another party of the country, given a new home and a better job. Your children will go to a first-class school and you and your whole family will share in the glorious future of the Great German Reich of

Adolf Hitler.' When my friend related this to me I wondered how many pacifists in Britain realised against what barbarity they were refusing to fight.

Early in February 1942, some time after I had arrived at the working party, I began to suffer from acute toothache and was sent to the local civilian dentist for an extraction. The dentist was the shortest, fattest woman I have ever seen and I think she must have been Polish as she had two notices on her waiting room wall which read, 'Here we use only the German greeting "Heil Hitler!"' and 'Patients are requested not to spit on the floor'. However, when I picked up a copy of *Angriff* I soon lost my grin from reading the notices, for I discovered that Singapore had fallen to the Japanese. Like most Britons at that time I had always had unquestioning faith in the strength of Singapore and so considered its loss in a far more serious light than I had the fall of France in 1940.

Once in the surgery there was little doubt about the nationality of my dentist for I was not left alone with her for a moment and my guard stood stolidly by the dental chair throughout the extraction. In spite of this she managed to give me a smile, a wink and a squeeze of the hand and was very gentle, giving me an injection, which was more than I expected in the circumstances.

That night I paraded for work wearing a Balaklava helmet (knitted by Dorothy) plus everything else I could muster to keep the cold out of my mouth. One of the guards laughed at my odd appearance but inexplicably disappeared into the camp office when I explained the reason. He soon came out with a broad smile on his face and remarked, 'I suppose you call me a Nazi bastard behind my back, but, go on, go back to bed, I've got you the night off work'. This man, Karl, was, in fact, a keen National-Socialist but a very decent chap in spite of that. Previously, he had worked as a brick layer on Hitler's new chancellery in Berlin and had twice spoken to his Führer during his surprise visits to the site. At Christmas every man on the site had received a hamper from Hitler as an expression of his gratitude for their efforts.

Karl told me how well he had always got on with British prisoners. On one work party each guard had had ten prisoners to look after and, one day, Karl had been very upset when only nine of his men reported, especially when he discovered that the tenth man had got fed up with working in his squad and had managed to transfer to another group, which was under the command of a most unpopular guard. Karl had always looked on his men as friends rather than as prisoners and had been quite hurt, until that same evening, when it was discovered that the tenth man had escaped during the day and had only made his transfer so that Karl should not be punished for his escape.

One afternoon most of the German workmen did not appear for the shift and our guard told us that they were attending a huge meeting which was to be addressed by the Gauleiter for Upper Silesia. The meeting was an appeal to them to work harder, and to ask them to volunteer to work longer hours for their Führer. This motion, needless to say, was carried unanimously and resulted in all foremen and non-manual workers having their working day extended from 8 to 12 hours. At weekends, as is usual on shift work, one shift always did double time so that all workers could change their hours of duty without interrupting the flow of work. For the non-manual workers this meant a 24-hour tour of duty on alternate weekends, and even we, as prisoners of war, could see the rapid deterioration in the efficiency of their work. The Nazis' solution to this situation was to send selected workers for a three-month course of 'Political re-education' at the local concentration camp. On their return to the plant these people would work like madmen and their example was seen as a warning to all other workers. It was believed that the Nazis had compiled a list of 'bad workers' and that whenever the production figures showed a decline the next two men on the list would be sent for so-called 'Political re-education'.

On another occasion it was all the Polish workers who were missing and next day one of them told me what had happened. Somehow the Gestapo had obtained a membership list of the Polish Underground Movement and had arrested the 12 local men who were on it. The previous afternoon every Polish worker had been forced to attend a meeting organised by the Germans in the main street of the town and had to have his name checked off on a police list as being present. The crowd had been surrounded by German soldiers with machine-guns and the local Nazi district Führer made a speech in Polish while gallows were being erected behind him. When his speech was finished the 12 prisoners were marched out and then the Nazi chose 12 Poles at random from the crowd and ordered them to hang their 12 fellow countrymen. My informer said that the 12 bodies were still hanging from the gallows in the main street and would remain there for 24 hours as an example to the local population. Our guards and the German workers just laughed at us when we enraged British prisoners of war protested about this barbarism, although one guard did agree with me that the Germans in Berlin would not believe how the Germans in Poland were conducting themselves.

Bad though the conditions were at Friedenshütte, the prospect of working down a local coal mine appealed even less to me although I realised that it was an ever-present possibility. Before prisoners were sent to the mines I was aware that there was always a brief medical inspection by a German Medical Officer. I wondered if wearing glasses would lead to rejection for mine work and determined to get myself a pair. We were paid 70 pfennigs a day for our labour (about seven pence), but, as we could not buy anything with it, I had amassed quite a large sum. Therefore I complained that my eyes were giving me trouble and that I wished to buy some spectacles. The very next day I set out with a guard to have my eyes tested. It was soon obvious that we were leaving Friedenshütte and, when I questioned the guard, he said, very shortly, that we were going to the next town, Konigshütte. This puzzled me as I was sure that Friedenshütte was large enough to support at least one optician, but concluded that they must order things differently in Germany.

As we were walking along a main road an extraordinary figure approached us, slinking along and looking furtively around him. He was a Jew, for he wore the six pointed yellow star on his ragged coat as required by Nazi law. Immediately it was obvious to me why he had not been imprisoned in the local concentration camp with all the other Jews. He was such a nightmarish figure that he was the perfect embodiment of the National Socialist idea of the Wandering Jew and of great propaganda value to them walking the local streets. He was a grimy figure with an unkempt matted beard, and so ugly he looked the personification of evil. As we passed I saluted him with a 'Shalom', the Hebrew greeting which means, I believe, 'Peace be with you'. As I expected, the old man was too scared to reply, but I hope the greeting gave him some morsel of comfort as it was probably the first civil word spoken to him for years. I had expected a demonstration of rage from my guard for addressing the Jew but was surprised instead by his look of panic. My guard's one objective in life was to get me as far away from the Jew as quickly as possible. Obviously he was scared that if anybody in authority had witnessed the incident, he would be held responsible for the conduct of his prisoner.

Shortly afterwards we reached the optician's where I was amazed to discover that he was a Jew too, but superimposed on his Star of David were the words 'Useful Jew'. I knew that practically every Jew in Upper Silesia was in a concentration camp, including all doctors, dentists and opticians. Why was this man exempted and why had he received from the Nazis the accolade 'useful'? I was almost certain that this obsequious individual must have been a traitor to his people to have received such favoured treatment. Anyway, he was obliging enough to confirm that I was slightly myopic and prescribed a pair of spectacles, which I paid for at once, and which were to be posted to me the following week.

On leaving the optician's it became clear why I had been taken to Konigshütte to have my eyes tested — my guard's girlfriend lived there and we were to pay her a visit on the way back to the working party. While my guard was having a tête-à-tête with her I sat with her mother in the kitchen, having, to my shame, given my word of honour to the guard not to escape for an hour. The time passed quite pleasantly for me, sitting in the kitchen with the middle-aged Hausfrau and drinking ersatz coffee and chatting. It ended with us poring over the family atlas so I could show her where I lived in England, but I quickly extended our researches to demonstrate the extent of Germany, Italy and Japan compared with America, Russia and the British Empire. The fact that the British Isles were supported by Australia, Canada, India, New

Zealand and South Africa as well as 'lots of little countries in Africa and hundreds of islands scattered about the world' certainly sobered my hostess. A week later I received my glasses and added them to my other possessions as an insurance policy against mine work.

As the winter drew to an end my thoughts turned more seriously to my escape plans but, once again, my plans were delayed. One night I felt suddenly very ill and reported to a guard who marched me to the nearest first-aid post. A Medical Orderly took my temperature and seeing it was sky high ordered me to bed. I remember no more until I recovered consciousness in the Medical Orderlies' room where, apparently, I had been carried on a stretcher. It so happened that the day before I was taken ill I had been reading Robert Louis Stevenson's short story *The Suicide Club*, and in my delirium, I raved with some eloquence, about the wickedness of suicide. When I returned to normal one of the Medical Orderlies treated me with great respect, bordering on awe, for he was a devout Irish Catholic and very superstitious.

I was extremely ill for a week and quite unable to eat or drink, to the great concern of the Medical Orderlies who thought I had pneumonia, but who had no way of treating me. Afterwards I discovered that the whole camp had been seething with indignation over the lack of medical care and there had even been talk of a strike to get me sent to a proper hospital. However, the proposed strike came about for totally different reasons when some prisoners returned to the camp with the news that they had actually seen some shell cases being loaded on railway trucks at the factory. With this news every prisoner refused to work and the atmosphere became electrified. Guards brandishing their rifles forced the men on parade but could not make a single prisoner go back to work. Eventually the Unteroffizier in charge came along with a civilian friend who claimed to speak English. The NCO made an impassioned speech in German which his friend translated, 'Here is munity!' he said. 'The National Socialist Government no like munity, but we are not baa-baas and we are not yet shooting!' There was a roar of laughter from the British, for the idea that anybody should imagine for a moment that they could mistake their guards for little lambs, was so amusing that the tension completely broke and the parade disbanded in disorder. Luckily I was having one of my lucid spells while this was going on, although I knew nothing about the situation outside, so when a Medical Orderly came in and asked 'What does barbar mean in English, Gayler?' I was able to tell him 'Barbarians.'

Next morning a German Major came to investigate my case. He cleverly arranged it so that when the men were called on parade the first thing they saw was me being carried on a stretcher to a waiting ambulance. As I was passing the Major he stopped the stretcher-bearers and apologised to me, in a voice loud enough for all to hear, for not having been given the correct treatment as soon as I had been taken ill. He told me that I was being sent to a first-class military hospital where I would obtain the best treatment in Germany.

I had once been told by a German that their Army Medical Corps had a magical treatment for VD and shell shock; a bullet through the brain. In the ambulance I got illogically concerned in case they used the same treatment on prisoners with pneumonia! During the journey to the hospital I must have fainted for when I came round I was in a hot bath being washed by a nun and an Englishman. When she saw I was conscious the nun said to the prisoner in German, 'He is very clean, ask him where he comes from'. The man did so and explained to me that most of the English patients in the hospital were accident cases from the local mines and they came in covered in coal dust. I joined these men in the ward and soon I was settled in a wonderful bed with real sheets and was interviewed by a German Medical Officer who diagnosed my conditions as inflammation of the left lung and prescribed electrical therapy.

The treatment of British prisoners in Hindenberg military hospital was beyond reproach. Even so the consequences of the war continued to be felt for there was a decided shortage of bedpans and urine bottles. Those men who could get out of bed would make commando-style raids on the German wards for these rare pieces of equipment; raids which were carried out in high good humour and returned with interest, by the German patients. I was amused to discover that there were three ways of 'lying to attention' in a German military hospital. For the low-ranking Medical Officer in charge of our ward we were supposed to lie on our backs and on top of the bed clothes with our arms at our sides. For the doctor in charge of the hospital we were to fold our arms, while for high-ranking visiting specialists we were to lie with our hands behind our heads. Needless to say the British patients were always too ill to observe these forms of military etiquette!

On the surface the staff of the hospital were all 100 per cent National-Socialist but on one occasion when the Mother Superior was making her rounds alone she pointed to a Crucifix on the wall and said softly, 'There is my Führer'. When I met such examples of anti-Nazi sentiment among German Catholics I could never understand the Pope's silence on the barbaric extermination of the gypsies and Jews by the German government. He must have been aware of what was going on, and when I tackled the Germans on the matter they would argue that they could be good Catholics *and* good National-Socialists, for the Pope was as anti-Jewish as Hitler. The Pope probably maintained his silence for excellent reasons but the result was that he badly misled many of his simple German followers.

One day an unusual number of nuns appeared in our ward busying themselves about the place and whispering together. When we asked what was happening they explained that they were hiding because an ambulance train had just arrived from the Russian front. These trains consisted of trucks upon trucks of wounded men they knew from experience that many would already be dead and all would be verminous, wretched and in agony. Even these dedicated women avoided the horror of these ambulance trains whenever possible.

The hospital had a visit from a number of Swiss representatives from the International Red Cross. Although they were accompanied by a bevy of German Army Officers I managed to snatch a brief private conversation with one of them and was delighted to learn that all British prisoners had been withdrawn from Friedenshütte. The Nazis had argued that they were not *directly* engaged on the production of munitions, but, fearing reprisals against German prisoners in British hands, had closed down the working party anyway.

After three weeks in bed on German military hospital rations supplemented by Red Cross food I was judged fit enough to travel by ambulance to Lamsdorf with some other discharged patients. As soon as we arrived at the Stalag we were examined by a British Medical Officer and, once again, I was ordered back to bed, this time in the so-called Convalescent Block. After the comfortable Hindenberg Hospital beds with their clean white sheets a Stalag bunk with a palliasse full of straw was a rude shock, but I was truly thankful to get back into any kind of bed for I was still much weaker than I had realised.

The next day I suddenly saw a man I knew pass my bed. It was Stephenson, the man who had received so many letters from his girlfriend at Spitzwald 18 months before. Steve's arm was in a sling and he explained that he had been employed at a very good working party at a saw mill in the village of Lamsdorf. The German food had been the best so far and with Red Cross supplies it had been quite adequate. The work had been healthy open air labouring and his employers, the Ziertz family, were quite kind people. Steve had accidently cut of the top of his left thumb with a circular saw, but had been promised that he could return to the Ziertz Firm when he was fit again. He urged me to join him if I recovered in time and I readily agreed, knowing from experience how appalling some work parties could be. Steve also brought me up to date with the Stalag news. He told me that, one morning during the winter, the British prisoners had been lined up awaiting work when the German foreman suddenly bent down, scooped up a handful of snow and dashed it into Steve's face, almost knocking him over with his furious rubbing, for the foreman had seen that the tip of Steve's nose had turned black and recognised this as the first sign of frost-bite. Steve had been sent to the village doctor who informed him that the foreman's prompt attention had certainly saved him from losing his nose.

Eventually Steve and I were both passed as fit enough to work by a German Medical Officer so the next day we were collected by a jovial-looking guard to walk down the road to the Ziertz Sawmill.

17

Ziertz

On leaving the Stalag we went through the ritual search when my cow-hide pack, the pride of my life, was pronounced to be German Army equipment and as such was confiscated. When I protested pitifully that I could not carry my pathetic possessions without it my searcher relented and said I could use it to convey my belongings to the sawmill on condition that the guard returned it to the Stalag next day. Upon arrival at the working party I offered the guard 50 cigarettes to 'forget' about the pack, but he said regretfully that he couldn't as the man who had searched me was his senior in rank and was bound to remember. If I wanted to retain my pack I should have offered him the cigarettes!

At 6:30 next morning I started work for the Ziertz family. We were fortunate in that we were employed on healthy open-air jobs which lacked the dull monotony of most work on which prisoners were engaged. We loaded huge wagons with wood, we stacked timber for seasoning in the open air and in drying rooms, we learnt to use every type of mechanical saw, from the huge frame ones for cutting up gigantic logs, to small circular ones for cutting up firewood. We spray painted the agricultural machines, which the sawmill produced as a side-line, and we learnt to sort the soft-wood timber. Over the entrance to the wood yard the name 'A. Ziertz' was written. One day a friend idly wondered what the A stood for and I suggested *Arbeit* (Work). The German peasants thought this was extremely witty and I heard it being passed round for weeks afterwards!

Being young, reasonably well fed and fairly treated we could not but help working with a will, although we did soothe our consciences with an occasional act of sabotage. The most successful of these acts was a strategically dropped cigarette-end on a pile of sawdust which was on the floor of a newly completed drying kiln full of timber. On the ground-floor of the building there was a brand-new Diesel locomotive and, at three o'clock in the morning, the whole thing went up in sheets of flame, which could be seen for miles around. The British were of course suspected and every man on the party was questioned by the police, but nothing could be proved.

While at Friedenshütte I had once got into the German workers' canteen and read a most interesting notice put up by the Nazi Party. It had said, 'German workers! You are now working with British prisoners of war. These men are tough front-line soldiers who will stop at nothing to help the war effort of the enemy. They will commit acts of espionage and sabotage, and will try to spread enemy propaganda. When working with them never speak to them except to give orders; never allow them to do skilled or technical work however willing they may seem; and never let them work unsupervised.' Naturally, human nature being what it is, all these orders were ignored. I related this to my companions at the mill and I pointed out that if we committed any illegal acts the men most anxious to shield us would be the Germans in charge, for they would be held responsible for allowing us to take the opportunity to injure the work of the Reich. A tall taciturn Australian electrician took my words to heart and completely wrecked a whole electrical installation. He went totally unpunished as the chief German electrician had dared not admit that he had left the prisoner alone and in charge. What story the German told the investigating authorities we never knew.

Herr Ziertz also owned a huge tract of the surrounding countryside to grow timber for his mills. As it took about 20 years for the trees to mature, the forest was divided into sections. In peace time the mature trees in one section were felled and then that area replanted. The workers at the mill were secretly worried because the Nazis, in pushing on with their war effort, had ordered the felling of immature trees too, assuring them that after the war had been won all the wood in Scandinavia would be at Germany's disposal.

One day when I was passing the guards living quarters I saw the Unteroffizier in charge sitting at a table with a really tragic expression on his face and a letter on the table in front of him. Now, at this period, it was not unknown for a guard's family residing in North or West Germany to be killed in a British air-raid with uncomfortable consequences for the prisoners in his charge. In case this had occurred again I went into the guards' billet and asked.

'Bad news, Herr Unteroffizier?'

'Yes,' he replied, 'my brother-in-law has gone mad!'

'How terrible for your sister', I said sympathetically.

'It's far worse than it sounds,' he continued. 'He was an Unteroffizier in the Army, like me. One morning he marched into the Company Office and announced that he had accepted Jesus Christ as his Führer and now his only enemy was the Devil and he could no longer follow Hitler or serve in the German Army. When asked if he meant he had become a conscientious objector, he agreed that he had!'

Now, the punishment for conscientious objection in the Third Reich was death but, because of his previous exemplary conduct, instead of being executed he had been sent to a concentration camp.

'He would be better off dead than in one of those places, Karl.' I commented soberly.

'Those are the exact words my poor sister said to my wife.' the German replied sadly.

When the war ended and every German seemed to be protesting ignorance of the existence of concentration camps, let alone what went on in them, I thought grimly that at least three Germans had first-hand experience of them: my friend the Unteroffizier, his sister and his wife.

Food was the eternal preoccupation with prisoners of war, and, although we had our parcels and reasonable rations from our employers, we were always on the lookout for methods of supplementing our diet. One Scot on our work party set snares and caught a number of hares, which were very welcome, although cooking them without our guards discovering what we were doing presented something of a problem. Most days our Australian electrician friend managed to milk one or other of the cows in a nearby field and our potato supply was unlimited for the old caretaker in charge of the store would let us 'borrow' the key for 50 cigarettes a time. For other vegetables we raided the local allotments at night, removing the bars from the window as I had learnt to do when I escaped, and replacing them on return. As Steve was the proud possessor of a sack neither he nor I had to lose any sleep by going on these expeditions as each man who borrowed the sack left a few vegetables in the bottom for us when he returned it.

We had two guards in particular who were quite decent fellows and splendidly corrupt. We could buy a loaf of German rye bread from the peasants quite easily for ten English cigarettes, while the price in the nearby Stalag was 100. However, then we were faced with the problem of smuggling the bread into the camp. This was solved by paying one of the guards 50 cigarettes to hide the goods in his pack while we were searched on entering or leaving the compound and this system resulted in a great deal of profit for all concerned.

Our guards also had a radio set and occasionally allowed us to listen to the German propaganda broadcasts in English. In August 1942 we were delighted when the news of the Dieppe raid was announced although we were equally depressed by its apparent failure. The Canadian prisoners captured on this raid were sent to Lamsdorf, in the inevitable cattle trucks, on the side of which the Germans had written scathingly, 'Churchill's Second Front'.

During my first few weeks at Ziertz I was very weak and my new friends did the bulk of my work for me, but as I quickly grew stronger I still dared not contemplate escape as I was still far below my normal physical condition. As the work at the mill increased, the labour force was supplemented by a group of Ukrainian forced labourers and then further still by a party of British prisoners, who came to the sawmill from the Stalag each morning and returned there at night. One day

Dodger Green, whom I had last seen at Friedenshütte, appeared on the Stalag work party and came running across the wood-yard to speak to me. When he came up close to me he looked into my face uncertainly and said, 'You are Bob Gayler, aren't you? Good Heavens, what has happened to you!'

When I told Steve about this meeting with Dodger he looked at me sideways and said, 'To tell you the truth, Bob, I had no idea who you were when you hailed me from your bed in the Convalescent Compound, but at least I was a little more diplomatic than this chap Green!'

Time passed slowly and winter came once more. A huge prison camp for Russians was established on the other side of Lamsdorf and we saw prison trains arriving at the railway sidings behind the sawmill. The poor wretches were so packed in the trucks that when the doors were opened prisoners were pushed out by the weight of the men behind them. We were outraged by the conduct of some German Army officers who screamed abuse at these prisoners and lashed at them with sticks as they scrambled out of the train. Soon after their arrival a working party of Red Army prisoners came to the sawmill to collect some timber, and we smuggled as much Red Cross food to them as we would spare. The Soviet government had refused to sign the Geneva Convention and, as it was Nazi policy to consider all Slavs as sub-human, the Russian prisoners were treated as expendable and were literally worked to death. I was standing near this miserable group of men when their German guard turned to one of them and snarled, 'Give me the whip!' The man reluctantly drew a dog whip from beneath his coat which the Nazi snatched and started lashing at his prisoners. He seemed quite nonplussed when every Englishman in sight immediately stopped work and came running, up shouting and threatening to have him hanged after the war was over. Afterwards we discovered that whips were standard issue for all Germans in charge of Russian prisoners.

On the other hand the Ukrainian civilian forced labourers were treated better than we were, having no guards and being free to visit the village in their off-duty time. We got on very well with them, but took them to task for having a portrait of Hitler hanging up in their billet. The laughed and assured us that there was a portrait of Churchill on the other side and that they would quickly turn it around when the British Army arrived!

On one occasion a most extraordinary person presented himself at the mill in order to collect some timber along with two local peasants. He was dressed in an unbelievable suit made of pieces of rag tacked together with huge stitches and he was fatter, dirtier and more cheerful than any other German I had ever seen. Our German workmates told us that all the tramps in the country had been rounded up by the Nazis into special camps and were hired out to local employers to contribute to the war effort. The general population seemed to look on them with a mixture of amusement and contempt, and this fellow certainly seemed typical of his class. I caught sight of his hands at close quarters and saw that they were as soft as a child's (under the grime) and when he helped us to load the timber he did a most amazing amount of groaning and grunting although his hands never actually came into contact with the wood! He went through the motions of working with every sign of enormous physical strain for the benefit of his employer, but accompanied them with broad winks to us. He left in high fettle with numerous English cigarettes and bars of chocolate hidden among his rags.

The bitterly cold winter finally passed and with it my third Christmas as a prisoner. We continued to send and receive letters from home fairly regularly and one even reached me via Portugal, Spain, France, Switzerland and Germany in the record time of ten days. Since it had to be passed by both British and German censors en route this was quite an amazing feat. Every three months we were allowed to receive a parcel of clothing from our families and in one of mine were my big leather cycling gloves which proved to be of great comfort when working in the wood yard.

At the end of January 1943 I was stacking some planks of tongued and grooved floor boards when old Karl, the German with whom I was working, suddenly stopped and I looked up to find tears streaming down his face. I asked him what was troubling him and he said, 'My boy is in Stalingrad'. He went on to tell me how a wounded German officer had been flown out of the city and how he had brought with him a letter from a brother-officer who came from Lamsdorf. The letter had said that the German forces were surrounded by the Red Army. They were short of food and ammunition and were faced with complete annihilation. The writer had ended by saying that the last thoughts of the Lamsdorf boys would be for their loved ones at home. The heart-broken wife of the officer had secretly circulated the letter during the previous evening to those non-Nazi families of the village who had sons or husbands at Stalingrad. This news was sadly ironic in view of the German newspaper banner headlines from a speech by Hitler who had said 'He who holds Stalingrad will win the war!' He was quite right too.

Our small party of British prisoners, knowing the contents of the Lamsdorf letter, followed the reports of the battle with bated breath and, a week later, the Nazis admitted that the city had been lost and Hitler ordered three days of national mourning. The rejoicing of my companions was dimmed for me by the picture of old Karl in tears for his son. The statistics from Stalingrad were appalling. The Germans lost 72,000, 42,000 were wounded and 107,000 taken prisoner. This was to be the turning point of the war.

In March, Herr Ziertz, the owner of the sawmill, and an officer in the German Army, came home on leave. It was most amusing to see how the German foremen conducted themselves when he showed himself in the mill. At first they all pretended not to see him enter and stood with their chests stuck out shouting orders to all and sundry. Suddenly becoming aware that their employer was standing at his elbow, each foreman would snatch off his hat, crush it to his chest, cringe and paw the ground with one foot. We all knew the phrase 'bowing and scraping' but I had never seen it literally acted out before. I suppose we were very ill-mannered, but all the English greeted this display of contemptible fawning with hoots of laughter and went around for the rest of the day greeting each other, the Ukrainians, the Germans and even piles of timber in the same manner!

Around this time, I received a special Invalid Red Cross parcel from England. It had been sent by my girl-friend, Dorothy, the year before when I had been in hospital with pneumonia. Even now, a year later, it was a great boon, but the enormous length of time it had taken to reach me only emphasised the terrible isolation I felt from my friends and relatives at home.

One of our men who was thin, even by prisoner of war standards, was known with true Army humour as 'Fatty'. Fatty fell in love with one of the local girls who was connected with the Ziertz family. At night he would get out of the window to meet her and soon, through their romance, we knew more about what was going on in the mill than any of the foremen. This girl was a leader in the *Bund Deutsche Mädel*, the Nazi movement for girls, and one night in Fatty's arms she told him that earlier that same evening she had given a talk to 200 younger girls about prisoners of war, telling them that no self-respecting German girl would ever look at one of these wicked enemies of the Führer, let alone speak to one. This girl had a younger brother and sister who were both great favourites with us. The little girl, named Malice, was chatting to me one day when she told me that she went to school in Oppeln every day by train, adding, as an after-thought, that she always travelled First Class.

'My,' I said, 'you are a grand lady!'

When she explained *'Mutti hat ängst uber meine Jungfrauheit'* I was quite startled. I could not imagine an English ten-year-old telling an acquaintance that, 'Mummy is worried about my virginity'. Also, it was incredulous that German gentlemen who travelled First Class could apparently be trusted not to rape little girls they met, while it was evidently rife in the Third Class.

Her brother, Hermann, was a sturdy little lad of eight, and one day came into our living quarters despite strict orders to the contrary. While talking to him I offered him a small bar of chocolate from my Red Cross parcel. He refused with horror, pointing to the inscription on the parcel 'Gift of the British Red Cross'. Now, the word 'gift' occurs in German, but translated it means, 'poison'! I wondered if that inscription was purposely chosen to discourage theft during transportation of the parcels through Germany?

Later, in the summer, Fatty came in from one of his amorous night-time expeditions with some serious news for us. We were to be replaced at the mill by Russian prisoners and were to be sent to do other work. When a German Medical Officer paid us a visit next day we knew his examination was to sort out those of us who were fit enought to go to the mines. Immediately I donned the glasses I had bought at Friedens-hütte for such a contingency. After we had been briefly examined and the officer had left, the guards told us that we were to be divided into two work parties and read out the names for each. I was elated to discover that my name was with those who were obviously the least fit for mine work, but my joy soon turned to consternation when Steve's name was included on the mining party list. Many friends were parted in this way and no amount of bribery could persuade the guards to alter the lists.

The Nazis started to make alterations to our billets for the reception of the Russian prisoners. The first act was to remove the three decker bunks on which we had slept, for animals like the Red Army men slept on the floor. Only one bed was left and this was for the Russian in charge of the party. We also made our preparations for our Russian allies by drawing a picture of Churchill and Stalin shaking hands in front of British and Russian flags. Below this we drew a diagram of how to remove the bars from the window, a map of the surrounding district showing escape routes and a map of the local allotments with illustrations indicating crops to be found in each. We hid these documents between two floor boards where they would not be seen by the Germans but where any man sleeping on the floor could not fail to find them.

18

Grosstein

On a hot July morning we set off in two separate parties, Steve and I promising to join forces once more if opportunity should ever arise. Naturally I took the precaution of wearing my glasses so I would not look too conspicuous among my companions, who were all either bespectacled or else in obvious ill-health.

At Oppeln Junction we changed trains and it was there that my attention was riveted on a train standing at the opposite platform. It consisted of French express coaches which were filled to suffocation point with Jewish families and their possessions. I was horrified to see that these people, about half of whom were children, were heavily guarded by steel-helmeted SS soldiers with rifles and fixed bayonets. The Jews had obviously been instructed to wear their best clothes and looked very smart despite the terrible overcrowding. One of my companions was callous enough to comment, 'You never see a poor Jew!' but soon became silent when I asked him where he thought these people were going.

At last we reached a small station, or rather a halt, called Grosstein, which was in the middle of open countryside and which had only a huge stone quarry in sight. We realised that this quarry was our destination. The British working party at the quarry was a small one and our arrival only brought the number up to 40. Once we had settled in we asked our new companions what it was like and the uniform answer was 'Bloody awful!' When I asked for details of our work all I got was a grim smile and was told I would soon discover that for myself next day and it would be a pity to make me lose sleep at night by talking about it.

The morning came all too quickly and after breakfast we went down to the quarry to work. On the previous evening charges of explosives had been set off in the rock face and so we found lumps of limestone of various sizes littering the floor of the quarry. Our task was to load a small tip-up truck with these lumps of rock and push it along the railway lines to the end of the quarry where it was hauled up by a cable to the top. Each prisoner had to fill five truckloads during his day's work, and as I managed to fill my first truck in half an hour this target

134

seemed reasonable enough. However, I soon discovered my mistake. The first load had exhausted the easily lifted pieces of stone in my section, so, for the rest of the day, I had to break up the larger boulders with a massive hammer, in true convict style. It took the new men of the working party from six in the morning until six in the evening to complete our task; although one strong and experienced New Zealander, who had been there for over a year, had finished his day's work by two o'clock.

When we staggered back to our camp that evening I commented to a companion that the sooner I left the better I would be pleased. He heartily agreed but told me that he had been there for two years already and the only ones to leave during that time were the seriously ill apart from one man who had been shot dead when trying to escape. Our new companions also told us about a mysterious 'British Free Corps' which had been founded by the Nazis and which any British prisoner could now join if he was willing to fight the Russsians. Apparently they had returned from work one day to find leaflets printed in English stuffed in their overcoat pockets, claiming that 'The authorities have given permission for a British Free Corps to be formed to help the European struggle against communism. All British subjects have permission to join, including British prisoners of war in German hands, who, as trained soldiers, will be given high rank in their own special unit. This Corps will not be used against Britain, only against Russia.' The men were sure their guards had known nothing about the pamphlets for when they saw them they had asked what they were and where they had come from. When the prisoners had explained that they were invitations to join the army, the Germans wanted to know which army, and one astute Englishman told them it was the Russian one! At this the guards had become very excited and gathered in all the leaflets whereupon they had been sent off to the nearest town but the prisoners had heard nothing more of the matter since. Some of the more simple and politically unsophisticated prisoners still harboured the idea that these leaflets had really been sent with the authority and approval of the British government and that, if things became too bad at the stone quarry, they could always get away by volunteering to join this anti-communist unit. Thus, I took it upon myself to pretend that the senior British authorities at the Stalag knew all about the 'Free Corps' and had instructed me to tell them that it was a Nazi Party trick which even the German Army did not know about (which was perfectly true), and, I went on to say, that everybody who did join would probably be executed after the war (but this I hoped would be untrue considering the political naivity of the majority of conscripted Private soldiers who were my companions). Later on I discovered that the Nazis at this time had been making secret overtures to the Soviet government for a separate peace, but, in order to convince the Western powers that they were still bitterly anti-communist they broke the tenets of the Geneva

Convention by forming the British Free Corps. This unit was purely a propaganda ruse and was never intended to go into action but still, for all I know, it served the purpose of its creators.

On my second day at Grosstein I managed to get a job at the top of the quarry pushing the loaded trucks of stone to a kiln where it was baked to make lime. My new task was not such hard work as the stone breaking but it was, as we agreed among ourselves, far heavier labouring than any democrat would wish to contribute to a fascist war effort! The following day was Sunday but since a railway truck full of coal had arrived for the lime kiln some of us had to work and unfortunately I was one of the five prisoners selected for this disagreeable task. That night I came to the conclusion that I must get away from the quarry at any cost so I smashed my spectacles under the heel of my army boot and reported sick next morning, protesting that being unable to see clearly I would be a danger to myself and everybody else if I went to work. I was sent to see the Medical Officer at the local Luftwaffe aerodrome with two other men who were ill. There the Medical Officer looked at me and then at my smashed glasses and said in despair, 'Jesus Christ! What am I supposed to do with blasted Englishmen who smash their glasses?'

Promptly I replied in German, 'Send me to the Stalag at Lamsdorf, Sir, where the Red Cross will supply me with new glasses at the expense of the British government'.

So, on Tuesday morning I set off to Lamsdorf with two other sick men and a guard. The senior guard who inspected us before we left picked me out to 'assure' me that I had a return ticket, and, as son as my eyes had been tested at the Stalag, I would return to Grosstein immediately where the glasses would be sent on to me. He even made sure that I took all my possessions back to our sleeping quarters, pointing out that as I was coming back that day I need not burden myself for the double journey. Even so I managed to retain a Red Cross box full of letters from home and a collection of textbooks for 'reading on the journey'.

On the train journey I was hanging out of our compartment window when a German Unteroffizier, who was looking out of the next one, suddenly turned to me and said in a very Cockney accent, 'Where are you going to, mate, Lamsdorf?' Stunned, I asked who he was. He pointed to a Union Jack sewn on the arm of his German Army uniform and answered, 'I'm in the British Free Corps'. He went on to explain that his wife in England had had a baby by a Free French soldier which was bad enough and so, as he was thoroughly fed up with being a prisoner, he had joined the German Army. Obviously I must have been the first Englishman he had spoken to since taking this disastrous step for he looked quite taken aback when I commenced to tell him, in no measured terms, of my opinion and he disappeared from the window like a rabbit into its warren. Much later it transpired that there were only in fact 30* members recruited for the British Free Corps out of the tens of thousands of British prisoners in German hands. On arrival at Lamsdorf I broached the subject of the Corps and found that not only was I the only one never to have seen one of their recruiting pamphlets, but I was also the only one ever to have met a member from that mysterious brigade.

At Lamsdorf we were subjected to the ritual search and then proceeded to the medical examination room where we were interviewed one by one by a German Medical Officer who had a British prisoner acting as interpreter. Knowing that I would need as much time as possible to think during this crucial interview I spoke in English and considered my next reply while the Englishman was translating. Having glanced at my broken spectacles the Medical Officer grunted, 'See he gets fixed up with new ones straight after his eye test' and he was already turning to the next prisoner when I asked the interpreter to tell him I was suffering from certain symptoms, which I knew would convince him that I had dysentery. I knew that the German medical profession feared the outbreak of dysentery or typhoid in the overcrowded prison camps for the prisoners would infect the guards and, through them, the entire local civilian population.

Predictably the Medical Officer at once issued the necessary orders, 'Get him admitted into a ward in the hospital at once and see that the lab does all the necessary tests'.

When we left the medical examination room our guard, who had followed the German parts of my interview with great interest, roared with laughter and said to me 'You rogue, telling an officer that story! You have got more nerve than I have!' My fellow-prisoners also congratulated me on my deception, one of them commenting that nobody could prove that I was *not* suffering from the symptoms I claimed.

The Stalag hospital consisted of a number of wooden huts containing only ten patients in each and, by prison standards, were luxuriously furnished, having double-decker bunks in place of the regulation three-deckers. I was directed to one of these by a British medical orderly and I got into bed. A British Army doctor materialised at my bedside almost at once and said sympathetically, 'What's wrong with you, old chap?' One does not lie to one's own people so I promptly replied, 'Nothing, Sir, I'm malingering'. I explained that I had been working for the Nazis for over a year, hated it and intended to do no more for them, if it was humanly possible. The Medical Officer chatted to me for some time and after hearing about my visit to Hindenberg Hospital a year ago gave me a thorough examination. His verdict was that I was as fit as I had any right to be after three years as a prisoner, but added that three weeks' rest on the best food that the hospital could provide would do me no

*Actually 58. Ed.

harm. He also recommended me to sun-bathe as much as possible and do gentle physical exercises to help strengthen my left lung.

I soon settled down in the ward and since practically all the other men seemed to be suffering from digestive troubles I enjoyed the luxury of virtually unlimited white wheat bread, in place of the heavy rye bread I had lived on since 1940. In addition there was also an ample supply of milk drinks from special Red Cross parcels and these were an almost unheard of luxury in a prison camp. The ward had a file of the Nazi English-language weekly *The Camp* and so I caught up with the recent war news, which was dominated by the fall of Mussolini in Italy. I was surprised by the change in the editorial tone of the newspaper since its early issues. In 1940 it had claimed to give us all the news, good and bad, pointing out that from the German point of view it was all good. Now, with an unexpected show of frankness, the editorials admitted that since it was written by Germans it obviously gave the German view of events.

In the afternoon prisoners from the main part of the Stalag were allowed to visit their friends in hospital and I was delighted when two of them turned out to be men whom I had known at Konin in 1940. We spent a few pleasant moments exchanging stories of our experiences and next day one of them was granted special permission to visit me and, unexpectedly, he presented me with a parcel of spare clothing, shaving kit and other toilet requisites to replace those I had been forced to leave behind at Grosstein. This was a gift from the Stalag branch of Toc H (a Christian organisation for service men) and I must have been in a quite weak condition because there were tears in my eyes when these gifts were placed on my bed. I could not help thinking that Christians always seemed quicker to organise themselves to help those in need than agnostics like myself.

I made an interesting friend at this time who was a fellow-inmate of the ward. He was a middle-aged Welsh Jew named 'Taffy' Rose. When the first British prisoners had arrived at Lamsdorf they had been inspected by a high-ranking Nazi Party leader. On parade this man had ordered, through a German Army interpreter, that all Jews should step out of the ranks. Although there were quite a number of Jews present, only Rose, with head held high, had obeyed the command. It so happened that as he was at one end of the parade and because the Nazi was looking along the ranks in the other direction, he was not seen immediately. It was the German interpreter who had shouted out, as if he was repeating the order, 'Get back in the ranks you bloody fool!' Taffy had obeyed promptly whereupon popularity of the German interpreter and Taffy's reputation for foolhardy courage were firmly established. At one time Taffy had been a commercial traveller in the West Country where, according to him, they do not like Jews and nor do they do like Welshmen. 'When a Welsh voice came out of a Jewish face I certainly did not get many orders at first, but, in the end, they bought from me because I'm a damn fine salesman, and I made some damn fine friends down there, too!'

While I was in the Stalag hospital the war news continued to encourage us to hope for victory within three years, especially when the fall of Sicily was reported. One of the worst features of life as a prisoner of war is the uncertainty of its duration. A criminal in jail can see the end of his sentence coming slowly nearer, but we could only see the period of wasted life behind us lengthening through the dreary years.

As is customary in British Military Hospitals, on discharge I was interviewed by the senior Medical Officer and asked if I had any complaints. Of course I replied I had none, but only a great deal of gratitude, plus one request. The officer grinned and said, 'Oh yes, you're Gayler. I've had quite a number of malingerers through my hands during my Army career, but you are the only self-confessed one I have met. What is it you want?' Again I explained that I was determined to do no more work for the enemy and would like his help as he could give me work that would keep me in the Stalag and so keep me away from a working party. He replied that if I wished he could discharge me, not to the working compound, but to the NCOs' compound. Under the Geneva Convention the 'Detaining Power' meant that NCOs were in a very favoured position for they could choose whether to work or not, as they wished, although it did permit the enemy to force all Privates to labour as required. 'Once in the NCOs' compound, it's up to you, but I would like to bet that you'll fix things up for yourself!' said the Medical Officer drily.

19

Stalag life

Taffy Rose and I were discharged at the end of July 1943 and, although he too was a Private, we were both sent to the NCOs' compound. As soon as we arrived the Sergeant Major in charge expressed his surprise that we had not been sent to the working compound, but dismissed the matter quickly to tell us the latest news. Mussolini had been arrested and Badoglio, who had taken over in Italy, would not deal with Germany, so it looked as if the Nazis had lost an important ally. This cheered up Taffy and I considerably and it was with lighter hearts that we turned to the problem of our own future.

As soon as I had established myself in barrack room 9a I went to the Stalag School. The school was a barrack room next door to the Stalag Theatre, and it was one of the most highly organised institutions in the camp. The headmaster, Mr Laurie, was a professional schoolmaster and an MA. Every member of his staff had the highest possible qualifications for his subject; anatomy and physiology were taught by doctors, every modern language by native teachers, art by professional artists, and so on. As soon as I arrived I asked for an interview with Mr Laurie and explained to him that, as a trainee librarian in civilian life I wanted to stay in the Stalag to study for the Associateship of the Library Association and showed him the collection of textbooks I had been able to bring with me from Grosstein. He informed me that the Stalag School had recently been recognised by the University of London and that if he helped me he would expect me to study seriously and to sit for my examination, 'if our chaps in Italy don't get here first!' He scribbled a note to the Warrant Officer in charge of the compound asking him to give me a staff job which would make me an official resident.

The Sergeant Major, when presented with the headmaster's note, asked me if I would be prepared to work as a compound sweeper and help to keep the compound in immaculate condition. I replied that I would much rather work for my fellow-prisoners than for the Nazis which made the Warrant Officer relax and say 'You will find it jolly hard work even after a German stone quarry for it will take you at least half an hour a day!'

When I returned in high spirits to my new barrack room and told Taffy about my good fortune he rushed off to the Compound Officer like a shot from a gun. When he arrived the Sergeant Major waved him away before he could say a word, saying 'I know what you want Rose, you want a cushy job like Gayler. I guessed you would be round here within 30 seconds of hearing Gayler's story so I've already put your name on the list of compound "sweeper-uppers" for I just haven't got the time to listen to you telling me how you want to study to become a Church of England padre of some other such rubbish!'

So, now there were five cleaners in the NCOs' compound. One was an able seaman (the only Naval man in the Stalag), one a marine named Gerry Hoon, who was to become one of my best friends, one other Private, Rose and myself. In all, five men who would otherwise have been working for the Nazis. As staff workers we were the 'bourgeoisie' of the community and as such slept in 'Cleaners' Corner' on single-decker beds. The 'aristocrats' of the compound were, of course the Sergeant Major in charge and his three clerical assistants, who all slept in 'the Office', a sub-division built in another corner of the barrack-room with walls made from Red Cross packing cases.

Now began the most monotonous period of my captivity in the Stalag. We all had to practise what we called 'Mental Escape' which meant never thinking of life outside the camp but concentrating only on our activities within our prison. With our Red Cross parcels the problem of physical survival was solved, but to endure the mental rigours we all indulged our hobbies and interests as far as possible within our strange community. Stalag life itself provided plenty of interest to one with an enquiring turn of mind, but the life of the individual was so dominated by boredom that unless he immersed himself in chess, yoga, reading, study or something, he would go crazy.

I soon settled into the routine of the NCOs' compound. Reveille was at 6:00 am with roll-call at 6:15. Roll-call meant everybody on full parade in the compound and it usually took until 6:45 when we went back to our barrack room for breakfast. This meal invariably consisted of German substitute coffee (without milk or sugar of course), together with the remnants of the previous day's bread ration and any Red Cross food we had in store. At 8 o'clock we five cleaners congregated outside barrack room 9a and started our day's work of sweeping up the compound, collecting the litter, and generally cleaning the place up. This only lasted until 9:30 or 10 at the latest, so Gerry Hoon and I usually spent until noon visiting friends in other compounds, preparing our midday meal of Red Cross food or bartering cigarettes (as we were both non-smokers) for any item of food we required.

The German lunch — a meagre quality soup — was issued at one o'clock and was again supplemented by us with Red Cross food. Those of us who knew what it was like to live on German rations alone often profoundly pitied the Russian or other concentration camp prisoners

141

who had only their rations of German food on which to survive which were inferior both in quality and quantity to those we received. After lunch I would go to the Stalag school for the afternoon and study from 2 o'clock until 5:30 in the library. There were three professional librarians in the camp, including myself, the others being an Air Force Sergeant and Dennis Merry, an MA who was on the staff of the Bodleian Library in Oxford. Dennis was the only non-native language teacher on the school staff for he taught Ancient Greek! Neither of my two colleagues showed any interest in working for professional examinations in Lamsdorf so I commenced my studies alone.

The school library was a surprisingly good one. The marvellous Red Cross had a special service to cater for the intellectual needs of prisoners of war and we were regularly sent many useful books and courses. Individual prisoners also donated books which they had received from home and even the Germans sent us a large collection of books in English from a Quaker library in Vienna which they had closed down. Needless to say no books of a political nature survived the scrutiny of the Nazi censors. With my study for the day ended at 5:30, I would return to 'Cleaners' Corner' for the issue of our German 'Bread and Spread' ration and the evening roll-call. Until 'Lights out' at 10 o'clock the evening was our own and it was surprising how everybody seemed to occupy himself.

There were prisoners in the Lamsdorf Stalag from all over the British Empire; Indians, Maoris, Canadians and Jews from Palestine, were among the less exotic and then, after the fall of Italy, we were joined by a large number of South Africans who had been captured first by the Italians in North Africa and who had now fallen into German hands. When these men were sent from Italy to Germany the Nazis had no camps ready for their reception and had housed them in some empty barrack rooms in a huge Stalag for Russian prisoners. Even these front-line South African troops, who had been through the horrors of active service and the privations of the prison compounds of the North African desert, were shocked by the conditions in the Russian camp. The Red Army prisoners had resembled walking corpses and were treated by the Germans in a fashion no civilized man would treat an animal. In such a place the life expectation for even the strongest and healthiest of the Russians could not have been more than a few weeks and the South Africans had realised that they must do something for their allies, however little. Since the South Africans were still unregistered and uncounted by the Germans they pooled their spare clothing and found that they could dress 20 Russians as South Africans. They had the heartbreaking task of selecting from thousands of men the 20 youngest who were fit enough to pass as South Africans. It was arranged that the lucky 20 should pose as Afrikaners who could speak no English and that a South African linguist who knew English, German and Afrikaans as well as Russian was never to be parted from

142

them. Thus, we had this secret minority in our midst and the subject which was listed on the school time-table as 'English for Afrikaaners' was, in fact, 'English for Russians', and these men were the most desperately earnest students at the 'akademie'.

The Russian pseudo-Afrikaaners were only one of the secret minorities in the Stalag. Another was the 'Swop-overs' of which my escape friend Roberts, was one of the first members. As previously explained these were Private soldiers and RAF men who exchanged identities so that the Privates could avoid labouring for the Germans and the RAF men could attempt an escape. Some irresponsible soldiers, however, bored with Stalag life after a few months, would complicate matters still more by making a further change of identity with yet another man, and this even unto the fourth or fifth 'generation'. The resulting complications can be imagined!

One unavoidable feature of swop-overs was the worry caused to relatives at home who, of course, could not be informed of the arrangement since all mail was censored by the Nazis. The result was that wives received letters apparently from their husbands in strange handwriting, while mothers received letters from their sons in familiar handwriting but signed with an unknown name. Nevertheless, the chance of getting a member of an RAF flying crew back to Britain was considered worth the worry caused to relatives.

Another minority group, although a very small one, was the 'Outlaws'. A few men in *Straff Kompanie* awaiting court martial, or already sentenced to a long spell in a Nazi punishment camp, had escaped from the punishment compound into the main camp. Since they were not on the muster roll of any barrack-room they had to sleep on any bed which happened to be empty and hide at morning and evening roll-call while a secret levy was made on all German rations and Red Cross issues to feed them. At intervals the Nazis would make special checks in the hope of finding the missing men while they kept us on parade for anything up to 18 hours so the camp could be thoroughly searched and every man scrutinised by the German staff of *Straff Kompanie*. They were rarely successful.

Marine Gerry Hoon, with whom I 'mucked in', was a public school man from Bristol who had been captured in Crete and was looked on as a 'young prisoner' by us old men of the British Expeditionary Force. He told me many extraordinary stories of the fighting on the island of Crete, of which two in particular stick in my memory. Apparently, a number of German paratroops were captured by the British, disarmed and put in a temporary barbed wire prison cage. Then some local Cretan peasants arrived fully armed and expressed their intention of killing the Germans. The British guards had been forced to defend their captives and to fire a few rounds over the heads of the Cretans to convince them that murdering prisoners was just 'not done'. Later, when the British guards were themselves taken prisoner, the Germans concerned in the incident had searched the island for them and took them to a local village for a rough and ready Anglo-German banquet. Then they gave each of them a written account of the incident which ended with a request to all Germans, with whom they came into contact while prisoners, to treat them well.

The other incident relates to a man in the Royal Army Medical Corps. During the fighting on Crete the man was amazed to see a Nazi stretcher party approaching his temporary hospital carrying a wounded comrade. The German patient was admitted to the British hospital and the stretcher party arranged to bring in other wound cases. Throughout the battle both German and British casualties were tended in the same hospital, while a 'left luggage office' was run where both sides left their small arms while the wounded were carried to the wards. The weapons were then collected by their owners when they returned to their business of killing each other.

Gerry and I managed to live reasonably well in Lamsdorf as, both being non-smokers, we could use our cigarette ration as currency to buy extra food to supplement our diet. From the early days of captivity there had always been a great deal of bartering Red Cross food items so that a skilled barterer could start with a single bar of chocolate as capital and, by making a small profit on each transaction, end up with the equivalent of a complete Red Cross parcel. Such an achievement would probably be considered admirable by a businessman but I considered it to be rather dishonest in the light of our circumstances. From these small beginnings a regular market had grown up, culminating in a registered 'Swop Shop' in every compound. These 'shops' consisted merely of two or three Red Cross packing cases with a blanket draped over them on which the articles for sale were displayed. If you wanted to sell anything you left it with the Swop Shop proprietor, telling him the price you wanted in cigarettes. When a purchaser bought it he paid the price and gave one extra cigarette to the shopkeeper for his commission. When the seller collected the proceeds of the deal he too gave the shopkeeper a cigarette, so these men made two cigarettes profit on each transaction and in time some of them became 'cigarette millionaires'.

The most famous of the shopkeepers in Lamsdorf was Scottie, who ran the Swop Shop in the 'Rackets Compound', which was where all the Stalag tailors, boot repairers and other staff workers lived. Scottie was very astute and soon employed a staff of fellow-prisoners to run his shop for him while he went after bigger game. Since the British government continued to pay men in enemy hands their full Service pay old prisoners calculated that they had a substantial sum mounting up to their credit in England (especially Padres, doctors and senior Warrant Officers, who were on far higher rates of pay than Privates). The government sent us a supply of printed forms by which we could transfer these credits to our families in case of need, and I made a practice of transmitting my Private's pay to my father every six months so he could invest it to earn interest for me. Scottie saw the possibilities of this situation and, by methods known only to himself, he managed to obtain from the nearby Russian camp a supply of watches, including some Red Army chronometers of the type issued to Generals and Military Commissars to time the commencement of battles. These were magnificent examples of watchmaking and all the professional jewellers in the camp were invited to inspect them and estimate their value. The consensus put the price at £300 each, whereupon Scottie offered them for £100 each and bought by credit transfer. He was reputed to have made thousands of pounds profit on the transactions from this scheme alone.

The Swop Shop in my compound was run by Jock, a huge bald ex-heavyweight Boxing Champion of the Black Watch. He lived in an office similar to the Sergeant Major's in another corner of our barrack room and it was rumoured that he had thousands of cigarettes plus a huge supply of food stock-piled under his bed. One night I was woken up to find Jock standing in the middle of Cleaners' Corner in an insane rage. His gigantic figure was stark naked and had an iron bar bent over each fist as a knuckle-duster. 'Come on, lads,' he bellowed, 'the thieving bastards have raided my bunk and stolen all my cigarettes!' He told us how he had woken up to find an open razor being held at his throat by a masked man and, as he lay helpless, two others silently ransacked his stock and absconded with his wealth. We followed Jock to the door of the dark barrack-room but I, for one, was very relieved to discover that the German sentries had realised that something unusual was happening and had half the searchlights trained on our barrck room door. I don't doubt that most of the machine-guns were included too. We were all well aware that it would be certain death to venture outside and of our small group hidden in the doorway I am sure that only Jock was disappointed. He led us silently back to his office for a 'brew-up' and some food, and told us that, in spite of their masks, he had recognised the three gangsters.

Next day, accompanied by three of the toughest men in the camp, with weapons hidden about their persons, Jock called on the thieves. Standing in the doorway of their barrack-room, his henchmen solidly behind him, he said quietly, 'I want my cigarettes and quickly!' There was a long silence and then their leader smiled ingratiatingly and said, 'Sure, you'll find them under that bunk, Jock'. Jock entered the room without a word, pulled out two large suitcases of his belongings and departed with his silent bodyguards.

Jock was the only man in the camp to own a pet. Jock's pet was a raven who always sat on his shoulder. At roll-call our German Unter-offizier always included the raven in his count and then subtracted him from his final total.

One thing I discovered from my close association with the Scots of the 51st Division was that although Robert Burns was considered by them to be their greatest poet, (indeed I was the only Sassenach to be invited to a Burns Night Supper in Lamsdorf) he was neither the most popular nor the most quoted. That honour was reserved for McGonigal, surely the worst poet who ever lived. His most famous, or infamous lines were quoted endlessly!

'The little birds fly in and oot
The Royal Albert Institoot.'
Or, 'The Tay, the Tay, the glorious Tay
It flows through Dundee every day.'

I was moved to uphold England's 'honour' with the words of one of our Poet Laureates, with the lines inspired by the illness of King Edward VII:

'Along the wire th'electric message came
He was no worse but much the same.'

Christmas came and went and 1943 found the Stalag covered with snow (to the greatest excitement of the South Africans). Once again, the harsh weather more or less confined us to barracks and our conversations were endless. One day I was discussing Stalag life with an acquaintance, who was a sociologist, and he startled me by remarking that every crime possible, in a womanless community, had been committed in Lamsdorf. When I expressed incredulity at this he pointed out that our community was, in fact, as large as a medium sized English town. It had been in existence for over three years now and although the inhabitants had been subjected to abnormal stresses and conditions he was very gratified by the small amount of anti-social behaviour in the camp. That there had been only *one* case of suicide amazed him. When I remarked that we had not had a case of murder in the camp he looked at me consideringly and said, 'Wait until spring comes.' I, in turn, looked at *him* queerly and wondered how he could so confidently predict a murder, unless he intended to commit it himself? For, I did not believe that his specialised knowledge of the general behavioural patterns of mankind could have been extensive enough to allow him to predict such a crime!

The possibility of accidental fire or fire caused by an air-raid was ever present in a prison camp so at the request of the Red Cross the Germans built a huge static water tank in the centre of the compound. This froze solid in the severe Continental winter, and when spring arrived and the snow disappeared the static water tank thawed. I realised what my sociologist friend had been hinting at when a man's body, in British Army uniform, was found floating in the tank, having presumably been frozen there since the previous autumn. According to the German camp authorities the only men missing were the outlaws from the punishment compound, and the corpse was still recognisable enough for the British staff and German guards from *Straff Kompanie* to agree that the dead man was not one of them. The whole incident was a complete mystery, although I felt that the sociologist, for one, knew more than he was admitting.

One day the Sergeant Major called me into his office and told me with an expressionles face that I was wanted at the Legal Department of the Camp Leader's Office. I was puzzled by this for, as far as I knew, the Legal Department existed to help men who had business and matrimonial problems in England, and, having neither a business nor a wife, I could not imagine why I should be wanted there. Also when I arrived the normally friendly Sergeant Major was acting in a strange manner, not looking at me when he spoke and turning away as soon as he had delivered his message. I went directly to the office, worried at all this mystery and fearing only bad news could be awaiting me.

Our British Camp Leader was one Regimental Sergeant Major Sherriff, of the Welsh Guards, probably the most respected man in the Stalag, respected by the British and Germans alike. His Office was in the Theatre Compound with the school and the church and, like them, was really only a converted barrack-room. I presented myself at the door labelled 'Legal Dept' and when I made myself known to a plump Sergeant he barked at me, 'Who is Tex Esden?' Mystified but replying promptly I said, 'He is a middle-aged Private in my regiment. He fought with a Canadian unit in the First World War and tried to join up with them again in this one, but they rejected him as being too old. So, he sailed from Canada to England at his own expense and joined the first British regiment that would accept him, which happened to be mine.' I hesitated, 'May I ask why you want to know about him, Sergeant?'

The Sergeant looked at me keenly and after a pause replied, 'Well Gayler, you know these stories circulating about the Germans introducing their own men into the Stalag as prisoners in order to get information about escapes and so on? Well, they are perfectly true and so we check up on all newcomers. You must admit that a middle-aged Canadian in a British Territorial Unit certainly deserves investigation!' In a flash the mystery of the body in the static water tank was solved for me, the man had been a proven enemy agent. Thus, my sociologist friend had been wrong, for it was not a case of murder but rather the execution of an enemy spy. I asked the Sergeant how he knew I was trustworthy and he answered, 'Oh, we know all about you, Gayler. Don't be in too much of a hurry to leave the camp once you have passed your examination. That's an order. We may have a job for you here one day. Now go down to the working compound and make sure that this character really is Esden, but mind don't say a word about all this to anybody, not even to your pal Hoon. That's another order!' I obeyed him explicitly.

At the time of the Dieppe Raid, in August 1942, the Germans claimed they had captured a British Army communiqué that ordered German prisoners to be taken, as soon as possible, to specially erected barbed wire prison cages and that until they reached these cages their hands should be tied. The Nazis waxed indignant over this 'insult to the German fighting soldier' and announced that in reprisal 1,000 British prisoners would have their hands tied together each day. Sure enough a battalion of fully armed German troops came to Lamsdorf a few days later and proceeded to the NCOs' Compound, where the hands of all the men were tied with, of all things, the string from our own Red Cross parcels. Two days later a supply of rusty old handcuffs arrived at the Stalag to be used in place of the string, which resulted in a great saving of time for the Nazis and greater comfort for the prisoners. On the first day the men were handcuffed an *ad hoc* committee was formed of all the professional criminals, policemen and locksmiths in the camp and, within two hours, members of this committee were giving lectures on how to pick locks, saying something to the effect of: 'Taking the sharpened key of a bully beef tin between the thumb and forefinger of the right hand, insert it in the key-hole of the left handcuff, prise up the ratchet and you will be able to remove this horrible shoddy example of German workmanship from your left wrist. Repeat for the right hand. This will not damage the handcuffs in any way and so you will be able to put them on again for the evening roll-call, in order to give our square-headed friends the pleasure of unchaining you!'

From then on the farce continued in the same daily pattern. Each morning the handcuffs were brought to our compound and handed out to the prisoners who put them on themselves. After roll-call we went into our respective barrack-rooms, took off the handcuffs and slipped them under the towels at the end of our bunks. The German NCO in charge of our compound knew quite well what was going on but for the sake of a quiet life he turned a blind eye to it. News reached us that questions were asked in the House of Commons concerning this affair and we all sincerely hoped that our government would not kick up too great a fuss over the matter or the German government would be likely to check up that its orders were being enforced in our Stalag.

Some very amusing incidents arose from this handcuffing. On one occasion a German General was shown round the camp with a huge retinue of subordinates. Our compound was given good notice of his approach so every man was in place and wearing his handcuffs when the party came in. However, Taffy Rose suddenly remembered that a friend was having a thorough wash-down in the bathroom and slipped out just in time to hiss, 'Put your handcuffs on. The Jerry officers are coming!' The man did so and, completely naked, stood to attention when the Germans passed through the washroom, as military etiquette demanded. The senior officer looked gravely at the naked Englishman, returned his salute, and made a remark in German which made all his companions laugh. As the last German was leaving he turned to the prisoner and remarked drily, 'The Herr General would like to know how you removed your shirt while still handcuffed!'

After visiting our compound the General continued to the School where he expressed approval at the diligence with which the German language was being studied in the class in session. The teacher, an Austrian Jew who had been captured serving in the British Army in Greece, deftly rubbed off the blackboard the German sentences which he had been using to demonstrate a grammatical point. The camp Commandant looked thoroughly relieved that this was achieved before the General happened to read them, for the first had read, 'Hitler and his gang of National-Socialist thugs are the grave-diggers of Europe'.

I suppose the situation regarding the handcuffs would have continued indefinitely, but for an incident one morning. As we were dispersing from roll-call a new Unteroffizier passed our compound and saw a man casually removing his handcuffs as he walked along chatting to a friend. The German, who did not know our little ways, ran screaming into the compound and grabbed the man but, before long he was surrounded by a mob of angry prisoners who all proceeded to remove their handcuffs and throw them at his feet. The Nazi quickly retreated from the compound and stormed up the main street of the camp to the German Administration section, leaving the NCOs' Compound to speculate about future developments. We did not have long to wait. Within ten minutes the German adjutant of the camp arrived with some 50 guards in full uniform — steel helmets and rifles with fixed bayonets. We were called on parade while the four other cleaners and myself carried out the handcuffs and dumped them in the middle of the parade ground before we returned to the ranks.

The German officer addressed us through an interpreter, saying, 'Any man who does not put on his handcuffs will be severely punished by the German camp authorities.'

Immediately our Sergeant Major rapped out. 'Any man who *does* put on his handcuffs will be court martialled on his return to Britain!' This counter-order was greeted with a great cheer from the ranks as well as from all the other compounds too. Then the German ordered 20 guards to handcuff the first twenty prisoners. This was completed in complete silence, whereupon the Germans turned their attention to the next 20 Englishmen. By the time they had got to the third 20 the first 20 men had already removed their handcuffs, linked them together, and thrown them into the middle of the parade ground. The struggle went on throughout the blazing heat of the day with no relief from 7 o'clock in the morning until 10:30 at night. By the end of the day the Germans had handcuffed just 20 men. In the gathering twilight the German adjutant ordered his men to fall in and collect up the handcuffs.

He stepped forward and said in English, 'Gentlemen, I salute you'. Our Sergeant Major called us to attention and returned the salute. The episode of the handcuffs was over, and we never saw them again.

However, two pairs of handcuffs were not handed in but retained by a couple of Australian prisoners who must have taken them home and presented them to their National War Museum in Canberra where, 35 years later, I saw them on a visit to Australia.

The Stalag at Lamsdorf was the prisoner of war's equivalent of Charing Cross Station or Shepherd's Bar in Cairo for, if you were there long enough, everybody you had ever known would pass by. One day I was walking along the Stalag main street on my way to the school when I met Len Stoppani. He was my artist friend from the Kensingtons and I had last seen him on the first day of our march in 1940, when he had remarked that it would at least be 'interesting' to be the prisoners of 'these efficient rogues'. I did no studying that day but took Stopper along to Cleaners' Corner where I introduced him to Gerry Hoon and we sat comfortably together exchanging experiences for the rest of the day. Next day he paid a visit to the theatre where he demonstrated his artistic skills and where he was given a staff post as a Scene Designer in the theatre and as Art teacher at the school. These were both to his 'very great content', as Pepys would have said. With Len working at the theatre Gerry and I were always certain of First Night tickets for the shows and we saw a whole series of excellent productions including 'Me and My Girl', 'Journey's End' and 'Macbeth'. For the production of 'Pygmalion' the Commandant provided an apple for each performance for Professor Higgins to munch as the action required. Bernard Shaw could not have imagined a production of his play in which the eating of an apple would have brought the performance to a standstill. This was just what happened, however, for none of us had tasted an apple in four years, so the whole audience rose to its feet to cheer as the apple was consumed with evident relish. After each performance there were always a few optimists at the 'stage door' to enquire what had happened to the core, but they were always solemnly assured by 'Higgins' that 'there was no core'.

One day a friend called to tell me that Steve was in the Stalag hospital and was enquiring after me. Since being parted from me he had been sent to a coal mine, just as I had feared, and now he had returned to Lamsdorf to have all his teeth extracted as he was in considerable pain from toothache. He gave me a vivid description of the mine where he had been working for nearly a year. He said that all the normal safety precautions had been completely ignored and the only thing that had mattered was to get as much coal as possible to the surface to help the war effort, irrespective of the cost in human lives. When there had been a fall in the mine the Polish workers had been forced into the danger area at gunpoint in order to salvage any equipment. All German workers had carried revolvers and were permitted to use them as they thought necessary. Steve had managed to discover a technique to avoid working for the enemy; he simply hid in a disused working, blew out his lamp, and went to sleep. However he did this once to often for he awoke one day to find himself surrounded by Germans with their lamps shining on him and they had given him such a thorough beating that he had been unfit for work for three days. He also told us of the theft of soap from prisoners at the pit-head baths. Eventually one man prepared a special tablet of Red Cross soap and left it in his coat pocket as usual while he changed into his working clothes. This tablet had numerous razor blades embedded into it and so pity the German thief who slashed himself to pieces under the showerbath that night!

Naturally Steve was anxious not to return to his working party, but he need not have worried for, next day, a member of his regiment paid him a visit and arranged for him to be employed as a camp bugler and to live in the Church-Theatre Compound. Having no teeth Steve was completely incapable of blowing a bugle and at first he was very puzzled at his good fortune. Soon, however, the real reason for Steve's good fortune became apparent for it came out that he was a cricketer of professional standard. The Church-Theatre compound team was very weak that season and Steve's regimental comrade had known that they could rely on a useful century from Steve in every match

Sport was, of course, a highly organised activity in the camp, being the major interest of many of the prisoners. Association Football had its devotees and the Canadians played Softball (a poor relation of Baseball), and they even made some British converts to this game. Cricket was played avidly and a special matting wicket had been patiently woven by its fans from the string of our Red Cross parcels. Rugby, however, was the game which thrilled me most, and, when the Wales versus New Zealand games were played with the gigantic Welshmen thundering down the field, handing off equally gigantic Maoris, the excitment was terrific.

The day came when I was instructed to report to the Headmaster's office. Mr Laurie sat behind his Stalag-made packing-case desk and waved a sealed envelope at me — my examination papers had arrived and he wanted to know when I wished to sit them. My immediate reaction was to say, 'This time next year', but then I thought that I would do better to sit that very afternoon, in order to get the ordeal over. The head laughed and proposed a date three weeks' hence, so that I could revise thoroughly. The day came and I took my examination in the company of candidates for the Matriculation General Mathematics paper, invigilated by the senior Roman Catholic Padre. I had no idea how I had fared until months later Dorothy congratulated me in one of her letters for passing (having had the news from my father) and my friends in Cleaners' Corner held a party to celebrate my success. Taffy Rose warned everybody that working class boys who passed examinations often lost touch with their humble backgrounds and invited all the plebeians of Cleaners' Corner to give me a good sharp kick up the backside should they dectect any affectation in my future conduct.

Not all letters from home contained such happy responses as mine from Dorothy. One day Steve handed me a letter from his girlfriend

Winnie who had written to him so much when we were at Spitzwald in 1940. In the normal course of things we never passed round our letters, so I knew at once what this one must contain. True enough the opening words were the classic, 'This is the most difficult letter I will ever have to write' and Winnie continued to say how she had fallen in love with somebody else and was going to marry him. As the years passed such letters became increasingly common; sadly many of them from wives to their husbands. The only possible way to deal with the situation was to laugh so, in one barrack room, a Stalag Rogues Gallery was established. There the unhappy man could go alone to stick the lady's photograph on the wall among the hundreds of others. There was always somebody on duty nearby who would invite the new member of the Heartbreak Club to a mug of tea and tell him how lucky he was to have managed to escape his entanglement, if not from the prison camp. On one celebrated occasion a recently captured Canadian prisoner was inspecting this gallery of female delinquents when he looked closely at a photograph and pulled an identical one from his pocket 'For God's sake don't tell her husband' he said in horrified tones, 'but I'm the reason for her picture being on this wall — I'm the father of her child!'

As my sociologist friend had pointed out, one amazing thing about Stalag life was that we had had only one case of suicide throughout the war. This isolated case was by one of the older men who had been convinced that he had cancer. One morning he started to climb the barbed wire fence around the camp, knowing that the guards in their look-out tower were duty bound to machine-gun him, which they did. Sadly when the British and German doctors held a post mortem on him they found no cancer nor, for that matter, anything else.

As a cleaner I sometimes paid visits to the German section of the camp where on one occasion, I met a friendly guard whom I had not seen for some time. He looked very grim and said we were both lucky, myself in particular, that we were not in the Russian camp on the other side of Lamsdorf. Apparently that morning a man had been missing at roll-call so the Nazis had brought in police tracker dogs, naturally thinking he had escaped. The dogs, however, started to dig in one corner of the camp, where they discovered the man's head and bones. He had been the victim of cannibalism. This, above all else, made me realise what the conditions must be like for the Russian prisoners, for eating the body of a comrade who had died of starvation indicated a degree of suffering beyond imagination. Such an action, we considered, was in no way a reflection on the Red Army prisoners but rather a condemnation of the Germans whose brutality had driven their prisoners literally insane with hunger.

One day an old friend from the sawmill working party at Ziertz passed through the working compound and told me he had recently seen Fatty, the fellow who had had the German girl-friend. Fatty had been sent to the coalmine with Steve's party but had suddenly been recalled to the Stalag for an interview with a German officer. Puzzled, he went to be interrogated and soon realised that the officer questioning him was, in fact, his successor in the lady's affections and that she had told her new German boyfriend all about her old English one. At the end of the interview the officer had said to Fatty 'Well, my friend, I am sending you to the hardest, toughest, roughest working party in Greater Germany where you will be sorry that you were every born!' Having already experienced the coalmine Fatty was understandably concerned at this prospect and his emotions can be imagined when he found himself gardener to a German sanitorium, where he was treated as one of the staff, living on first class hospital rations and having no guards or barbed wire within miles of him! It was here that my friend had met him and he said that Fatty firmly intended to stay in his paradise for the duration of the war. So much for the 'toughest roughest' working party. It must have been their mutual girl-friend who had engineered all this. Fatty even continued to receive his Red Cross parcels at the Sanitorium although he was no longer in need of them and, I imagine, he had quite a pleasant time in his garden.

Another of my old friends whom I met up with in the Lamsdorf Stalag confessed to me that he was head over heels in love with a beautiful German girl of aristocratic family. She had promised to wait for him until after the war, but he was very worried because her father was a German inspector of prisons in Upper Silesia and was known to be high on the Polish Underground execution list. Later, after the war, I met a mutual friend who knew all about this Anglo-German love affair. He assured me that the girl had been the most beautiful woman he had ever seen off a cinema screen. However, to his knowledge, she had promised herself to at least 12 British prisoners and, he said, his mind reeled when he contemplated the number of German boy-friends she must have had in addition! So, I doubt if my first friend had any cause to worry, for she could obviously look after herself and probably her father too.

One compound in the Stalag was inhabited by Jewish prisoners. These men were German citizens but who had escaped from Germany at the start of the Nazi takeover and had settled in the Near East, mostly in Palestine and Egypt. On the outbreak of war they had volunteered for the British Army and had been captured in Greece. These Jews were treated in strict accordance with the Geneva Convention as the Germans feared that Nazi Party members in British hands would suffer in acts of retaliation if the Jewish prisoners were mistreated by them. It is certain, however, that none of these men would have survived if Germany had won the war. The gas chambers would have claimed them as they had done so many thousands of other Jews.

One of these Jewish prisoners was so worried about his sister, who lived in Breslau, that he actually escaped to visit her. When he knocked

153

on the front door she nearly fainted when she found her brother standing outside her door in British uniform. He was quickly bustled inside and he explained how and why he came to be there. In her turn his sister then explained that her husband was an officer in the German Army serving on the Russian Front and that, in spite of Nazi pressure, he had refused to divorce her. (Under Nazi Racial Laws if one partner in a marriage was Jewish there were grounds for divorce.) Thus, the wife of a front-line officer, she was treated as an honorary German but only 'While the war continues and they still need Johann's services' she explained bitterly. Luckily her brother and husband were the same size and build so the escaped prisoner had spent the next two weeks living a normal civilian life wearing his brother-in-law's suits and, though well aware of his activities, not one of his pre-war acquaintances denounced him to the Nazi authorities.

At the end of a fortnight his sister had tactfully told him that as he had no food ration coupons housekeeping was becoming very difficult and he realised that it was time for him to return to Lamsdorf. So he donned his British uniform and marched in to the local police station. There he stood to attention, as Nazi etiquette demanded, and said 'Yid Cohen reporting.' The jaw of the policemen behind the counter dropped to his knees as they had been reporting Breslau as 'Jew-free' for two years. Cohen had then slapped his prisoner of war identity disc on the counter and said boldly, 'I demand to be sent back to my prison camp, and, I warn you, if a hair on my head is injured 20 SS men in England will be shot'.

He was sent to Lamsdorf under escort forthwith where he related to us his amazing story. He was also able to tell us that he had discovered that there was at least one Jewish regiment fighting for Germany on the Russian Front. This was a special Jewish unit in the Roumanian Army, that country being an ally of Germany.

It was during the first week of June 1944 that I was walking by the Stalag cook-house, when a friend employed there shouted to me jubilantly 'The Second Front has started! Tell everybody! According to the Krauts its no Dieppe Raid this time, but the real thing!' We all danced up and down imagining this would mean victory within a few weeks, but once again our hopes were shattered and, in fact, the war lasted nearly another year.

About this time there was an exchange of German and British Red Cross personnel. One of the lucky ones to be exchanged was my old friend the Medical Orderley, Frank Sturrock. By extraordinary coincidence, he was sent to the Royal Herbert Military Hospital in Woolwich on his return to England. There he met my girl-friend Dorothy who was a VAD (Red Cross Nurse) and he was able to give her a detailed account of the conditions in the Stalag and of some of my experiences.

The summer passed slowly and the routine of Lamsdorf life

continued. To keep busy Gerry and I learnt fencing with home-made foils from an expert Scottish instructor. An arts and crafts exhibition was held and dominated by Stoppani's portraits and chess sets carved from toothbrush handles on Ancient Egyptian themes! The beautiful display of poppies in the garden of the Indian compound came to an end and a satisfactory supply of opium was manufactured from the poppy heads by the devotees. With the coming of Autumn the Stalag Casino moved indoors with its Crown and Anchor tables although the Australian Two-up School bravely carried on in the open air. We all followed the war news from hour to hour on our secret radio sets and so we were far better informed of the war's progress than our guards. Indeed, when a German expressed disbelief in a rumour passed on by one of his comrades he was often told, 'It must be true, one of the prisoners told me so!' German radio-location vans operated round the camp in vain for whenever they discovered the position of one of our sets and made a raid they only ever found men playing cards or reading books in the barrack room concerned. The radio set had already been dismantled and was safely at the othe end of the Stalag by the time the Germans arrived. Our look-out service was excellent.

Early in October 1944 the German in charge of the NCOs' compound told me, with an amused smile, that Sonderführer Lange wished to see me. This news was a unpleasant shock for me as I knew Lange was the Nazi Party representative at the Stalag and he was responsible for the conversion of the British prisoners to National-Socialism and for subjecting us to Nazi propaganda whenever possible. I reported to his office in the German section of the camp with great trepidation. I found him to be a man of intelligence and of considerable charm, but was from our point of view probably the most dangerous man in Lamsdorf. I was astonished when he said to me, 'You have been working hard in the Stalag as a cleaner for over a year, Gayler, and we would like to reward you by sending you to a holiday camp in Berlin for a month'. When he saw that I was for once lost for words he elaborated. He said the German authorities wished to demonstrate the admiration they felt for people like me who had really got on with a necessary job and did what needed to be done. Dazed, I murmured a few words of thanks for the high opinion in which I was held from such an unexpected quarter, when he suddenly asked if I had heard a rumour about a Jew having been sent to this holiday camp and that some of the British prisoners were very upset about it. I had enough wits left to me after my surprise to realise that any comment I made about this story would be taken by Lange to indicate my pro- or anti-Nazi sympathies and, as at this point in time I did not intend to let him know anything at all about me, I replied that I had no knowledge of the rumour. He waited for me to say something more but after a long and awkward silence jovially told me to prepare to leave for Berlin in three days' time. He shook hands with me and wished me a happy holiday.

With my mind still in a whirl I took a long walk round the Stalag, wondering what Dorothy and my father would think if they knew I had just shaken hands with a Nazi Party member who was sending me away for a month's holiday. Casually I went in and out a number of barrack rooms in different compounds until I was certain that I was not being followed or watched. Then I made my way to the Theatre Compound and into the Camp Leader's office and its Legal Department. The staff there were extremely interested by my story and gave me some sheets of foolscap paper and told me to go to the school library and write out a detailed account of my interview with the Sonderführer. I did this and when I handed it in I was instructed to return to the Legal Department that afternoon. I was permitted to tell my friends about my interview and my impending departure for Berlin but I was ordered to say nothing whatever about my subsequent visit to the Camp Leader's Office.

When I returned to the Legal Department at 3 o'clock I was astonished to be presented with three typed copies of my statement and asked to read and sign each one. I was invited to sit down and was told more about this mysterious Berlin Holiday Camp. It was thought to be used as a recruiting centre for the infamous British Free Corps and the British government would be most interested to learn anything I could find out about the place. It was further thought that the German organisers of the Free Corps now realised that they were losing the war and wished to convince the British that the British Free Corps never had existed. When I asked how I fitted into this scheme it was explained to me that Lange was a highly intelligent fellow who had my record at his disposal. He would know me as a Private who had been twice in *Straff Kompanie* and as the leader of a successful strike. 'All that stuff about Nazis rewarding honest labour is so much poppycock!' said my interviewer. 'Lange probably hopes that you will come to us on your return from Berlin and assure us that his bosses, who run this precious Holiday Camp, are jolly nice guys who would never *dream* of breaking international law by getting Englishmen to join the German Army.' To my great relief I was instructed, that even if the Free Corps was in fact still recruiting members I was, on no account, to join but to do my best to return to Lamsdorf with all the information I could collect. I was told that it was believed that all German members of the English Section of the Ministry of Propaganda were students of the English language or history and were pro-British, while the English members, such as William Joyce, were Fascists and pro-German! Further, I was warned that all the British members of the Holiday Camp staff were known peacetime members of the British Union of Fascists and I was not to trust them. As I left the Legal Department I was cheefully waved off with a 'Have a good time and don't for God's sake let the RAF kill you in an air-raid!'

20

Berlin and the last of Lamsdorf

On the appointed day I left Lamsdorf for Berlin in the company of five other prisoners all of whom had come from different working parties. Our guard was a member of Sonderführer Lange's staff, a pleasant young Feldwebel (Sergeant) who spoke excellent English and who said that his greatest desire was to work for a better understanding between our two countries. These words caused many memories to pass before my eyes. The Englishmen who died of starvation in Schubin in 1940; the Polish patriots being publicly executed at Friedenshütte; the French Jewish families on their way to the concentration camps and of the Russian prisoners being whipped at Ziertz. I felt that Germany would have to change rather drastically before I could share my guard's desire for friendship between our countries, and that Nazis, such as he, would have to be deprived of all vestiges of power.

Our party had a reserved third-class compartment as far as Breslau where we changed for Berlin. I was a little concerned at the efficiency with which the rail service seemed to be operating for, as a result of air-raids and of troop movements I had expected far more interruption to normal traffic. However, huge notices at all the important railway stations cheered me up, for they announced that from August 24 1943 the Führer had given complete responsibility for the Home Front to Himmler, (the leader of the SS, and without doubt the most feared man in this National-Socialist Paradise). The poster must have been a constant reminder to the public of the political terror which dominated their lives and which would, I hoped, bring about the eventual downfall of the Nazis.

We reached the outskirts of Berlin in the early hours of the morning, nearly 24 hours after leaving Lamsdorf, for the train had had to slow down to walking pace at regular intervals because air-raid damage made it necessary to relay some part of the track every day. On the outskirts of the city we were surprised to see so many people on their allotments so early in the morning, but we suddenly realised that complete families were living in the tool sheds to escape the nightly bombing of central Berlin. The men we saw were not there working on their allotments but setting off to business in the City.

When we arrived at the main station we went directly to the U-Bahn, the Underground Railway, and then out to a suburban station. It was odd to be in the middle of a crowd of people dressed in civilian clothes once more, although in fact about half of them were wearing some kind of uniform or other. One couple near me in the crowd consisted of an effeminate blonde German boy stroking the arm of a squat primitive-looking oriental woman, and I wondered how this fitted in with Nazi racial theories, but I suddenly remembered that Goebbels talked of Germany's Japanese allies as 'the Aryans of the Orient'.

At last we arrived at our station which was named Grossburen and a short walk through a wood brought us to our holiday camp at Genshagen. Although it had the usual barbed wire fence round it a tall hedge had been planted inside the camp so that the wire could not be seen by the inmates. Another nice touch was that none of the German staff of the place carried rifles, being armed only with revolvers in their holsters. In fact, a considerable effort had been made not only to house us in reasonable comfort but also to create an illusion of freedom. There was a placid atmosphere in the camp and all the guards wore bright smiles and spoke English with varying degrees of fluency. While at Genshagen we still received our Red Cross parcels although the German rations alone were sufficient to live on. The Englishman in charge at the camp was Quarter Master Sergeant John Brown, whom I hated on sight for he took great pains to salute, shake hands and smile brightly at all the Germans he met. He was in my view, a typical pro-Nazi.

During our few weeks' stay in Berlin I never heard the British Free Corps mentioned on any occasion, although various Nazis who chatted to me seemed anxious to hammer home the idea that a German, like an Englishman, was above all things loyal and would never dream of trying to influence anybody to be a traitor to his own people. From this I deduced that the Lamsdorf Legal Department was right and that the men who had organised the British Free Corps had realised that Germany had lost the war and so were trying to establish that they had never been guilty of breaking the Geneva Convention by recruiting British prisoners for the Nazi cause.

Various entertainments were provided for us at the holiday camp, including one or two lectures which had a distinct flavour of propaganda for they were concerned with the 'Strength through Joy' movement which provided cheap holidays for German workers. Some of the talks, however, were of a non-political nature and very interesting. I remember especially one on the electron-microscope given by a Colonel in the SS. He spoke excellent English and an American prisoner next to me told me that he had known him in New York. When I asked if he was friendly with him the man said 'Gee, no. I was only chauffeur to the American scientist who was his buddy!' Another

158

speaker who talked to us was Max Schmeling, the famous boxer, who was then an officer in the Physical Training Corps of the German Army. Rumour had it that he had recently beaten up Goebbels after the latter had attempted to make love to Max's actress wife. He seemed a jovial character and cheerfully informed us, when no other Germans were about, that he hoped to settle in America after the war.

During my month there we were not confined to the camp all the time but taken on various visits to places of interest in Berlin. The first visit was to the Olympic Stadium which Hitler had had erected for the 1936 Olympic Games. It was very impressive for it included not only the stadium itself but the finest swimming pool and open air theatre that I had ever seen. The size of it can be imagined when one remembers that a million people were present in the stadium when Mussolini made a speech on one of his visits to see Hitler. The stadium had suffered practically no air-raid damage and so it was being used to store furniture from bombed-out houses. As our party left the stadium in the mid-afternoon an air-raid warning was sounded so our guards hurried us to the nearest shelter, which happened to be in a Russian prison camp. As we went through the too-familiar barbed wire gates we saw a formation of American planes flying over us at incredibly high speed and in perfect formation. While we were watching them excitedly a Russian hurried over to us and asked if any of us spoke German. He requested me to get our party down into the air-raid shelter at once as none of the Red Army prisoners would take cover while the British remained above ground, although having been in Berlin longer than us, they desperately wanted to. Once we had taken cover I managed to seek out the man who had spoken to us. He was a high-ranking officer in the Red Air Force, and so I took the opportunity of asking him quietly in German what he thought of communism. His reply was that it was far *too* successful and that the British and American capitalists would inevitably declare war on Russia 'as soon as we have beaten this lot', indicating the nearby Germans with distate. I enquired which side he thought would win this future Third World War and he said he did not know, although he was certain that the Red Army would sweep as liberators through Europe to Gibraltar overnight. 'After all', he continued 'the biggest single political party in France is the Communist Party, the only real opposition to Mussolini in Italy, or to Franco in Spain is, in both cases, the illegal Communist Party'. The air-raid ended and we wished our Russian friends (and possible future enemies) farewell and continued our interrupted journey back to our camp.

These trips into Berlin proved to be very interesting and it seemed incredible that such bustle and activity could continue in a city being bombed by the Americans by day and by the British by night. On the whole the people seemed to be well dressed and well fed, although the city itself was so shattered, that an undamaged building was the rare exception.

The routine in our hoiday camp was very different from that of a normal prison camp. In the morning we followed our personal inclinations, some men reading and talking with new friends made at the place, some of us physical fitness enthusiasts starting a class under an expert South African instructor, while others followed their own particular hobbies. The afternoon usually offered a musical entertainment by some first-class German artist, and on one occasion the recital was given by an English opera singer who was married to a German doctor. This was the famous Wigan-born operatic singer Margery Booth, her husband being Herr Doktor Strohm. This lady was charming, talented and beautiful and after her recital the man next to me commented 'Well, Bob, her husband is the only Kraut I have ever envied!' The German officer who introduced her to us said that we must all feel great sympathy for her, as indeed we did, for she was seeing the nation of her origin in a struggle to the death with the nation into which she had married.

During the evening there was nearly always a film show, usually of German films but sometimes of American ones. These included a number made during the war and some contained such crude Yankee propaganda that even we were ill at ease watching them!

Another one of our sight-seeing expeditions was to Potsdam, where we visited the Garrison Church and where we were reverently shown the lectern at which Hitler had stood when the German government had met there after the Reichstag had been gutted by fire. We were also shown the vault where Frederick the Great is buried. In peace time the gates are kept closed, but as war was raging the gates of the vault were wide open, presumably to let Frederick's war-like spirit free in the land to inspire his fellow countrymen in their struggle. After we left the church, I asked with assumed ingenuousness, if I might see the home of Professor Einstein as I had been told that it was a famous example of modern domestic architecture. I knew full well that its celebrated Jewish owner was one of the most hated men in the world to a Nazi. However, the guard did not flinch, but smiled sadly and said that it had been completely destroyed by a British bomb. I suspected this was a lie but it was a fairly clever story to invent on the spur of the moment. During our Potsdam visit we also went to Sans-Souci, where, had we known it, the leaders of the United Nations were to hold their famous Potsdam Conference a year later.

While we were waiting on a station platform during our return trip I happened to find myself standing between a South African prisoner and a one-armed German soldier from the Afrika Corps. The South African suddenly leant across and said to me, with a grin of satisfaction, 'I helped to knock his arm off, Bob!', whereupon the German replied instantly and in better English than the South African's, 'And I helped to stick him behind the barbed wire, Bob!' There was a moment of tense silence and then we all broke into laughter and the two men who had fought on opposite sides in North Africa were soon exchanging experiences. Another amusing incident on this trip occurred when one of our men was left behind on the platform. The poor fellow found himself totally alone in the middle of wartime Berlin in British Army uniform, with no contacts, no money, no idea where to go, but with a lively knowledge that local mobs were believed to have hanged enemy representatives out of hand. His chances of escape were admittedly poor, so, as he was rather lacking in initiative he marched smartly up to the highest ranking German officer he could see, saluted, and said in broken German 'I am an English prisoner and I have lost my guards'.

The officer looked at him angrily and rapped out, 'Well, get as far away from me as you can! I'm on 24 hours' leave and I don't intend to spend it sorting out your troubles!' After attempting to surrender himself to numerous other servicemen the prisoner had finally got on to the following train and found our party waiting for him at the next station. The guards were so relieved by his arrival that they stood us all a drink of beer at their own expense and bought the unwilling escaper, who was a pipe-smoker, a magnificient *meerschaum*.

On another of our trips into the city, a smartly-dressed lady stopped us and asked, in a very upper-class English accent, 'Excuse me, are you in the British Army?'

The most senior prisoner came to attention and said, 'Indeed we are, Madam!' Whereupon the lady replied, 'Good Heavens, here already'. and, chuckling at her own wit, she disappeared into the crowd.

There were a few permanent British residents at this camp, who were employed in doing menial tasks at the Ministry of Propaganda. Those who had to empty the wastepaper baskets sifted through the contents and had their own methods of passing anything of interest on to our own Secret Service, while sometimes they managed to 'liberate' recent British newspapers for us to read. Thus, I realised that the Lamsdorf 'Legal Department' was not correct in their assumption that all the British staff at Genshagen were fascist traitors for some were obviously loyal democrats.

At last my visit to this extraordinary prison camp ended and my party made its way across war-torn Germany back to Lamsdorf. I left Genshagen without regret for, although there had been comparatively few air-raids during my stay, I guessed that a new wave of intense bombing would soon be due and the holiday camp would be a most unpleasant place to be.

Lamsdorf had changed little during my absence. In Cleaners' Corner an 'outlaw' had been sleeping in my bed but vacated it as soon as I returned. From Cleaners' Corner he moved to an empty bed in another compound, but just before Christmas he had the misfortune to be recognised as an escaper from *Straff Kompanie* and was promptly marched down to the German administration block for identification. Then he was escorted through the Stalag to the Punishment Compound by an officer and an armed guard and, as he passed our compound, he made a sudden desperate dash for the nearest barrack room but was shot dead at point-blank range. Naturally we were all shocked at the death of our fellow-prisoner but, at first, we even felt sympathy for the German guard for having to do his duty and shoot an escaping prisoner. However, our sympathy was short-lived, for the Nazi walked over to examine the body and laughed proudly at his handiwork. We all swore revenge for our comrade's death.

My first duty on my return to the Stalag was to report to the Legal Department on my experiences at the Berlin camp, but I was surprised that nobody was in the least bit interested and, after two or three desultory questions and a brief word of thanks, my interview was over. A long time after the war I discovered why their attitude had changed so dramatically. It appears that the British camp leader at Berlin, Quarter Master Sergeant John Brown, whom we all hated as a pro-Nazi, was, in fact, in direct contact with the British Secret Service and he received the DCM for the information he was able to pass to England about the camp, the activities that went on there, the effects of the bombing of Berlin, the locations of various secret arms factories and other matters of great interest to our armed forces. Mr Brown has written his own record of events which deserves to be far better known than it is. In his book *In Durance Vile* (London, Hale, 1981) he tells how one of his Secret Service contacts was the opera singer who entertained us, Margery Booth! Near the end of the war she was arrested, taken to Berlin Gestapo Headquarters and interrogated and tortured for three days, but outwitted the secret police and at last they had to let her go. When released she escaped to Bavaria where she was able to hand in John Brown's secret papers to the British authorities. These papers proved to be of great value, being used in the post-war trials of William Joyce, John Amery, members of the British Free Corps and other traitors. For her services Margaret Booth was given back her British nationality, surely the greatest reward one can receive. This brave woman certainly upheld the tradition that all female spies are beautiful!

Back at the Stalag, Lamsdorf was covered with snow once more and, needless to say, the fuel shortage became desperate. One wealthy Canadian rancher who had thousands of cigarettes sent to him used unopened packets of them as fuel to brew tea and cook his Red Cross food! My Berlin trip had made me quite a celebrity and I gave a number of talks about my experiences, including one to the Stalag Branch of NALGO (the National Association of Local Government Officers, as it was then called).

A sensationally successful series of talks on 'The Psychology of the Normal Man' was given in the Stalag School by Dr Cronental, a pupil and personal friend of Freud. These lectures were so popular that each talk had to be repeated four or five times to accommodate different audiences. Cronental had been an officer in the German Army in the

First World War and afterwards had qualified as a doctor. He had specialised in psychoanalysis until the Nazis came to power when, as a Jew, he had been imprisoned in a concentration camp. In the early days of the Hitler régime the Nazis were still sensitive to international opinion and so a few doctors were released from these camps under pressure from the British Medical Association. Cronental was lucky enough to be one of these. When he and his wife returned to their home they found that it had been looted by the local Brownshirts, and that his psychoanalytic case histories, the harvest of his professional life's work, had been burnt in the middle of his consulting room floor. They had left Germany for Egypt and on the declaration of war he had volunteered for service in the British Army. Subsequently he had been captured in Greece as a Sergeant in the Royal Army Medical Corps.

Dr Cronental told us that, from the psychological point of view, the white English-speaking members of the British Empire were the healthiest people in the whole world. To support this statement he pointed out that such people comprised the biggest section of the population of the Stalag, yet they provided only ten per cent of the cases in the mental section of the Camp Hospital. His explanation for this state of affairs was based on the following reasons: (i) The Black Death in the Middle Ages had hit England harder than any other country, killing off all the weaklings leaving only the fittest to breed; (ii) Britain has not lost a war for nearly a thousand years, and has never suffered under an army of occupation. No prisoner who had seen a fraction of the German Occupation of Poland would be tempted to underestimate the importance of this; and (iii) because of the geographical position of the British Isles we had, at intervals throughout our history, received infusions of the best types from the continent, the Huguenots were an example, while at the time he was talking to us the very best of the French and Polish nations were represented by the Free French and Free Polish forces in Britain.

The winter of 1944–45, held a new hazard for us in Lamsdorf. The night soil in the latrines had frozen solid and so the huge rats that lived on this filth were becoming mad with hunger. A number of men were bitten while relieving nature and one poor fellow had to be castrated in the Stalag hospital in order to save his life.

As Christmas drew near the Compound Cleaners had certain extra duties to perform, one such being to destroy the illegal stills under the supervision of the British medical officers who feared that the virulent home-made spirit would cause blindness and possibly even death. Some of these stills were very elaborate with the prunes from our Red Cross parcels being used to distill the spirit; Gerry Hoon and I used our prunes as food, including the kernels of the stones as nuts in our 'Christmas cake', which Gerry had made from our black bread ration.

On the last day of 1944 sensational news swept through the camp that artillery could be heard in the distance at the Eastern end of the Stalag. The Eastern Front was nearing Lamsdorf and the Red Army was approaching to liberate us! That night we saw the New Year in and at midnight there was a triumphant march round the roads of the Stalag headed by a kilted Scot playing the bagpipes. A small group of grim German officers stood in the snow watching us. For the fifth time the prison old-timers heard the words 'We'll be home this year!' and, for the first time, I dared to believe it.

For the first few weeks of the new year (1945) Stalag life continued as usual although there was always a small crowd of men at the far end of the camp straining their ears to reassure themselves that the sounds of distant battle were still audible, even if it was getting no nearer. On the morning of January 22, however, Gerry and I were sitting in our class at the school when the Headmaster came in and announced that we must all return to our barrack rooms at once. When we reached the NCOs' Compound we found all in confusion as the Germans had just ordered everybody to prepare to leave the camp within half an hour. We hastily packed our belongings and formed up on the parade ground. Within a matter of minutes we were moving off without even a backward glance at the NCOs' Compound which had been our home for so long. We marched along the Stalag main street for the last time and, as we passed through the main gate of the camp with the tattered swastika flag still flying above it, each man was issued with a loaf of the usual black rye bread.

21

The march, 1945 edition

Passing through the village of Lamsdorf I saw some of the Germans with whom I had worked at the sawmill. They were in a state of absolute panic and said wildly, 'When the Russians get here they will burn the place down and murder us all!' I tried to cheer them up, but thinking how our own troops would react if they liberated the local Russian camp and discovered the horrors of which the Germans were guilty I was privately inclined to agree that they had cause to worry. Along the icy roads, between landscapes of incredible beauty with their mantel of virgin snow, our long column of guards and prisoners marched westwards. After the first few miles men began to throw away their less valued possessions. I saw a copy of the Concise Oxford Dictionary face down in the slush. I had coveted a copy of this work for years but the swopshop price had been 1,000 cigarettes and so I could never afford it. Now I was too exhausted to pick it up.

Day after day we marched westwards, slipping and sliding on the icy roads. At night we were herded into the barns of any nearby farm we were passing as darkness fell. Gerry started to have trouble with his feet and was soon limping badly while a small pimple on my left wrist quickly developed into a huge boil and I had to carry my arm in a sling. We rationed what little food we had but by the fourth day our supplies were exhausted and we were relieved when we were each given a packet of German Army crispbread. These were packed in cardboard cartons incorporating a field postcard. I was childish enough to fill in mine with a stub of pencil to 'Herr Adolf Hitler, Reichkanzlei, Berlin' and tell him in pithy, soldierly and, I trust, grammatical German what I thought of him and his country. I posted it in a roadside postbox and have often wondered how far it got on its journey!

After a week's marching Gerry and I were both in a very poor condition and, when we halted that night, I said that I did not think I could continue much longer. Gerry agreed and suggested that we should escape from the column the next morning after a good night's sleep. Our plans agreed, a great feeling of relief swept over me and I went to sleep in the straw that night blissfully content. Next morning, in the chaos of everybody forming up in line, Gerry and I unobtrusively edged towards a sparse wood next to the farmyard and made our way through it to the snowcovered fields beyond. Once more I was free in Nazi Germany.

We made our way across the fields acutely aware of the tracks we were leaving behind us in the snow. Since Gerry's feet were in such bad condition I walked ahead of him so that he could follow in my footsteps. Suddenly I disappeared from his sight into a ditch full of snow, which caused us some merriment and against the dazzling whiteness we realised how dirty and bearded we both were. There and then we had the most painful wash and shave of our lives. We rubbed snow on our hands and faces until it melted and then attempted to shave, a process which really only amounted to pulling the hairs from the skin of our faces with the maximum of discomfort. Looking a little less villainous and consequently, we hoped a little less likely to be shot on sight, we continued on our way. Our objective was the nearby town of Schweidnitz. In the open countryside we felt rather conspicuous and feared we could be shot by any German or Russian who wanted to practice his marksmanship, while in a town we hoped to take cover in an air-raid shelter or, considering our condition, in a hospital, until we were liberated by the Red Army. Also we hoped that the people of the area would be so full of their own affairs that our nondescript figures would excite no interest until the front line reached us. We struck out boldly along a road signposted in the direction of Schweidnitz when we were suddenly hailed by an unsmiling German woman, who was obviously used to dealing with wartime foreign workers, for she addressed us as if we were slaves. Not liking the look of her I told her that we were Frenchmen and had been instructed by our employer to make our own way to Schweidnitz where he would meet us to arrange for our evacuation. She watched us continue on our way through narrowed eyes and we had not gone far when we were challenged again, this time by a very well-dressed middle-aged man riding a beautiful chestnut horse. When I told him we were Frenchmen he commented that we both looked in a bad state and escorted us to a nearby building where we were greeted by an Unteroffizier who was in charge of a French prisoners of war working party stationed there. The Unteroffizier yelled for the cook, who was the only prisoner not out at work, and this man came bustling in shooting a rapid series of questions at us in French. I gave Gerry a malicious grin for now it was his turn to be spokesman, but Gerry's French was strictly of the 'Plume de ma tante' variety so we were forced to admit to the German that we were English prisoners but sick and in need of attention. This news was greeted without comment by the German, and he obviously thought we were quite fit for he ordered me to take my arm from its sling and remove the bandage. Once the pressure of the bandage was released the huge boil, which covered the whole of the back of my wrist, burst and discharged a stream of blood and pus. This evoked cries of sympathy from all present and the Frenchman produced hot water, soap, ointment and a clean bandage for me. Attention was then turned to Gerry who removed his boots and bloodsoaked socks to reveal his feet which were in a terrible condition. These were ministered to as well and we were given a welcome meal of hot soup and bread. The Unteroffizier then said that he would escort us to a prisoners' hospital in Schweidnitz, which delighted us for such a place had been our objective and we knew that a German guard would guarantee that no over-enthusiastic Nazi would shoot us out of hand.

On our way to the town, which was only a short distance away, we listened to a revealing tale of woe from the German. He had been badly wounded on the Russian Front, while his wife had been seriously hurt in a Berlin air-raid and their home had been destroyed. Now he was bitterly resentful that only the most fanatical Nazis were being sent to the Western Front for Hitler was well aware that the one ambition of the ordinary soldier was to give himself up to the British or Americans as soon as possible. Thus he and his like-thinking fellows were left to face the Red Army, for he said, 'Only a madman would surrender to the Russians!' In reference to the attack on Hitler's life on July 20 1944 he commented that, 'Hitler lives so another million Germans must die!' although he said nothing of the Russians, Jews, Americans and British who would also perish.

When we reached the town we were conducted to a church hall in a back street which acted as the Prisoners' Hospital. There was no barbed wire round the building and the only German staff were two elderly little Privates. The patients we found there were a motley collection of French and Russians, who seemed to have nothing wrong with them, except for one smiling little Tartar who was an NCO in the Red Army and was suffering with rheumatism. Why the rest had been sent there we could never find out, but whenever an odd prisoner of war was found at large in the district it seemed that there was a standing order that he should be sent to the 'Hospital' for the lack of anywhere else suitable. Like Gerry and myself all the inmates were very thankful to find this temporary haven and the last thing they wanted was to escape, especially as there was an adequate supply of food!

The day after we arrived there was an influx of more prisoners, including a Maori, some South Africans, a very tough little Greek Sergeant and a Cockney on a stretcher who had been wounded on his rump in an air-raid. There was also a Greek of the village idiot type in the group dressed in British uniform and who was a great embarrassment to the Greek Sergeant. This man, a mentally retarded giant, had broken into a British Quartermaster's store near Athens when the German Army had occupied the place and he had arrayed himself in the best clothing he had ever possessed, a British Army uniform. As he was leaving some German front-line troops entered the building, saw him and, assuming he was an Englishman, had forced him into a passing column of British prisoners. These men quickly recognised him for what he was but knew the Nazis would execute him as a looter if they discovered his true identity. Therefore they had passed him off as one of themselves. After innumerable adventures, all of which were far beyond the giant's comprehension, he ended up with us in Schweidnitz.

We were all very worried when a German Medical Officer paid us a visit. He quickly examined everybody and marked most of the men, including Gerry, as fit to march, by easy stages, to Görlitz, the town which seemed to be the destination of all prisoner of war columns which were marching westwards. The medical examination of the Greek giant was the most amusing of all. The Medical Officer asked me, in German, what was wrong with him. I translated the question into English, a South African translated from English into Italian and the Greek Sergeant translated from Italian into his own language and then, back came the answer, 'He doesn't know.' The German tried again, 'Ask him where he has any pain.' In German, English, Italian and Greek the question passed along the chain and back came the answer 'Everywhere'. The Greek Sergeant then sent a brief observation of his own along our line of communication. He commented that his compatriot's chief weakness was in the head, with which the Medical Officer and his corps of interpreters heartily agreed. The German estimated the size and weight of the giant and gave him four small pills and watched him swallow them. Then he said cheerfully, 'He will not give you much trouble for the next 12 hours!' Sure enough the poor old giant spent most of the them in the WC and his groans and wails could be heard reverberating throughout the building.

Next day one of our little old German guards said that we must take the Cockney with the air-raid wound to the local military hospital for an operation. As none of us were very strong he permitted eight of the fittest men to carry the wound case between them on a stretcher and ordered me to go with them as interpreter. We set off through the practically deserted town. The shop windows were nearly empty of goods but had slogans whitewashed on them, such as, 'We believe in victory!' and 'To arms! The Silesian Homeland is in Danger!' We left our companion at the hospital and returned to the church hall and on our way back we passed a group of pitiful and ragged old ladies carrying shovels and pick-axes. Our guard grimly told me that because they were Jewish these old ladies were employed on the heaviest labouring jobs in the district.

On the following morning the men classified as 'fit' by the Medical Officer set off and my heart sank as Gerry turned to wave to me as they disappeared round the corner. I cursed my luck at being the only Englishman left at the 'hospital' but found some consolation during the next few days when I struck up a firm friendship with a young Russian officer of my own age from Stalino. He spoke really beautiful German and his knowledge of military strategy was very impressive, considering he was only a Lieutenant. As far as I could discover he had received a highly specialised education as a Red Army officer but knew practically nothing outside his own subjects. One of the South Africans was rather amused at my comments on this and observed that if I questioned most young British officers about modern literature and art I would get equally blank stares!

All the Russians I met assured me that the food in the Red Army was terrible, for they explained it had been good food until ruined by their cooks. This, I think, must be the universal grumble of all soldiers. Their stock complaint about their army diet was that there was always too much of one thing and never enough of another. Yet they could have no complaints about their clothing which they all agreed was first class, especially their winter issues which consisted of a quilted jacket, a long overcoat and another heavy greatcoat to wear over that. One their feet they wore light slippers as well as socks, a pair of leather boots up to their knees and then huge felt topboots. I commented that I wondered that they could move in such an array of garments. They grinned and assured me that they could still move their trigger fingers, which gave them an immeasurable advantage over the Nazis who were too cold to move even that much!

Sitting round the table at night we were a strange company — Greeks, Russians, Maoris, South Africans, Germans, French, Belgians, Palestine Jews and British were all represented. With the sound of battle in the distance we all realised that all any of us wanted was a decent home and job, good schools for our children and, above all, peace in which to enjoy life. A Jew looked at one of the Germans and said, 'We must all be mad, every one of us,' and the whole table agreed with him.

In the middle of the following morning an order came that all British Empire personnel declared as unfit to march must leave for Görlitz by train immediately. We hobbled to the local station, passing girls from the local secondary school who were digging tank traps at the edge of the town. A column of gigantic Tiger tanks passed us, moving up into action at the front and, as vestiges of snow still remained on the ground, the tanks were camouflaged with white chalk for white paint would burn furiously if they were hit.

At the station our small party waited for hours on the empty platform for no train came into sight until long after dark and even then we had to fight our way into a compartment already full of refugees. Our guard got chatting to some of the peasant women who recognised from his dialect that he came from the same part of Upper Silesia as themselves. When he proudly named his native village a chorus of voices informed him that it had already fallen to the Russians whereupon he entered into a long whispered conversation, which he took good care I was unable to overhear.

As our ancient train slowly rumbled westwards through the night the spirits of our German travelling companions seemed to rally, so during one of our many prolonged halts I asked Otto, our guard, if he thought that the advance of the Red Army was faster or slower than the progress of our train. This effectively brought the small-talk of our companions to an abrupt end.

Early next morning we drew into a station where the train was searched by military police, presumably for deserters. As soon as we were seen we were ordered off the train and we disembarked with better grace than one might imagine when we saw that our places were needed for young mothers with babies in their arms. The road to Görlitz was pointed out to us and we followed it all day, occasionally making sure of our way by asking people we met, but they invariably spread out their hands, shrugged their shoulders, saying, *'Ich bin auch Flüchtlinger!'* (I am also a refugee). When darkness fell we wearily made our way to a farm near the road but found it was full of refugees. There we were given some dry bread and a little milk and then settled down in the straw of the warm, but stinking byre, to sleep. Just before we went to sleep I nodded to our guard's rifle, which he had hung on the wall, and said, 'Aren't you scared that we will shoot you during the night, Otto?'

The German replied soberly, 'Only God knows what the next day or two holds for us, Robert. It might be best if none of us had to wake to face it.'

Next morning we were awoken by the cows being milked and I quickly slipped outside to discover what was going on but all was still and silent. Just as I was about to return to the cow-shed an old woman came out of the farmhouse so I struck up a conversation with her and asked her why she had left her own home. I pointed out that every government, democratic, communist or Nazi, needed farmers on the land and that she would have been far better off in her own four walls than wandering across Germany as a refugee. She explained that she had had no choice for as the front line came near armed SS men had forced everybody to abandon their homes and march to the west taking whatever they could carry with them. The SS would no doubt have shot anybody foolish enough to disobey them, for as soon as the villages were empty the Nazis were burning them down, so nothing of value should fall into Russian hands.

On our march that morning we asked the way of an old labourer who assured us that we would reach Görlitz by nightfall. When Otto asked him where he was bound the old fellow stood to attention and said with a beaming smile, 'Off to report to the *Volkstürm*, Herr Gefreiter!' The *Volkstürm* was the German equivalent to the British Home Guard and Otto gave a cry of welcome and dramatically shook the old man by the hand to welcome him to the armed forces of the *Vaterland*. As we watched him hobble on his way none of us gave much for his chances of survival in action against the Red Army.

Resting by the roadside at midday a party of about 30 concentration camp prisoners and their SS guards passed by. With their gaunt faces and shaven heads, marching through the bitter coldness of the mid-European winter in their thin blue and white striped uniforms and wooden clogs they looked like mere caricatures of men. As was his wont Otto asked one of their guards if we were on the right road for Görlitz and the huge beefy SS man assured him that we were and that they themselves had been on the road for two weeks. He grinned as he added that they had set out with some hundreds of prisoners and that soon, with a bit of luck, they would have none. Looking at the poor devils who were all that remained there was not much doubt that he was right.

On the outskirts of Görlitz we passed a Hitler Youth Camp and saw boys being called out on parade by their leaders. It was like a scene from an anti-war propaganda film for every boy had a rifle slung on his shoulder and some of them were so small that their rifle butts practically touched the ground. I thought that, if the Russians I had met were a fair sample of the Red Army, they would be quite unable to bring themselves to fire on the Germans if they knew of the old men and small children that Hitler was sending to the front to oppose them.

At last we reached the Görlitz Stalag. We shook hands with Otto and wished him well. Any German soldier at that time needed all the luck in the world what with the Russian Army bent on revenge sweeping down on him. As we entered the camp we discovered that although it was a huge camp it was not so well-built as Lamsdorf had been. The barracks were of wood instead of brick and the roads were unmetalled which, since the thaw had just started, were a sea of mud. All the allied nations were represented among the prisoners, including a large number of Russians and walking down the main street to the British Compound I was startled to see a French Scoutmaster in full uniform. There were a large number of Scouters among the French prisoners for the Germans had permitted them to send home for their uniforms and to carry on their Scouting activities within the confines of the camp and they did a great deal of good in Görlitz Stalag.

When we reached the British Compound I was cheered to see many faces I knew from Lamsdorf. I asked if anybody had heard any news of Gerry Hoon and at once somebody said,' Yes, he's here!' Come along and I will take you to him!' As I followed my guide he remarked over his shoulder,'Gerry has thrown himself at the feet of Jesus'. Now Gerry was a member of the Church of England but only to the extent of taking Communion once a year at Easter. It flashed through my mind that circumstances had proved too much for him and that he had developed a religious mania, but as I was led into a barrack-room I understood. Until recently the room had been used as the Stalag Church but it was now full of men sleeping on the floor. Under a huge mural painting of the Last Supper, literally at the feet of Christ, my companion gently kicked a sleeping man who had his head hidden under an overcoat.

171

'Wake up Gerry', he said, 'here's Bob Gayler to see you!' and up sat — Steve! When Gerry had arrived at Görlitz he had met Steve there and as mutual friends of mine they had joined forces. After Steve had greeted me he lost no time in arousing Gerry, who was sleeping next to him, and the three of us rejoiced at being together once more and they even managed to make space for me to sleep next to them.

The next week was spent in idleness and in increasing hunger. I explored the camp and found it to be a place of indescribable squalor and deprivation. Every morning a cart would pass outside our compound laden with corpses of the Russian prisoners who had died during the night. The scenes in the Russian Compound were shocking but, although it was out of bounds to British prisoners, I managed to get in and have a look around. I saw the undertaking squad carry out numerous corpses from the various barrack blocks and load them on the cart which passed our compound every morning. Some of the poor fellows had died in grotesque positions and, since rigor mortis had set in, the undertakers often had to jump on the rigid bodies to get a full load on to the cart. I was informed that they were buried en masse in a huge pit near the camp.

While in their compound a Russian described to me the manner in which their Stalag had been evacuated. All the prisoners had been marched out as we had done at Lamsdorf while the guards mounted extra machine-guns all round the camp. Then they set fire to the buildings, forcing the men who were hiding to run out. They had been machine-gunned as they emerged to escape the flames. Another Russian told me that this was standard practice in the evacuation of all Russian Stalags.

As day followed day our hunger grew worse and I calculated that it would be only a matter of three weeks before my companions and I were in the mass grave. We all had the colourless white faces with the bright red noses and blue lips which, as survivors of 1940, we recognised as the hall-mark of starvation and prolonged exposure to the cold weather. As hope was fading a rumour swept the camp that a Führer-Befehl (a personal order from Hitler) had been issued that all British prisoners were to be moved right across Germany, as far to the west as possible. Personally I discounted this story for I could not see the Germans' motive for undertaking such a big movement of prisoners at a time when the roads and railways were already full of refugees and troops. It was suggested that Hitler imagined he would thus inhibit Anglo-American bombing if he let it be known that we were in the target areas, but none of us thought for a moment that consideration for our lily-white skins would be allowed to interfere with the strategic requirements of our armies in the field.

However the rumour of a move was true, for we were given a hurried medical inspection by our own Medical Officers. All the men were in a very bad condition but, under German orders, the doctors had to sort

172

out one fifth of the sickest prisoners; we guessed that the majority of us were destined to march across Germany while the rest would go by train. I had thought that both Gerry and Steve were certain to be selected for the train party while I would march, but, in fact, it was Steve and I who were classified with the sick and Gerry who was marked 'Fit to march'.

When Gerry left with the huge column of 'fit' prisoners I nearly wept, for he looked so much worse than when we had last been parted at Schweidnitz three weeks before. Steve was elated at not having to march and confided to me that he had been marked unfit because the Medical Officer who had examined him was one of his own regiment, but I was aware that Steve had been marked unfit, not because of any regimental loyalty, but because like the rest of us he looked as if he had only another week to live. It gave me a great shock to realise suddenly that I too had been classified with this sickly minority.

Next morning the train party marched, or rather limped and shuffled, to the local railway station, leaving the prisoners of all other nationalities behind in the Stalag. I was surprised to observe that a bridge over which we passed had an armed guard on it and then saw that a charge of high explosives had been attached to it. I realised that the Red Army was expected to arrive in the very near future.

At the station our party, a thousand gaunt scarecrows, climbed into the usual cattle trucks. I smiled to myself as I scrambled aboard, remembering how outraged I had been as a small boy when I was told how my father had travelled in this type of transport during the First World War while on active service in France. However, our allocation of 50 men per truck was a little less luxurious than the conditions our fathers had enjoyed, but I reflected wryly that we had to expect more men in each truck for we were so much thinner! Before our train started there was an issue of 49 loaves of bread per wagon along with the information that it was not known when we would get any more food. Every man in my truck had the insane fear that he would be the 50th man and would get no bread, but an RAF Flight Sergeant shouted out, 'I'll go without my loaf, if you will all give me a little bit of your bread.' Our relief was so great that we willingly gave a generous slice and in the end the volunteer got the equivalent of over three loaves, which we did not begrudge him as he generously shared it with his muckers.

At last we started off and somebody commented, 'The last train from Görlitz, non-stop for God knows where!' but as he said 'non-stop', the train stopped! We all laughed and our mood lightened a little as we thundered westwards.

22

The journey to the west and Fallingbostel

Our hunger was so great that every scrap of bread in our truck was eaten within 12 hours for, once eaten, it could not be stolen. The progress of our train was slow because it was stationary almost as often as it was moving, which was indicative of the chaotic conditions of the German railways. The first big city through which we passed was Dresden and an RAF man who was next to Steve and myself told us that it had suffered one of the heaviest air-raids of the war and at a time when it was crammed with refugees. Years later I read that this raid on Dresden had been Churchill's 'Thunderclap of destruction' and had been aimed at impressing the advancing Russians. More people, most of whom were women and children, were killed in Dresden on February 14 and 15 1945 than were killed in all air-raids on Britain throughout the entire war.

It was Wednesday February 21 when we passed through Dresden, and on that very day Hans-Georg von Studnitz, an official in the Press Section of the Foreign Ministry in Berlin was writing in his diary.

'Since the Dresden attack there has been a lot of talk about reprisals against prisoners of war. The idea is said to have emanated from Goebbels and to have been submitted to the Führer as a serious proposition. The Foreign Minister and Supreme Headquarters have opposed the idea, on the grounds that it might well place in jeopardy the lives of the million German prisoners in British and American hands and even to lead to the introduction of further horrors such as the use of gas. Furthermore, any such move on our part would inevitably cause the remaining neutral countries to break off diplomatic relations with us. Strempel has prepared a memorandum warning of the disastrous consequences of such measures.' (Studnitz, *While Berlin Burns*. London, Weidenfeld & Nicolson, page 248.)

It is certainly of interest to know the weighty political considerations which have prevented one from being murdered.

Once through Dresden our journey continued in a westerly direction. I became seriously concerned about Steve whose condition was deteriorating rapidly. The extraction of his teeth at Lamsdorf had given

174

him a cadaverous appearance but, even allowing for this, he looked seriously ill. In the middle of the afternoon of the second day of our journey we stopped just outside the railway station of the town of Halberstadt and we were not at all happy to see that there was an ammunition train standing on the track next to ours. It was not exactly what one would choose in a country already suffering badly from heavy air-raids. After about an hour the ammunition train moved off, to our great relief, and our guards opened the doors of our trucks. Steve produced the last of our Red Cross food from his overcoat pocket which contained just enough tea for a 'Brew up' for the two of us. I judged that this was the time to use it for Steve was in urgent need of a stimulant. So, I got out of the truck and made my way to the engine where the German engine driver was giving boiling water to all who needed it. Standing in line for my ration of water I looked about me. In the field by the railway truck a gang of concentration camp prisoners were working, and their SS guards were soon chatting to our Army guards although I noticed that they did not take their eyes off their prisoners for a moment. In the distance there were two aeroplanes circling in the clear blue sky which were a source of apprehension to us all in case they were not German. Having collected a dixy full of scalding water on my precious tealeaves I was slowly walking back along the train to my wagon when suddenly I saw with horror that the two aeroplanes were speeding towards us. Gently putting my tea down on the ground I dived under the nearest truck and looked out to see the leading plane diving directly at me. It was apparently in flames, but once I heard the hammering of guns I realised that the flames were from the nozzles of the machine-guns mounted in the foreedge of its wing. It screamed overhead closely followed by the second. There was a moment's silence and then the crackle of rifle fire and I grinned with contempt as I scrambled out from under the wagon, thinking that any guard who hoped to bring down the planes with rifle fire must be extremely optimistic, as they must have been ten miles away by now. However I was sadly mistaken for the firing was not at the aeroplanes but the SS guards were, in fact, shooting down their fleeing prisoners. As I watched an Army guard knocked up the rifle barrel of an SS guard as he took aim and shouted, 'Stop for God's sake! If you shoot an Englishman by mistake we will all be hanged!' I ran along the train and was relieved to find Steve laboriously climbing down out of our wagon. I helped him down and together we joined the mass of prisoners of war and concentration camp inmates in their flight across the field away from the railway.

We reached a row of trees which, as infantrymen, we had instinctively made for as affording the best cover from the air. We stopped, panting, when Steve and I came face to face with one of the concentration camp inmates. Like all his fellows he was a living skeleton, in fact, compared with him Steve and I were positively obese! The poor chap had protrud-

175

ing, glazed eyes, and was muttering to himself. He looked quite demented, as indeed he probably was, considering the ghastly life he had been leading. When we spoke to him he turned away unhearing and wandered aimlessly off, still talking to himself. On his jacket he wore a large pink triangle to indicate he was in the concentration camp because he was homosexual.

I had been very puzzled by the raid, for if the planes' object had been to kill us the correct tactic would surely have been to fly along the length of the train and machine-gun it, not to fly across it. Now, on higher ground, we could understand the reason for what had happened. On the next line to ours there was a locomotive and the first plane had dived with all guns firing to try and damage it beyond repair, while the second fighter had given similar treatment to the engine of our train from which I had collected my boiling water only a few moments before. This sport was known as 'Loco-busting' by the airmen.

After an hour or so most men gradually started to make their way back to the train and we returned as well since escape was out of the question in our present physical condition. We found that all the men in and under the wagon next to the one where I had taken cover had been killed, about 30 in all, most of them men who had been prisoners for over four years. The German engine driver who had given us the hot water was also dead. Judging by the damage done the ammunition used by the planes must have been .505, rather the .303 we used in our Service rifles.

Suddenly I remembered our can of tea and found the empty dixy on its side where I had carefully put it down, the earth still damp beneath it and the doors of the railway wagon next to it closed for it was full of the newly dead.

Hours later, long after darkness had fallen, a British Medical Officer came to the door of our truck to ask for volunteers for a fatigue party. We were all well aware of what it was for, and the officer said it would be a very short task and he needed only the four strongest men among us. As I still felt reasonably fit, and thought I was without doubt one of the men needed, I made my way reluctantly to the door to join the funeral party.

The dead were handed down from their wagon, each wrapped in a blanket. With a man holding each corner we carried our dead comrade along the railway tracks to the station. It seemed incredible that a man so thin could weigh so much, but then I realised that it was our weakness that was causing us to stagger under our burden. In the pitch dark of the blackout we blundered up the slope at the end of the station platform and out into the road. There we could dimly make out the horse-drawn carts silently waiting for their load and where two Germans relieved us of our burden and silently swung it up on to the wagon. I half expected to see the man next to me cross himself or hear a muttered prayer but all was silent and somehow dream-like.

Returning to the station I left my companions in the darkness and determined to explore in the hope of finding some food. Seeing a glimmer of light I pushed my way through a door covered by a blanket and found myself in a small waiting room where three German soldiers were sitting round an iron stove. They knew the job I had been doing and as soon as I entered one said 'What a fine lot the RAF are, killing their own men'. I answered defensively that 'It was not the RAF. They were American planes!'

'Oh, you speak German, do you?' said my questioner. 'Here, have some porridge, you look as if you can do with it' and he gave me a huge billy-can full of *Haverflocken* made with real milk and sugar, which tasted better than anything else I had been given since I had been captured.

My three companions watched me in silence for a few minutes until one of them said, 'Just like the RAF to send the simple Americans over to do the dirty work in daylight and then sneak over under cover of darkness themselves'.

'You can say what you like about the RAF' I answered with composure, 'I'm in the infantry myself.' This was received with great amusement for in the German armed services there was little love lost between the Army and the Luftwaffe. At this moment an air-raid warning sounded so I quickly finished my porridge and followed my hosts through a door and down a flight of steps into a crowded air-raid shelter full of civilians. We sat there in silence, all straining our ears for sounds of bombing and I suddenly became aware that I was the only representative of the enemy forces present in the shelter. Eventually somebody said, 'Damned Englishmen, they should all be hanged.' To make a point I invented a little sister of eight who had been killed in London during an air-raid in 1941 and said that it was us, the little people, who suffered in wartime, for the people in power looked after themselves. Such criticism was dangerous stuff in Nazi Germany, but there was a murmur of agreement. Then the siren sounded the 'All Clear' and I quickly left and made my way back to the train.

Steve was very relieved at my return and asked where I had been. I could have bitten off my tongue when, even in the darkness of our wagon, I could sense his envy when I mentioned the porridge. To our great relief the train moved off later that night and by noon next day we reached Hanover where we were left in the sidings for over an hour. We waited nervously in our locked cattle trucks knowing we were a sitting target for any plane but eventually we moved off without incident, now travelling due north and I wondered if Hamburg or Bremen would be our destination. After a very slow journey punctuated by long halts we reached the town of Fallingbostel on the Luneberg Heath. Here we descended and were marched through the gates of a German prison camp. This was Stamm Lager Nr XI B, Fallingbostel.

23

Fallingbostel

Our new camp resembled Lamsdorf and Görlitz in that it had been functionally built but this one was hopelessly overcrowded with prisoners of every nationality, including some Polish women from the Warsaw rising. As we were in such a shocking condition a number of barrack rooms were vacated for us, the inhabitants being moved into tents where their lives were made miserable by the thick mud underfoot. There were, of course, no Red Cross supplies in the camp and the German system of rationing was breaking down. The daily issue of food by the Nazis was reduced to one small loaf of bread between ten men and about half a pint of soup each, which was really little better than coloured water. Once more we were back to the conditions of 1940, except that on some occasions the German rations failed to materialise at all. Again I experienced the agony of being unable to sleep at night because of hunger.

For three weeks we lingered on under these conditions. Oddly enough Steve seemed to grow no worse and even explored the camp and, in the midst of this scene of misery, he managed to prevail on a French dental mechanic at the Stalag hospital to make him a set of dentures. The men in our barrack room attempted to boost Steve's morale by telling him how much improved he looked, saying such things as, 'God help the girls when you get home, old man!' One of them commented to me privately, however, that until now Steve had looked like a man with no teeth who was about to die, now he only looked like a corpse with a full set of teeth. Steve said that apart from the dental material the only medical equipment in the hospital was a few bandages made of crêpe paper.

Although there was no food in the camp and the death rate was mounting day by day, film shows were put on in the theatre which was also where hundreds of men slept by night. We saw a number of very early short Charlie Chaplin films including 'Easy Street', but I do not think this classic clown has ever raised so few laughs as from that gaunt and apathetic audience. Another source of entertainment and education available was the Stalag library which still functioned. The most im-

178

mediately useful book I borrowed was *The Modern Epicure* by Fletcher in which the author advocated living on a very small quantity of food by chewing every mouthful until it was liquid. I experimented with this scheme and am sure it helped me to survive, although my companions said that I probably used more energy in chewing than I gained from digesting the food.

At this point I got into a long and serious conversation with one of the German guards. With the world in flames, with civilization crashing about his ears and with victorious enemy armies sweeping through his country this plain and nodescript individual was dominated by a single thought; his thinning hair. The only extent to which the earth-shattering events around him impinged on his consciousness was to attribute his impending baldness to the wearing of a steel helmet. I feared for the future of Germany, a country which all but lay in ruins, for if many of the inhabitants were as divorced from reality as this specimen, the future boded no good for them. Rumour circulated through the camp about conditions in the surrounding countryside. It was said that a local farmer's wife had been raped by a number of SS men and that the local population went in greater fear of the SS than we did. There was also a story that the British were advancing rapidly and that the SS were establishing a stronghold near the Stalag to ensure that we would die with them.

Just when the situation was really desperate for us a miracle happened. A fleet of huge white lorries marked with the Red Cross emblem drew up outside the camp and were admitted. They were driven by heroic Swiss drivers, who had passed through both the British and German fighting lines to bring food to us under the flag of neutrality. There was an immediate issue of one parcel between two men and naturally enough, our revels were wild and ecstatic. With each meal we ate the shape and colour of our faces seemed to change and the influence on Steve was particularly dramatic.

Once more it was impressed upon me how narrow the margin is between starvation and repletion. We also enjoyed a good wash with the soap in the parcels, the only interruption to our high spirits being when two gaunt and grimy Americans came to the door of our room and offered to exchange their soap for food. They quickly retreated at the reception they received, their most bitter critics being two American negro soldiers who were extremely ashamed by these two white men who had disgraced their country in the eyes of the British.

After the arrival of the Red Cross supplies events took place rapidly. First the German Commandant called his men on parade and told them that the British were advancing so quickly that he had orders to withdraw all German personnel, leaving behind only a skeleton staff to maintain discipline among the prisoners. He pointed out that those left behind would be taken prisoner by the British, and so he called for volunteers. Every man on parade stepped forward and the Commandant was forced to select the minimum number of the oldest men to stay. He sent them on duty outside the barbed wire and withdrew with the rest of his men to join the retreating German armed forces in the area. We were left alone and unarmed between the opposing British and German armies.

The Prisoners' Representatives of the various national groups in the camp met in an emergency committee under the chairmanship of the British Camp Leader and the most senior British prisoner, Regimental Sergeant Major Lord of the 1st Airborne Division, as he was the representative of the Liberating Forces. As soon as the committee went into session the doors flew open and the German armed guards marched in and insisted on surrendering to the Camp Leader. The Committee refused and sent them back to continue to patrol outside the wire although each German was to be accompanied by an unarmed prisoner. The last thing the committee wanted was for the prisoners to get out of the Stalag and roam about the district causing havoc while the British Army advanced and they certainly did not want any local Nazi Party Leaders getting into the camp to hide in British or Russian uniforms. The committee was about to resume its deliberations when the doors flew open again and this time a squad of Russians marched in, all wearing Hammer and Sickle armbands. They were members of the secret Communist Party Organisation in the Stalag and they had come to arrest the Russian Camp Leader, whom they denounced as a Nazi collaborator, and who they wanted to replace with one of their own Party members. As they withdrew they passed a number of Frenchmen with Cross of Lorraine armbands. These were members of the Free French Underground Movement in the camp and they, in turn, replaced the existing French Camp Leader with one of their own men.

To maintain discipline within the camp each nationality formed its own corps of Military Police. One had only to look in the wrong direction with the wrong expression on one's face to have, say, a Pole tap on one's shoulder and call a British policeman who would say, 'For God's sake, old chap, do play the game or there will be hell let loose, won't there?' Another Englishman and myself had to be rescued by these police from an angry mob of Jugoslav prisoners who had the idea that the British government was planning to send King Peter back to their country as a capitalist puppet, while they wanted Tito and a communist régime. Why they should shout abuse at British fellow-prisoners about this I could not understand, but I was very glad to walk away under the protection of British and Jugoslav policemen.

A number of painters appeared on the roofs of the buildings in the Stalag and painted Red Crosses and 'Prisoner of War Camp' in every language they could think of on the roofs. They had just completed their task when a British fighter flew low over the camp. We all dived for cover but were neither bombed nor machine gunned so I expect the painters felt properly gratified by their handiwork.

Outside the Russian Compound a huge hoarding was speedily erected, which had been made in secret under the noses of the Germans. It bore a gigantic portrait of Stalin and had a row of Red Flags along the top to decorate it. Immediately after it had been erected the *Fallingbostel* branch of the Soviet Union Communist Party published a list of Russians who had collaborated with the Nazis and the prisoners on this list promptly escaped from the camp to rejoin the fleeing Germans. In view of Stalin's edict these were probably the luckiest of the Russian prisoners for he had said 'Russian soldiers taken prisoner are traitors to Mother Russia and can expect death at the end of the war!' Yet, it is always so difficult to discover the real truth in wartime that I wonder if Stalin ever said this, or if it was another product of the German Ministry of Propaganda. After all, Stalin's own son was taken prisoner.

Another example of this, for instance, is that all the German soldiers firmly believed that the Russians had claimed that 'All German girls and women are the just spoil of the Red Army soldiers', but I have no doubt that this was an invention of Goebbels' fertile imagination to help make the German Army fight to the bitter end.

An air of apprehensive excitement hung over the Stalag. In our no-man's-lands between the two embattled armies I was very conscious that I had arrived at a cross-roads in my life. I started to walk alone round our silent compound determined to arrive at a philosophy of life, or, at least, a scale of values by which I could live when I was free. I reviewed my life but after hours of meditation and miles of walking I had to abandon my pilgrimage. Spiritually unsatisfied, but determined after my recent experiences I would at least ensure my share of the good things of life in the future, I retired to bed to the accompaniment of the sounds of distant battle.

While we were at our Red Cross breakfast next morning we heard a huge cheer go up from the next compound. We dashed outside to see a gigantic British tank of the 8th Hussars lumbering by. Suddenly it stopped and a soldier appeared from the conning tower — such a man as I had never seen before — a superman with bronzed face, flashing white teeth and sparkling eyes. It dawned upon me how ill everybody in Germany looked (including the SS men who were supposed to be the racial élite of the new Nazi world state).

The Guardsman shouted out, 'Are you British?'

'Yes!' I screamed. Our interrogator looked concerned for I suppose we were an odd looking crew to his eyes.

'How long have you been here?' he asked.

'Since Dunkirk' somebody shouted and a look of horror came over the man's face. He disappeared into his tank and then re-appeared and threw over everything he could lay his hands on. Tins of corned beef, cigarettes, packets of army biscuits and a copy of *Picture Post* came sailing over. I suddenly realised that I had spoken to a free Englishman and his arrival must mean that I, too, was free. I had been a prisoner for four years, ten months, four days, one hour and ten minutes; or, about one fifth of my life.

Almost simultaneously with the arrival of the tank a jeep containing a United Press photographer and a Church Army worker reached the Stalag. They cheerfully informed us that they were well in advance of the main body of British troops and had been fired on twice by the enemy during the morning. After they had left there was a lull, rather a long anti-climax, until a large party of British officers arrived late in the afternoon. As they drew up in their trucks outside the main gate Regimental Sergeant Major Lord turned out the British guard to salute them. In our eyes the guardsmen seemed so smart that they could have been on duty outside Buckingham Palace. They were immaculate in scrubbed belts and gaiters and well-ironed battle-dress. As H. Essams wrote about the British Army in *The Battle for Germany*, 'If leadership, comradeship, discipline and self-respect are the basis of high morale, then all were present here'. As the officers entered the camp Sergeant Major Lord called the milling throng of prisoners inside the gate to attention while a tall and very dirty Russian, leaning against the corner of a building grinned at me and said in broken German, 'You Englishmen will have to jump about smartly now that your officers are here!' At that moment a short, fat Russian officer came into view in the middle of the group of British officers and, in a flash, the Russian's face lost its smirk and he was standing to attention as stiffly as the rest of us.

The period which followed was one of confusion. We were disinfected, registered, medically examined and then once more registered and disinfected, in spite of our vigorous protests. At last, during the afternoon of the following day, those of us who had been prisoners the longest left the Stalag in a fleet of lorries.

24

The last lap

All that afternoon and evening we travelled across occupied Germany and once, after dark, our driver even got lost and took our lorry right up to the advancing British front line. By good fortune he soon found his way once more and so, in the middle of the night, we reached a tented camp where we slept until dawn.

The next day was one of the most frightening days of my life. I can remember waking up in the tent that morning but can recollect nothing else until I became conscious of riding through the deserted streets of Brussels in a lorry late in the afternoon. I must have suffered from amnesia for some 12 hours. A psychologist could probably explain why I have completely forgotten my first day of freedom, but I can only suggest, in the words of Sir Osbert Sitwell that, 'The intensity of the emotion killed memory'. Steve has since told me that during my missing day we made our way from the camp to Osnabruck and flew in RAF transport planes from the captured Luftwaffe airfield to Brussels where we were taken by lorry to a YMCA hostel and I must be one of the very few people of my generation who has no recollection whatever of his first journey in an aeroplane!

That evening in the hostel we were entertained by an ENSA dance band which we considered far inferior to the one at Lamsdorf. Next day we were taken to the Brussels airfield and climbed into a Dakota aeroplane. It taxied to take-off but sank in the soft mud near the runway. Frustrated, we all got out and feverishly helped me to push it back on to firm ground. At last we were inside it again and were soon airborne without further mishap. We flew over war-torn Belgium and saw the earth scarred with tank tracks and noted how they converged at bridges to cross rivers and then fanned out again. Then we were over the sea and I studied the skyscapes along the shining wings of our plane for some time before we looked down at the vast expanse of sea. A pier came into view, a promenade and a town which I recognised as my childhood holiday haunt of Felixstowe. I turned to Steve and shouted hysterically above the roar of the engines, 'England, Steve! It's England!'

However, Steve was sitting on the floor of the plane, his face the colour of putty. Steve took no notice, for he was being very, very sick.

Epilogue

One of the planes bringing ex-prisoners home to Britain crashed into the North Sea with the loss of all on board; surely the most unfortunate victims of the war. My particular friends and I were lucky enough to return unhurt and, within a few months, we all married. We have spent the intervening years in working at our careers and bringing up our children, of whom we are all inordinately proud.

Steve made such a miraculous recovery that within three weeks of reaching home he had met a very attractive Scottish nurse, swept her off her feet and married her. With his days of professional soldiering behind him he quickly achieved his ambition to become a Civil Servant and is now a pillar of Her Majesty's Stationery Office and spends blissful weekends during the Season umpiring cricket matches.

Stoppani, the artist, returned to complete his training at the Royal College of Art and his work has subsequently been exhibited by the Arts Council and many other important bodies, while Gerry Hoon is now in charge of the Insurance Department of British Oxygen.

George Lang, having joined the Westminster Bank, quickly passed all his banking examinations. One day I was speaking of him to a retired bank manager who curled his lip and commented that qualifications were all very well, but it was personality which counted for senior posts in banking. When I told him that as a prisoner of war George had always spoken to the guards as if *they* were the prisoners, the banker roared, 'That's my boy, he'll go far!' and he did, he became a tutor at the bank's Staff Training College and subsequently manager of their Wembley Park Branch, and, thereafter, of a series of larger and more important branches.

Walter, the German soldier who offered to escape with me to Russia, survived the twin dangers of being a soldier in wartime and a democrat in a Nazi state. In war-torn Europe he traced his Polish girlfriend, married her and is now owner of a thriving chain of gentlemen's outfitters in West Berlin.

After marrying my wartime girlfriend, Dorothy, I was fortunate enough to get a government grant to go to University College, London. Now I am responsible for the cataloguing of the British National Bibliography at the British Library.

As we were all Private soldiers, the lowest possible form of military life, I often wonder what happened to our Lance-corporals!